Dating & Relationship Principles *for* Marriage

5 Proven Steps to Saying "I Do"

STEPHEN C. C. HAMMOND
AND EBUN HAMMOND

Copyright © 2023 by Stephen C. C. Hammond and Ebun Hammond

The moral right of the authors has been asserted.

All rights reserved. No part of this book may be reproduced in any form without permission in writing from the publisher, except in the case of brief quotations embodied in critical articles or reviews.

Scripture quotations taken from the Holy Bible, New International Version Anglicised Copyright © 1979, 1984, 2011 Biblica. Used by permission of Hodder & Stoughton Ltd, an Hachette UK company. All rights reserved. 'NIV' is a registered trademark of Biblica UK trademark number 1448790.

Where people, products, treatments including medical or psychological, legal descriptions, websites have been mentioned, these are given for general information purposes only and therefore should not be treated as recommendations. The advice and strategies contained herein may not be suitable for your situation. The reader is strongly advised and expected to do their own research including seeking professional medical, therapeutic and or legal advice first before doing anything mentioned in this book. Neither the publisher nor the author shall be liable for any loss including incidental, consequential, personal or any other damages.

All names and recognisable details have been changed to protect the privacy of individuals where their stories have been mentioned.

A CIP catalogue record for this book is available from the British Library

ISBN - Paperback: 978-1-7392773-0-7
ISBN - Hardcover: 978-1-7392773-1-4
ISBN – EBook: 978-1-7392773-2-1
ISBN – Audio: 978-1-7392773-3-8

Printed in the United Kingdom and other places through print-on-demand technology.

Cover design by: Jennifer Stimson

Published by Love Dimensions Limited, United Kingdom

For more information, or to book an event, contact:
https://www.lovedimensions.co.uk

Contents

Introduction 1

The 5 Steps to Saying, "I Do" 9

STEP 1: Preparing to Date 11
    Chapter 1: Principles of Love Attraction 13
    Chapter 2: How to Get Your Most Compatible Date Match 27
    Chapter 3: Differences Between The Sexes 47
    Chapter 4: Men Chase & Women Challenge 65

STEP 2: Start Dating 89
    Chapter 5: Getting Started 91
    Chapter 6: How to Stand Out & Get Noticed 109
    Chapter 7: Where to Meet People 125
    Chapter 8: Where to Go On Dates & What to Do 135
    Chapter 9: Online Dating 151
    Chapter 10: Long Distance Relationships 167
    Chapter 11: Let's Talk About SEX 173

STEP 3: The Courtship Stage 197
    Chapter 12: Courtship – Assessing Suitability for Each Other 199
    Chapter 13: How to Have a Happy Marriage 215
    Chapter 14: Let's Talk About COMMUNICATION 227

STEP 4: Getting Engaged 249
    Chapter 15: Getting Engaged 251
    Chapter 16: Safeguarding Your Marriage 265
    Chapter 17: Let's Talk About MONEY 279

STEP 5: Marriage – Getting Ready to Say, "I Do" 287
    Chapter 18: Wedding Preparation Ideas 289

Chapter 19: Marriage Preparation...293
Chapter 20: Sexuality & Fertility..307

And Finally 325
   Chapter 21: Dealing With Toxic Relationships..........................327
   Online Bonus Chapters (Access Password Here)........................337
      1. Dating & Single Parenthood..337
      2. Divorced, Widowed, or Was in a Long Term Relationship 337
      3. Dating For Over 50s..337
      4. Dating & Disabilities...337
      5. Dating & Mental Health..337
      6. Interracial & Interethnic Relationships..............................337
      7. Age Differences...337
      8. Faith & Beliefs...337

Thank You...339

Acknowledgments..341

References..343

Introduction

This book focuses on intentional dating and relationship making for marriage. With the use of science (from neurology, psychology, biology and social science), we will show you how you can find the right man or woman of your dreams for a happy and lifelong marriage. A sailing ship will catch the wind to propel it forward, but the rudder steers it in the direction that the captain wants to take it. A person in an intentional relationship is like a sea captain who steers their ship in the right direction to get to their expected destination. Being intentional means you are steering your relationship with a clear direction in mind. In this case, since you are reading this book, we can presume that your intended destination is marriage, and for that matter, to have a happy marriage. In this book, you will learn exactly how to do this. We hope you will enjoy reading it and are inspired by it as we felt privileged to write it. Our hope is that you will not only benefit from the information presented within these pages but also will want to share this information with those you care most about: your family and friends.

Apart from learning about intentional dating, another distinguishing feature about this dating and relationship book that sets it apart from others is the amount of attention given to the subject of sex; in fact, we have two chapters dedicated to it, in addition to lots of sections throughout the book. This is because, we feel, having this knowledge will bring about healthier and happier marriage relationships. Besides sex, we also discuss communication and different strategies for effective conflict resolution in relationships. Additionally, we consider in depth the subject of money and different ways couples can make decisions around their budgeting and finance.

Everyone who aspires to be married hopes to live happily ever after in their marriage. We think this is a reasonable and sensible expectation when things are done the right way from the start. There is no reason why your dream of meeting the right person and having a happy marriage cannot come true for you. Marriage requires a lot of work and effort to make it successful. The preparation and training ground for marriage success needs to be done in the dating, courtship, and engagement stages of the relationship. Also, to give a marriage the best possible chance of success, it is essential to make the right choice of a partner. Although there is no Mr or Miss Perfect, there is, however, a Mr or Miss Right out there that is the right fit for you. Despite high divorce rates, marriage as an institution has consistently remained the ideal in society, and people still want to get married. Even if you have had unsuccessful relationships in the past, you will learn all the necessary secrets you need this time to go on to have a happy, lifelong marriage.

Our definition of a happy marriage is where the goal of each spouse in the relationship is to create an emotionally positive and intimately loving environment for a couple to grow, flourish and be happy in. It should also be enriched with a good sense of optimism and humour. A happy marriage makes each spouse relax and be comfortable around the other, and at the same time enjoy the value and benefit of being in each other's company. Such a relationship is based on emotionally interdependent feelings of love, respect, kindness, and trust for each other. If this is the kind of marriage you are looking for, then this is the perfect book for you.

Introducing the 5 Steps to Saying, "I Do"

In this book, we have broken the stages of a relationship leading to marriage into 5 Steps. Each Step has critical and valuable information to help you meet the right life partner. Unfortunately, there are no shortcuts to this process. Within the Steps, are a wealth of tips and good habits that you will need to incorporate into your relationship for it to become a fruitful, happy, and lifelong marriage. These are very important, and you will need to practise them. They are all based on scientifically sound research and experience, and have been proven to work in the real world over and over again. When you apply them, they will also work for you.

STEP 1: Preparing To Date

You may have heard the expression, "preparation is the key to success." Like any other area of our lives, this is also true for successful dating. If you need to cook a meal that you have never made before, you would rightly need to follow a recipe to avoid making mistakes. That is what we mean by preparation. In this Step, you will learn about the importance of attraction and compatibility, two widely misunderstood themes in dating. You will also learn about the differences between the sexes and how these crucially play into how each sex expects to be treated by the other in a relationship. There is a lot more to this than you may think at first! All of the information in this first Step will prepare you to be more effective in your dating. It will also act as a foundation on which the other Steps progressively build.

STEP 2: Start Dating

This Step is all about introducing you to the wide and fun world of dating. When you initially start to go out on dates, this can involve meeting one or more people in a week. This carries on until, as time goes by, you have filtered down your selection to only one person you want to get to know and spend more time with. This is because, in the dating stage, you are not yet exclusive. Getting to being exclusive with each other means that you both have strong feelings for each other and are both becoming emotionally attached to each other. When a couple are involved in a sexual relationship this does not mean that the relationship is therefore an exclusive one. If a couple have not developed deep enough attachment feelings for each other, then monogamous exclusivity, either emotionally or sexually, is unlikely to be honoured. You will discover, in chapter 11, why it takes around 2-3 months for a man to emotionally fall in love with his lady. As the lyrics to the song "You Can't Hurry Love" implies, love is not something you can rush. The dating stage of a relationship may not be able to tell you if the person you are dating will be the right marriage partner for you. However, you will know if the chemistry is there to want to continue to build the relationship so that you can see where it is going. At this stage, it is up to you if you want to only see one person at a time. We advocate multiple dating because it avoids the risk of over infatuation, being obsessive, or being overly invested in your feelings for one person who may, in the end, disappoint you. If you are part of a religious community, the concept of multiple dating may not apply because, by its nature, religious communities are generally socially close-knit, and they usually have a set of dating guidelines in place for their members.

The dating period may take at least 2-3 months, but sometimes longer, before courtship can begin. It is natural that at this time, you and your partner are likely to be on your guard with each other because you don't want the new relationship to fail. This can understandably make you feel anxious to ensure the relationship has the best possible chance of working. During this time, you may also find yourself making an extra effort to please each other as you get to know each other. It is likely that the initial chemistry attraction you have for each other will remain strong and intense throughout this period. In some cases, these feelings can actually continue into marriage.[1] You are also both likely to be significantly more conscientious of how you dress, behave and conduct yourselves around each other. In short, during this period, your guard will remain high to ensure that you impress at all times. It is only after about 3 months that both of you may begin to naturally drop your guard enough to let the real person in each of you come out. Once emotional attachment feelings are strong in each of you for the other, and you have decided to be exclusive with each other, you are both ready for the next Step, which is courtship. Courtship gives you the space to let your guard down and learn about each other more.

STEP 3: The Courtship Stage

Courtship is often misunderstood by many people nowadays. This is not a surprise. Before dating took over, courtship was the original method by which couples met and got to know each other. The purpose was to find out if they were suitable to be married to each other. In this book, we introduce a very fresh, modern 21st Century perspective on courtship. The courtship stage begins when you both choose to be exclusively committed to each other while you get to know each other more. It is also the stage where you decide whether you want to take the relationship toward marriage. The period for dating to courtship normally takes at least 2-3 months, but sometimes much longer. Less than this could mean it may be difficult to know for sure that your partner is as deeply committed to the relationship as you are. Also, feelings of intense infatuation can often get in the way to cloud normal rational thinking, before natural feelings of love, trust and companionship begin to take over. However, the courtship period generally can take at least 6 to 9 months to know a person well enough to be reasonably confident for a proposal to be made and accepted. During this period, each will meet and get to know each other's family and friends better.

In Chapter 13, we introduce the secrets to having a happy marriage. Why are we talking about how to have a happy marriage even before a marriage proposal has been made? We are doing this because when you understand what is needed for a happy marriage, you can begin to put into practice right now all the habits and behaviours necessary to make your marriage, when the time comes, to be happy and successful. Learning lots of new good habits and behaviours can take time for them to eventually become part of you. By learning these valuable secrets now, your relationship will be significantly enriched as a consequence, even before a proposal has been made and accepted.

STEP 4: Getting Engaged

Engagement is the stage in the relationship where you deeply know in your heart if you are meant for each other. For these feelings to be genuine there is no room for lingering doubts. If there are, then you are not ready to get engaged because being ready to be engaged is the same as being ready for marriage. Deciding to spend the rest of your lives together is not simply about your parents or family's choice. Although they may have a special input as well. However, it fundamentally comes down to your decision, and nobody else can make this for you. Engagement is the exciting stage when a proposal is made and, hopefully, accepted. Besides any cultural observances that may need to be followed, it is also popular for a man to propose by giving a jewelled ring to his lady as a token of his love, affection, and intention to marry her and to also ward off other suitors that she has been spoken for. On the other hand, not everyone places a high importance on an engagement ring. We discuss the role of the engagement ring throughout this book but only to ensure that a man has demonstrated his seriousness to get married to his lady.

However, an engagement ring is not compulsory of itself, but is sincerely given by a man to demonstrate his love and intention to follow through with getting married to his lady. In chapter 15, we provide a checklist for a lady to ensure her man is indeed the right man for her. We also offer men lots of tips and ideas on how to make their marriage proposal as romantic and memorable as possible for the couple. Chapter 16, is dedicated to giving you proven and useful strategies to help you safeguard your marriage from infidelity and failure.

STEP 5: Marriage

All the previous steps lead up to the principal motivation for writing this book, getting to say, "I do." This Step focuses on marriage preparation, including wedding planning, sexual intimacy, and fertility. We also focus on how you can keep the passion alive in your marriage, including looking at the kind of things to expect to come up in your marriage, as well as how to grow in your emotional interdependency with each other.

About Us

Stephen and Ebun are both passionate about the topic of marriage, and about helping couples experience happiness in their marriage. Stephen has a BA in Film, Radio, and Television, and Ebun has an MBA (Cardiff Met). Prior to Stephen and Ebun launching Love Dimensions, Stephen worked as an administrator and lifelong learning tutor. Stephen has also been an ordained minister since 1996, and performed marriages, renewal blessings and taken many couples over the years through the process of pre-marriage counselling. Ebun is a qualified secondary school maths teacher in the UK. Prior to this, she was a project manager in the e-payment sector. Ebun has also been actively involved in charities that support family well being and welfare, for nearly two decades. Together, over the years, they have coached and supported hundreds of people from faith and non-faith backgrounds and cultures, to help fulfil their life goals and dreams, including getting married and staying married. We have been married since 2016, and live in the United Kingdom.

The 5 Steps to Saying, "I Do"

STEP 1: Preparing to Date

Chapter 1: Principles of Love Attraction

We start off our step by step journey in seeking and finding lifelong love by looking at the subtleties of attraction. That is, delving into what kind of things have the power to attract others to us and why. Understanding romantic attraction has been a complicated puzzle that story tellers, poets, song writers and scientists have been trying to work out and piece together for thousands of years. We may not know all the answers yet, but mankind certainly has a good understanding of most of the principles that are involved in love attraction. Science has come a long way, as you will discover throughout this book, in also understanding the biological, neurological and psychological forces at work within us in discovering what makes a person become attracted to another and why. The purpose of this chapter is to share with you various principles of attraction and how you can make the best first impression to your date. But first, let's begin by looking at different types of attraction.

Physical & Sexual Attraction

This works subtly different between the two sexes. Men are more sexual in what they look for in a date. This should not be surprising, because although the principal hormonal influence for the sex drive in both men and women, is testosterone, it is in abundance in men. In fact, men have around 15 times more than women.[2] That is why it seems in the dating space, men always have sex on their minds. This doesn't mean women do not think about sex, but if their focus is on having a relationship leading to marriage, then a one night sex hook up is not generally going to be the first thing they are thinking of. Instead, they will be interested in friendship that has the potential to grow into a long-lasting relationship. Each man is different, and likewise are men's preferences when it comes to the kind of lady they are physically attracted to. These preferences can cover things like a lady's physique, ethnicity, skin colour and tone, hair colour, etc. The reality is that a lady will not have any idea what a man really likes unless he actually comes over to her and introduces himself. Therefore, a lady will be taking a huge risk if she tries to make the first move. She may look at him and he may look and smile back at her. But perhaps he is just admiring her from a distance, because he thinks she is very pretty or simply flattered that she noticed him, and that may be all. Also, he may already be married or already in a serious relationship. If she does try to ask him out, then research has shown that his instinctive perception of her will be that she is making a sexual advance to him. When all she may want to do is to make friends.[3] [4] We will deal with many of these scenarios in Chapter 4: Men Chase & Women Challenge. Also, in Chapter 6: How to Stand Out & Get Noticed, we will discuss many different strategies on how a lady can hint and show strong interest in a man, without having to chase him.

Ladies too can be attracted to men for their physical looks. A lady may even rate a man highly for having an athletic body on apps like Tinder. However, subconsciously, what she is doing is looking at the symmetrical features on his face and body. She is looking to check that both left and right sides are the same as each other. The subtle message that women may pick up from this is, if there are any differences, it may suggest genetic issues that may be passed on from a prospective partner to any babies they might have together in the future. However, men should not pay too much attention to this, because ladies who are interested in marriage generally treat physical attributes to be superficial in comparison to personality, interests, values, beliefs, education and economic status. Also, marriage data suggests that the average age gap between a bride and groom is 2 years, with men in the vast majority of marriages being the older spouse.[5][6]

When a lady is interested in a significantly older man, it is usually linked to his power and ability to provide resources. Examples of this could be an aging rock star or a successful but overweight businessman in his fifties or a significantly older but wealthy politician. These may all find no difficulty in getting the attention of highly attractive ladies in their twenties or thirties, because of their social status and access to wealth.

Men are attracted to youthfulness and beauty in a lady. That is why in most marriages the man is older than the women, to ensure a higher likelihood of her fertility. However, as a man gets much older what is important to him may not be how fertile a lady is, but that she looks after herself to maintain her physical attractiveness (her youthfulness and beauty) for him. Every behavioural science research study on human mating attraction all come to the above same conclusions. In short, and as blunt as it sounds, men are attracted to women as sex objects, and women are generally attracted to men who look and behave as achievers; success objects.[7][8]

Economic Attraction

Economic attraction is particularly of interest to women, who may be looking for a life partner she would one day like to have children with. Therefore, she will want to see that he is a man of his word, reliable, and comes across as the kind of person who can take responsibility for his actions. All of these character traits may not have a direct bearing on economic status, but do have profound economic consequences in the workplace and career progression if he is lacking in any of these.

Economic attraction can also work both ways, especially for a couple to join up resources so that they can acquire more together. For instance, these days, for a couple to get onto the property ladder, both may need to be working so that they can prove their creditworthiness and ability to pay mortgage. A single person, is likely to find it much harder to do this on their own. Occupations and career aspirations could therefore be quite important here.

Intellectual Attraction

Intellect also has an attractive appeal, because it may signify higher earning potential when linked to either having a degree or other professional qualification. Intellect is also a compatibility area. For more information on compatibility, see Chapter 2. A well-read person maybe highly attractive because they are also likely to be able to engage in informed discussions with others who also share the same area of interest. Your intellect can be a powerful tool of attraction, especially if you have a passion about a subject area you have an interest in. This could be, for example, topical issues, such as current affairs. Also, a person can come across as being attractive if they are seen as being patient and generous to share their knowledge, skills and experience with others.

First Impressions Last

When you meet your date for the first time, the impressions you make on them through your appearance and behaviour is what will influence how much they desire you as a potential life mate. If you and your date do not find each other attractive, then it will be

Chapter 1: Principles of Love Attraction 17

difficult to go on to compatibility. Which we cover in detail in Chapter 2. People have different ways of measuring or regarding what they find attractive about others. However, there are many common areas that everyone do generally agree on of what is either regarded as attractive (or unattractive). Dating can be like going on a job interview, because at the interview stage, first impressions last, and you only get one shot to make a lasting positive one. When an applicant prepares for a job interview, they will naturally do their research to find out more about the company and what the job entails, so that they can have a good idea of what to say or talk about at the interview. When they attend the interview they will be smartly and appropriately dressed, as well as being respectful in their tone of voice, speech and body language. They make the extra effort to do all this because they want the job and in order to get it they need to impress the panel of people at the interview. It is exactly the same with preparing yourself before going on a date. You want your date to have a very good first impression of you that will make them want to see you again.

Below are a list of proven successful tips that are guaranteed to make your appearance and personality stand out among the competition. Some of the suggestions are a bit obvious but are given anyway, to avoid presumption.

1. Dressing for Success

Ladies: Dress well with smart clothes that fit and naturally accentuate your body without them being skin tight. Look stylish and elegant. Ideally dress modestly, because you want to project "loyalty" to your date. Try mixing and matching clothes, as well as different colours and tones that blend well with each other. You don't have to go for brand names. You can mix and match brand names with much lower cost clothing. If money is an issue, you can find loads of highly desirable pre-owned brand names at bargain prices on apps and websites like Vinted and Ebay.

Men: Whether you choose to wear a suit or go casual, dress smartly, unless it is simply not appropriate because of the activity (for example, rock climbing, hiking, running, etc.). Looking smart carries a sense of confidence and projects an image that you have what it takes to be successful and going somewhere in life. Make sure your clothing is ironed, because this also reflects on your appearance and how others may treat both you and the lady you are with.

2. Good Hygiene & Grooming

Having good hygiene is essential. It is also something that both men and women look out for. If you perspire easily, make sure that you keep your body smells in check because body odour can be very off putting. Besides, your daily washing routines, consider using a suitable body deodorant or perfume. Also, having a good set of white looking teeth is a very attractive feature. Therefore, it could be a good time to get your teeth and gums checked out by your dentist, and at the same time, asking them to give your teeth a professional clean. If you have gaps visible in your teeth, consider getting these filled with implants and any broken teeth capped. Also, bad breath is very off putting and could indicate gum disease. Therefore, use mouth wash before leaving your home or workplace to go on your date. If you smoke or vape or you feel you need a drink before meeting your date, consider taking some mints or chewing gum with you, or using a fresh breath spray before you meet them.

Ladies: Try to ensure that facial hair, hair under the arm pits and hair on arms and legs are all kept at bay (unless you know for sure that your partner does not mind it).

Men: Make sure that your scalp hair, beard and moustache are regularly washed, groomed and tidy looking. Also make sure that eyebrows are suitably trimmed and not wild looking (including removing hair above the nose between each eyebrow) and no hair is visible from either the nose or ears. Also, women's smell abilities generally outperforms men. Therefore, consider wearing a men's perfume that has been highly rated by women. A simple internet search will indicate which ones to try.

3. Makeup

Ladies: should wear just enough to enhance. If you are older, you can apply creams at night to tighten your skin and this will bring out a more youthful look to your face. Also, consider wearing red lipstick, because red has consistently proven to work as a powerful dating attraction colour.

4. Jewellery

We advise it is okay to wear jewellery, but not over excessively, because otherwise it can look untidy. Also, try to keep the wearing of rings to no more than three, but we strongly suggest not wearing them on either your left of right ring finger. Otherwise you could give the impression that you are either already in a relationship or have just come out of one.

Ladies: As a suggestion only, consider when you go out wearing largish earrings. They will get you noticed from across the other side of a room.

5. Smiling

Always smile. Do it compulsorily, even if it does not feel natural to you. To emphasis, develop the habit of smiling wherever you go, whether you feel like it or not. When you smile, you project a happy and joyful look. Which will radiate warm and positive feelings to those around you. Happy people attract other happy and positive people to themselves, because they are always attractive to be around. Happy people always attract other happy people to them. Learn what makes you happy. This goes with learning to smile all the time (unless there is a genuinely sombre reason not to). All of this may sound fake, but this is what actors, performers and presenters have to do every day. If your livelihood depended upon it for survival you would do it. How much more then, when wanting to create a positive impression with others. If you are going through struggles with your mental health please see our bonus chapter on Dating & Mental Health, where you may find some helpful suggestions.

6. Positivity

Always think, act and speak positively about yourself and the people around you. As the old saying goes, "If you don't have something good to say, then don't say it". Having a positive and hopeful personality enriches all relationships and will make them happier and long lasting.

7. Enthusiasm

People who are enthusiastic are great people you want around on your team. They project the feeling of positive energy that they want to get things done. We all know there are days that may seem easier than others to be enthusiastic, but enthusiasm conveys great zest for life. It also conveys the message that the person is up for an adventure. Enthusiasm can be equated to being passionate. Such a person is easily trusted because they come across as being passionate about both the things they stand for and what is important to them. We are not talking about a huge water fountain. Just a trickle of positive enthusiasm and energy is enough to come across as being excited about the date you are on and more importantly the person you are with. Enthusiasm also has the power to quickly turn what could otherwise have been a disaster date into a fun or laughable experience.

8. Humour

Humour is a highly attractive and appealing quality. We discuss the serious science behind this fun attraction in more detail in Chapter 3: Differences Between the Sexes. But for now, while it is no secret that romantic comedies appeal more to women than men, guys love a lady who laughs at their jokes on a first date.

Men: Here's a tip for you. You don't have to tell jokes to show a lady you can be fun to be with. Just don't come across as a person who takes life too seriously. The more you relax, smile and laugh, the more likely your date will laugh along with you.

9. Voice & Tone

Try to make your voice as engaging as possible, by avoiding monotone in your speech, because monotone sounds flat and boring. You can sound highly engaging by using different subtle high and low pitches in your voice as you say your sentences. This is guaranteed to make your voice more interesting to listen to. When you listen to the radio, you can hear the different tones in speech of the presenters. This makes them very appealing, interesting and attractive to listen to. Also, if you have a stammering/stuttering problem, then always speak deliberately slowly. Try getting into the habit of always putting deliberate pregnant pauses in either midway or at the end of your sentences to turn your speech into manageable chunks. This will help you to slow your speech down. Using pregnant pauses will also make you come across as a more thoughtful person. This strategy will help the brain to slow down so that your mouth and tongue can catch up with what you are trying to say. When you do this, you will be pleasantly surprised to see how wonderfully patient and generous people will be to you.

10. Body Language

Using open body postures (with smiles) will make you come across as being warm and friendly, open, honest and sincere. The opposite of coming across as being open is, for example, crossing arms or have legs pointed towards the door. Both of which, can suggest feelings of defensiveness or disinterest. You can find examples of 'open body postures' using the 'Images' tab in an internet search engine.

11. Avoid Making Cynical or Sarcastic Comments

These are extremely unattractive and off putting. Sarcastic people sound funny at first, but in time they come across as bitter and cynical about life and in the end are not fun people to be around.

12. Avoid gossip

If you like gossip no one will trust you with their secrets. Wicked people use gossipers to spread false and malicious information about people they do not like. Therefore, do not gossip about anyone or anything for any reason. Our advice is to stay away from people who do. Otherwise, they will make you look very unattractive to be around.

13. Avoid Swearing or Using Offensive Language

This includes any words that either sound offensive, rude, distasteful or disrespectful to another or demeaning, devaluing or dehumanising of another. It might sound cool or funny to the user and maybe make a person feel they are being authentic, but we think any use of bad or offensive language is wrong in any situation. After all, you are meeting on a date the person you hope could be the mother or father of your children. Children are naturally influenced and copy the words that their parents use (whether in your presence or behind your back). No right minded parent should want that for their children. Therefore, using any kind of swearing or offensive language is never attractive.

14. Confidence Gets You More Dates

Confidence has a huge role to play in the dating game. Confidence in both men and women is a strong love attraction for both sexes. It is not a surprise that an average looking man who has a confident personality will stand a better chance of attracting a date from a lady who is viewed as being more attractive than he is. This is because confident people often give a feeling to those around them that they are success achievers. Confident people who are risk takers always score well when it comes to mate attraction and dating.

15. Having Good Social Skills

People who can engage in conversation easily with both men and women are more likely to have strong social skills leading to a higher quality of social life. Also, women are naturally attracted to men who display high leadership skills or already hold positions of leadership. Learning social skills and leadership skills are big topic areas, and so cannot be thoroughly dealt with here. However, there are loads of free articles on the internet that teach you how to improve your social communication and leadership skills as well as many videos, available on Youtube. There are no short cuts to this. The more time and practice you put in, the quicker and more positive the results you will experience. This applies equally to both men and women.

How to Improve Your Confidence & Social Skills

For a quick way to get you started in improving both your confidence and social skills, you could try this. The next time you go to the supermarket, ask the person at the checkout till, "How is your day going?" You can also ask your cab driver the same question on the next journey you take. You could follow this up by asking, "Is this your main work or are you doing something else as well?" Or, you could try a good open ended question like, "What are the things you most like and dislike about your job?" The more you practise, the easier it will be to think of more follow up questions to ask. Doing this regularly will also help you to build up your confidence to network more easily with others and at the same time, increase your social circle of friends. Therefore, develop the habit of regularly saying hello and smiling to people wherever you go. Try your best, when you can, to turn this into a fun experience. Remember, smiling is contagious. Don't be afraid to fake it if you have to. Don't be put off if someone doesn't positively respond back. They are probably going through a hard day or may have lots of other things on their mind at that time. Forget about it and just carry on to the next person you meet. If anyone challenges you, "Why are you so happy?" Just respond by saying and asking, "I like to be happy. What makes you happy?" Practising these exercises all the time will help you to be ready for when you meet up with someone who you really do like, as well as help to reduce your feelings of stress and anxiety.

Men: this may sound a bit obvious, but if you are a man reading this and you get a positive response, don't forget to try to get the lady's phone number, because you never know where it could lead! Just tell her that you would love to check up on her and see how she is doing later. If she likes you, she will be flattered and may give you her number. If not, don't worry about it and move on.

Ladies: please take care with the exercise of smiling in random public places, unless you are attending a social gathering, function or other event with family or friends. This is because of the higher risk of attracting the wrong and unwanted attention of a dangerous person. If you are approached by a man in a social gathering, never agree to be alone on your own with him. However, if a man smiles at you and you like him, then smile back and wait to see if he has the courage to follow through. If he doesn't, it might be just his way of being friendly to you. Just accept it as a compliment and move on.

More Ways to Help Build Up Your Confidence

The more you practise your social skills the more confident you will be in conversing with others. The basic meaning of confidence is to have the mind-set to put something into action, because you would not do something unless you had sufficient belief you could do it in the first place, no matter how large or small the task. If you feel you need more help in developing your confidence then consider taking up classes in any of the following:

- Public speaking
- Acting
- Stand-up comedy
- Singing
- Dancing
- Debating

Also, consider joining a local Toastmasters club to learn how to do public speaking. If you feel you are not confident to confront people, then consider doing a course to help you learn to be assertive. The good news is that learning how to have an attractive personality is not difficult to do. In the same way as learning anything you are not familiar with, it just takes practice. When you do, you will be glad you did, because the results you achieve when you go dating will be amazing.

How to Avoid Attracting Bad People

In our experience, if a person lacks confidence, or has low self-esteem, or a low sense of self-worth about themselves, this can make them particularly vulnerable to attracting an abusive, controlling or unstable partner. This is because abusive and controlling people thrive off partners who have a low sense of self-worth.

When a person comes out of an abusive relationship or marriage breakdown or experiences the loss of a life partner, it can affect their confidence, because of emotional or physical trauma they may have gone through. It is therefore vital, that such a person first of all ensures they are emotionally in a good place before they begin to date again. This is because emotional hurt, loss, suffering and pain take time to heal. If these feelings are not dealt with, such a person may find it difficult to trust and get close to someone new or worse, end up with the wrong person. For more information on recovering from a traumatic relationship or bereavement, please see our bonus chapter on Divorced, Widowed, or Was in a Long Term Relationship. If you are still in a bad relationship, then we encourage you to read Chapter 21: Dealing with Toxic Relationships. As you read through this book, it will help you to build positive and constructive relationships, and at the same time, show you how to recognise and avoid people who could be bad for you.

Chapter 2: How to Get Your Most Compatible Date Match

The Importance of Compatibility

Having compatibility in a relationship means that a couple have similar things in common with each other. This can include sharing the same values, beliefs and interests as each other. Research studies have consistently found that having similar things in common are high factors that predict relationship success,[9][10][11] and that is why we place strong emphasis on compatibility here. Compatibility, therefore, provides a powerfully secure and natural foundation on which to build a relationship into a lifelong loving friendship.

We strongly believe that in a relationship, you can never have too much compatibility with each other, but having too little could make the relationship difficult to sustain in the longer term. Therefore, it is important for the couple to ensure they have some things they can actively do together (apart from bringing up children). Having similar interests and activities you share in together, can help to keep the love connections between you growing strong. Otherwise, a couple may simply fall out of love and drift apart without understanding why until it is too late.

Sandy and Peter were in their late 20s when they first knew each other. In fact, if you met them at the beginning of their relationship, you would think they had been close friends from childhood. They would end each other's sentences and it felt like each could almost mind read what the other was thinking. They would laugh and joke about the same things, and they seemed to hardly ever have any arguments. They also really enjoyed each other's company. On the face of it, the couple looked like a perfect match for each other, and both their friends and families commented on it as much. After two and half years of being in a relationship together, eventually, Peter plucked up the courage to ask Sandy to marry him. She immediately replied, "Yes! I thought you were never going to ask." After another year, they bought their home together and got married. But, within a year of their marriage, arguments began to surface, and Sandy became emotionally distant from Peter. He asked her, "Why are you not being as affectionate to me as before? It feels like you are either avoiding me or not wanting to get close to me for some reason?" She replied, "I just don't feel any connection with you like we had before. It feels like we have nothing really in common with each other. I think I just need some space." Peter was shocked at this, because he believed that as long as two people were in love with each other, then that would be enough to get them through anything. Sandy and Peter eventually went their own separate ways. Many relationships like Sandy and Peter's unfortunately end up exactly like this. Let's now see how compatibility could have been used to avoid this.

Compatibility is like the roots of a tree in a relationship. The roots are meant to provide anchorage and stability, to weather the storms as well as take water and nutrients into the body of the tree. The water that the roots draw from and on which the whole tree depends, is like love that flows into all areas of a relationship. The nutrients are essential because they are what is used to feed the tree. In human terms, nutrients are the same as keeping up the dynamic in the relationship. Practically speaking, this is about emotional needs being met; listening and being responsive to each other as well as showing gratitude and appreciation for each other. The branches of the tree are what is needed to hang the leaves and the fruit from. When you see new branches emerging it is evidence that the tree is flourishing, and the same likewise, the relationship is growing and flourishing. When you see a tree with no leaves, it is because either the windy storm season has come and the old leaves have fallen off or it is a near dead tree. In relationship terms, no leaves and no fruit, may indicate that the relationship has run dry, because the roots of the tree were too shallow to access the needed water much lower in the soil. Also deeper roots will enable the tree to survive through the stormy seasons and resist being blown over. When a couple is actively engaged in the same hobbies and interests or involved in cultural and other community activities together, they put compatibility into action and show that the relationship, like a tree, is strengthened by its deep roots. Compatibility, therefore, provides good ground for a couple to grow deeper in their relationship together.

Areas of Compatibility

There are many areas in which couples may be compatible with each other. Below, we have outlined ten, which we feel are important for you to consider. Our list, as well as the comments under each of them is not meant to be exhaustive, but simply to provide a guide for you. It is not important for you to relate with every compatibility area mentioned. Just for you to be aware that the more compatibility areas you do share with your partner, the stronger the relationship is likely to be later on in your marriage.

1. Social Compatibility

Social compatibility is an umbrella term, and can be defined here as when two people enjoy participating in the same activities together. This could be:

- Enjoy going to a pub or restaurant or party or attending family or other gatherings together.
- Participating in sports, social and recreational activities together.
- Learning a new hobby or educational activity together.
- Getting involved together in community charity work, such as volunteering at a local food bank, night shelter, hospice, a museum or other places of interest.
- Engaging in political, community activism or conservation work together.
- Regularly participating in cultural, religious or other community activities together.

2. Personality Compatibility

Our personality is made up of many habits that are connected to our behaviours, and these can affect whether people either warm to us or shy away from us. For example, if a person has the habit of keeping their home constantly clean and tidy, this will be attractive to almost everyone. But what if the person they are dating isn't as conscientious. Is this likely to end up being a deal breaker for the tidy person? Also, if a partner always leaves the dishes to dry naturally instead of drying them immediately after they have been washed, or a partner always squeezes the toothpaste tube from the middle, would either of these be very annoying to you? Everyone has a mixture of good and bad habits. Some bad habits or behaviours in your partner may annoy you, but would not be enough to break off the relationship. However, some people may regard some habits or behaviours as deal breakers. It may be worthwhile to discuss or even negotiate with a

Chapter 2: How to Get Your Most Compatible Date Match

partner to see if change is possible. Other types of habits and behaviours can be destructive, such as addictions or if a partner is abusive.

If a person has a warm, friendly, open, agreeable and considerate personality, with a positive and hopeful outlook on life, this will make others feel safe and welcomed around them. If a person is seen as being generous, kind and charitable with their money and resources, that personality will endear people naturally to them. By contrast, if a partner's personality comes across as being negative, pessimistic or depressive, it can put a heavy dampener on a relationship. In the same way, if a man comes across as being stingy or tight with his money or has an unstable work record or has children from different women or has an emotionally unstable personality, any of these could be reasonably interpreted by a lady that he will not be a reliable future contributor and provider. If a person comes across as being rude, or selfish, or controlling or abusive or angers easily, any of these behaviours are unacceptable and will make a partner feel unsafe around them. If you or someone you care about is involved in a toxic relationship, please see chapter 21, for more information.

Everyone potentially has positive and negative aspects in their personality. The key is to ensure that your positivity radiates while any negative aspects are kept under control and in time replaced by positive ones. This is why we strongly advocate in this book that for a happy marriage, both partners should be reasonably positive and hopeful in their personality, as well as having the ability to show love, kindness, empathy and understanding for each other's feelings.

3. Introvert & Extrovert Compatibility

Being either an introvert or extrovert is also a personality compatibility trait. However, we felt it would be more helpful to our readers to treat this as a separate compatibility area. An introvert is a person who is generally shy at public and social events or will try to avoid them altogether. They generally prefer to socially interact with people they know very well, such as family and close friends. On the other hand, extroverts are generally socially confident and can easily interact with strangers in public, or at social events, or any other type of gatherings.

Having one partner that is an introvert and the other an extrovert, is very common in relationships. For many relationships this does not present as a problem, but not always. For example, some people seem to naturally appear to be the life and soul of the party, or can, as the expression goes, "work a room", meaning they can interact and talk to almost anyone. By contrast, some people are more reserved and would rather sit quietly and away from the glare of others at a social event, or even simply prefer to stay at home. If an extrovert partner is content to attend social functions alone and their introvert partner is happy with this, or, if the introvert partner is happy to go along to functions and events but would rather prefer to blend into the background and the extrovert partner is also happy with this, then all is fine. This probably reflects the attitude of many spouses in their marriages, especially when one of the spouses also has a high public profile to maintain, like a performer, politician or a sports personality. However, if an extrovert partner feels they need their introvert partner to be present or actively involved at most social gatherings, and their introvert partner is either unwilling or does not feel comfortable with this, it could suggest the relationship is incompatible. Stephen and Ebun would describe themselves as both introvert and extrovert. We value our own company and we value doing things socially, either together or separately with others, but overall, we are probably more extrovert.

4. Educational Compatibility

This compatibility area is often defined by educational attainment or subtly by class status to do with which type of school a person attended. People who are educated at an independent fee paying school are more likely to have greater access to economic advantages and opportunities than those that go through a normal government state school system. They are also more likely to be attracted to others who share a similar socioeconomic background to themselves. This may ultimately affect their preferences in terms of who they feel they would be most compatible with. Similarly, those who either have a university degree or a professional qualification are more likely to feel compatible with each other. University degree holders may start their working life with lower pay in the same way as non-degree holders, but in 10 years they generally achieve better salary outcomes through greater career opportunities and promotions.

Compatibility based on degree level education presents an interesting problem for ladies. In the UK, university students are made up of around 56% women and 44% men.[12] Interestingly, by comparison, the sex gap in American universities is even greater: 60% women and 40% men.[13] To mitigate this, female university degree holders looking for love may need to broaden their search by putting greater weight on other compatibility areas rather than demanding that a male suitor must also have a degree. For example: social, economic or religious compatibility. Also, as an alternative to having a degree, an acceptable male suitor could be someone who works in a professional trade or runs their own successful business.

Jane's story illustrates various features that combine social and educational compatibility areas. She is a digital marketing sales executive and met her husband Mark, a sales director for a very large company, at a golf club. Jane grew up in a socially deprived inner city housing estate, and received a state school education before progressing on to graduating at university. As her career progressed, she eventually moved to a quieter and more up and coming part of town. Jane originally decided to give golf a try after watching the highlights of a championship tournament on

TV. She thought it would be fun and good for exercise because it involves a fair bit of walking to fully go round the whole course and also requires some skill to play as well. She eventually found a golf club that she liked and was only an hour's drive away from home. After a few lessons, she found she really enjoyed the experience and decided to join. The membership fees at the club was not the cheapest around but did have a larger membership base than most. After sometime, Mark, who was also a member, noticed her and introduced himself. He also went to university, but had a private school education background with a polished accent to match. Nonetheless, he became attracted by her appearance, well-spoken manner, smile, and lively personality, which he thought was her most adoring feature. After two years of dating each other, they got married.

5. Economic Compatibility

The expression "bring to the table" is often used informally in negotiations to look at what benefits or financial value, each side will contribute to make sure a deal happens. In terms of economic compatibility, "bring to the table", could be an apt description about the earning potential or access to financial resources and wealth that each person can bring to a new relationship. For example, ladies may be interested to know the potential financial worth of a man as a provider and protector for her and any children that may come about from a marriage union.[14] Although, these days, it is very common for wives to be co-breadwinners with their husbands, so that household finances can remain as healthy as possible. Nonetheless, wives expect husbands to be achievers in the workplace so that their earnings will increase in line with the demands of a growing family. The alternative could be financial hardship, which can place an immense emotional strain on marriages. In some cases, a lady may earn more than her man. This should not be a problem because they both will be working as a team towards the same goals. Irrespective of who earns more in the relationship, practical discussions will need to take place when making decisions concerning household finances. For more information and advice on the topic of managing finances, please see Chapter 17: Let's Talk About MONEY.

Below are some examples of how economic compatibility can have a role to play in mate selection.

- David, a young man who is completing a trade apprenticeship, plans eventually to be a self-employed contractor. He also hopes one day to set up his own business that will have other contractors working for him. He is looking for a lady who also has similar goals and aspirations. This is because he wants to get a mortgage at some point to buy his own home. However, he knows that his earning power alone will not be enough, at least in the shorter to medium term, until his business, which he plans to start in a few years will be successful.
- Janice, a working professional is looking for similar, so that they will be able to put their joint financial income and resources together to make it easier to create wealth and provide for children they have in the future.
- Rachel, who has been running a successful business for the past three years, is looking for a relationship that can lead to marriage. She is looking for someone who is ideally at least currently holding a management position or is also successful in business like herself.
- Rita, a 21 year old recent university graduate, would ideally like to be married in her early twenties because she is hoping to have children while she is still young. She is looking for a man of a similar age, who can demonstrate he has a promising career ahead of him. For this to be a reality, she accepts that she will have to be a working mother and co-breadwinner with her future husband.
- Richard, a retired older man is looking to settle down again, having gone through divorce some years before. He

already has grown up children and does not want to start a family all over again. He is concerned that getting married again does not endanger the inheritance he wishes to leave to his children. Therefore, he feels that the ideal lady for him will already have her own source of income (either pension or still working). He does not mind if she already has children of her own. Therefore, to facilitate what he is hoping to achieve in a new marriage, a prospective spouse would also have to agree to a prenuptial agreement.

- Paul, is a student who lacks financial ability right now, because of his full time studies. However, this is likely to change as soon as he graduates and begins his career. He says, "I will then be actively seeking career advancement opportunities to earn more". He is hoping he will meet a young lady who is also a student with high-flying career ambitions.

Other considerations to factor into economic compatibility of a prospective partner are things like debts or any spousal and child maintenance payments that are made as a result of a previous relationship. These outgoing expenditures may be seen as taking away essential resources from a new relationship, and could therefore be looked upon as possible deal breakers by some.

Men: From reading the above, you may feel a bit overwhelmed with some of the things mentioned. However, if you think about them now, then when they are brought up as part of a discussion in a new relationship you will at least already have had time to give some thought about what you are going to say. The reality is that one of the reasons for divorce is if a husband is not able to hold onto sustained work and income or does not want to advance their earning potential (for example, by avoiding promotion and taking on extra responsibilities at work or do further education and training to increase their chances of career advancement and higher earning potential). We strongly recommend men make a 3,

5 and 10 year plan of where they see themselves over that time. Then work out a pathway of numbered steps showing how you intend to reach and fulfil your goals. Although, already married, this is something that Stephen regularly does with Ebun, because it demonstrates leadership, aids future planning, and also gives vision, direction and purpose of what they both ideally would like to achieve in 3, 5 and 10 years' time. In other words, for marriage, every man needs a plan. What's yours?

6. Religious Compatibility

Religion plays an important role in many people's life. If it plays an important part in yours, then we strongly advocate that you find someone who equally shares the same religious beliefs and values you do. This is because religious beliefs often impact many areas of a married couple's life. This can include: family worship, rituals and practices; raising children in a particular faith; celebrating religious cultural festivals; and rites of passage ceremonies such as celebration of a birth, coming of age, marriage, and death. Many potential daters will not consider marrying someone who is not of the same faith as they are. This is for a good reason because, for many people, their faith has a deep and significant meaning to them. If a person is married to someone who does not share their religious beliefs this is very likely at some point to cause major strains and tensions in the relationship. This can be especially so, when trying to decide which faith and values a child should be brought up in. Also, if both spouses do not place an importance on their religious faith before marriage, but one of them later on becomes devout and serious about their beliefs, this too will inevitably present serious conflicts and tensions in the relationship. These issues should be discussed and agreed before marriage, in order to avoid potential problems later on. Research has found that those couples who regularly attend the same place of worship, are more likely to be happier with their marriage.[15] Please see our bonus chapter on Faith & Beliefs, for further information if this is a key area of compatibility for you.

7. Cultural Compatibility

This encompasses quite a broad range of things, such as following and adhering to:
- Particular cultural and religious festivals and event days.
- Cultural social and moral norms and values.
- Traditions and customs.

Cultural compatibility in a relationship is therefore about a couple together participating in the same cultural and religious traditions, customs and practices, because these have significant meaning to them both. If you are interested in beginning a relationship with someone who is from either a different race or ethnicity to yourself, it is worth doing your research to better understand their cultural heritage, values and beliefs. Because the more you know and understand, the more you will come across as being respectful and understanding. Our bonus chapter on Interracial & Interethnic Relationships, discusses this area in more detail.

8. Intellectual Compatibility

Intellectual compatibility is where a couple enjoy sharing and engaging with each other on similar informed topics of interest. However, this does not have to be academic, such as having a mutual interest in science research, but usually means that they may have a keener and deeper interest in finding out more background information behind daily news stories and current events on TV. Couples with intellectual compatibility also generally have similar world views and opinions on politics, current affairs, climate change, etc., and like to talk about them and usually are ready to share their opinions with others as well. If there is no compatibility on views and opinions (particularly religious or political ones), then there's likely to be a high occurrence of very hot headed debates around the dinner table!

9. Political Compatibility

It has become clear to almost everyone that since the world financial crash of 2008, the world has become a significantly more politically polarised place. There is a huge range of polarising positions and opinions, such as:
- Covid-19, and whether vaccinations and mask-wearing was justified.
- In the US, the right for citizens to own and bear firearms.
- Political oppression and human rights violations around the world.
- The Black Lives Matter movement, and "taking the knee" at sporting fixtures to highlight racism.
- Whether reparations are owed because of the transatlantic slave trade.
- The topic of immigration.
- Climate change and the world's huge economic dependency on fossil fuels.
- Brexit – the continuing debate on whether or not is was good for the UK to leave the European Union.

Feelings can also run high on political party affiliations. For example, in the UK and the US, there is mostly a two main political party system: in the UK, the two main parties are Conservative and Labour; in the US, the two main parties are Republican and Democrat. Even our political leaders seem to have a polarising effect on people. Along with these are a whole range of minor political parties. Many of which are single issue based. In the UK, for example, there is also the Scottish National Party, which is currently the third largest party in the UK Parliament. They advocate their strong desire that Scotland should leave the United Kingdom. The family dinner table in some households is no longer as calm as it used to be, with families split down the middle over one political opinion against another. Obviously, politics is something for daters to navigate for themselves, but we advise that you use a lot of graciousness, kindness and show some respect for the opinions of others, and focus more on what unites rather than what divides.

10. Future Plans

This is about having a similar vision of where a couple see themselves in the next 3, 5 or 10 years' time. For example, some people never see themselves either ever getting married or having children. Others may see themselves moving abroad or wanting to travel the world in the next 2 or 3 years. Could any of these be a problem if one of the daters were hoping to be married by then? Discussing early on in the dating period about future plans and the timelines that go along with them is a useful way to sound out whether the other dater's plans are compatible with your own. Many dating coaches sound caution about bringing out the 'marriage' word too early on in the dating stage. This makes sense, because it can make a person come across as being too emotionally needy or desperate. The way to tackle this is to say something like, "I am looking for someone who is kind, considerate and loving to grow a relationship with, and see where this goes from there."

Other things to take into account when considering future plans:
- If one or both of you are currently a student consider how after graduating, career progression and salary expectations may impact on your future life plans and the timelines to achieve them. Do these plans and ambitions sound realistic? If one of you is looking at doing a full time course of study or training in the near future, how would this economically impact the relationship or marriage (if by then you were married)? It is worth noting here, that many graduates start their careers near the bottom of a company's career progression ladder. However, in time, with a combination of ambition and job progression,

Chapter 2: How to Get Your Most Compatible Date Match   41

higher earnings are achieved.[16] As career progression is made a person will also acquire transferable skills that will potentially lead to job promotions and higher salaries being achieved. As their career advances, they also do not necessarily have to stay in just one sector of the job market. Salary figures from the UK Department for Education show that, graduates earn £10,000 more per year than those who don't go to university, and also have higher employment rates.[17] We are stating all these because we believe, even if a person is currently at university, they can still make viable future plans linked with reasonable expectations of what they hope to realistically earn in the future.

- If one or both of you are required to travel away for working commitments over the next few years, could the relationship or marriage cope?
- If you are in a long distance relationship with someone abroad, are the timelines for developing a meaningful relationship towards marriage realistic for you? If your partner is abroad, are you both able to satisfy the spouse settlement visa requirements for them to join you? Please see Chapter 10: Long Distance Relationships, for more information on this.

What of Sexual Compatibility?

Although many may feel that sexual performance should be treated as an area of compatibility, we have our reservations. So called, sexual compatibility may apply to those seeking short-term casual relationships, but it cannot apply to those seeking marriage. Although we absolutely believe that the enjoyment of sex in marriage is vitally important and also needs to be satisfying for both spouses. It should also be recognised that as we get older, our bodies go through changes where interest in sex may diminish or performance issues because of health problems may also arise.

The point we are trying to bring out here is that marriage has got to be so much more than having sex, or indeed, rating how well two lovers perform. The marriage contract you will enter into has an assumed undertaking within it that both of you will remain sexually exclusive to each other for as long as you both shall live. When one spouse dies, the other is only then free of their legal and moral obligations, and can then choose to marry someone else. The reason why we are emphasising these things is because this book's focus is about dating, getting married and staying married. Sex ultimately plays a huge role in this, and why give plenty of room to discuss the subject throughout this book.

You may be young, fit and healthy and probably think there is no reason why you cannot have a sexually active life into your 70s or 80s, and some people do. However, this is not always the case, and we deal with that in greater detail in Chapter 20: Sexuality & Fertility, and also in the bonus chapter, Dating and Over 50s. After reading those chapters we would ask you to reflect on how much sex really is important to you as a compatibility area. Or, whether it is more important for you to have a fulfilled happy married life, of which sex can be an integral part. In the Bible, sex is treated as a moral right and duty in marriage for both wife and husband. That is, neither spouse should deny sexual access of their body to the other (1 Corinthians 7:2-5). However, there is no licence for rape in marriage, under any circumstances, only mutual consent. Anything in marriage that is not done with mutual consent will be a disaster for the marriage, and eventually lead to its inevitable failure.

What Happens If There Is No Compatibility?

Can a relationship still work even if a couple seem to have not much in common with each other? Yes, but only a slight yes. Just because we are all different and unique to each other does not mean we cannot get along. However, in a marriage, for the relationship to be long lasting and have a chance of experiencing happiness, then they would be strongly advised to find regular activities (beyond raising children) that they can do together. If a couple do not ensure they have enough things in common at the beginning of their relationship, then over time strains will appear and they are highly likely to grow apart. The takeaway here is that there should be enough regular activities and interests that you both have in common on which to build your companionship. This cannot be treated as an option. This is why, if you want your relationship to work and experience the best possible chance of happiness, you need to find common interests that both enjoy and can do together.

Complementary Relationships

It is not in everything that a couple will have similar things in common. Sometimes, opposites do attract, and bring a positive benefit to the relationship. For example, if you put two magnets together, the North Pole end of one magnet will pull and stick to the South Pole end of the other. The magnetic power of both magnets together will be stronger. Another analogy we could use is a 'team'. When a team is made up of a group of individuals with a range of talents and skills the team will be stronger and more effective. Simple examples of how a couple can complement each other in a relationship are:

- One partner is more practical minded. For example, they may enjoy or be good at painting and decorating or fixing and constructing things. The other partner may be more intellectually driven. For example, good at numeracy and bookkeeping or problem solving, or maybe good at thinking ahead and making plans, such as saving and investing for the future. However, the reality is that people are more likely to be a combination of any of these.
- One partner may be good at saving money, and the other likes to enjoy expensive holidays. Could this couple come

up with an agreement that will satisfy both of them?
- One likes to drive and the other doesn't (or cannot). Maybe this is not a problem in your relationship right now, but could it one day? If so, is there a plan to deal with this?

A red flag to watch out for is when two people appear to have an opposite kind of personality to each other. For example, one person has a cheerful and upbeat attitude on life, and the other is negative and critical about people and things. Another opposite kind of negative relationship could be if someone has low confidence and a low sense of self-worth, they can unwittingly attract a confident but abusive and controlling partner. Whether a person feels they are naturally optimistic or can be a bit pessimistic at times, we say that an essential ingredient for a successful happy marriage is a combination of where both partners have a reasonable amount of positivity and hopefulness in their attitudes towards life. Reasonable being more than 51%, but not excessive. An overly optimistic person can come across as being unrealistic in their goals and aspirations.

Making a Needs Wish List

Now that we have explored a broad range of compatibility areas (some of which may apply to you), let's take a moment to look at what you would like in an ideal life partner. These are the kind of things that would make them compatible with you. Take a pen and paper and write on it the things that are important for you to see in a prospective partner. This is your 'Needs Wish List'. Making a list like this could be useful, especially if you have had experience of bad relationships in the past, and want to avoid them in the future. The list may also be useful to you if you would like to try online dating. For more information on online dating, please see Chapter 9. To get you started, here is a list of things that may or may not be important to you to see in a desirable partner. Borrow from it and add your own.

In my Needs Wish List, my ideal partner will:
- Always/sometimes like to go to parties and other gatherings with me.
- Drink/smoke or not mind if I drink/smoke.
- Like to travel and explore different places abroad.
- Like playing board games.
- Be into soccer or other sport.
- Have the same faith and values as me or faith is not important to me.
- Be a meat eater/vegetarian/vegan or doesn't matter.
- Like to be spontaneous or plan ahead of time.
- Want to have children or get on well with children.
- Love pets.
- Be interested in current affairs, such as the news and documentaries.
- Love going out to the movies/theatre or prefer to stay in for a movie night together.
- Be educated to at least degree level or not relevant.
- Be into fitness or regular exercise or not at all.

Having made your Needs Wish List, now put a 'C' for compulsory against any that must be in the relationship. Everybody's Needs Wish List will be different.

Try turning your list into some sentences. For example:
- "Must/Ideally be a non-smoker/drinker."
- "I am looking for someone who is also a practising Christian/Muslim/..."
- "I am a vegan vegetarian, and would like to date the same."
- "Is a tidy person."
- "I am interested in keeping fit, going running, and doing

weight training. Hoping you are the same."
- "I like to cook, I hope you do as well."

Make sure your list is put in positive language and you review it frequently. It is important to be realistic with your expectations. It is also very useful to find a friend who knows you reasonably well and whose judgment you trust to go through your list. Also, doing a Needs Wish List is a great way to work out if your needs are unrealistic or do not go far enough. If you are doing this exercise for online dating, not everything you are writing down may need to go into your online profile. However, it is a helpful guide for you to know what kind of person you may be looking for.

Chapter 3: Differences Between The Sexes

In this chapter, we will be taking a look at the biological differences between men and women. As you will see in Chapter 4: Men Chase & Women Challenge, and indeed, the rest of the book, these differences affect the way men and women communicate, behave and emotionally interact with each other. Although it may seem that the information we have presented here is a lot, the reality is that science is still, in many ways, only at the beginning. No one actually doubts that some differences do exist between the biological sexes, but determining exactly how much and how far these differences go is still a work in progress. In this chapter, we start at the beginning of a human life. Where our sex is determined as part of the written code at the point of conception. We then move onto how male and female brains work slightly differently (but not smarter) in the way that information is processed. We also briefly discuss how the main sex hormones, testosterone and estrogen, affect our bodily functions and behaviour. Also, we will look at the differences in the way that each sex normatively communicates, and how our sex seems to influence the subjects that we choose to study at school, and later in college and university, and then how this translates into the type of occupation pathways that men and women may choose. This is very interesting stuff and worth reading. We end this chapter discussing the differences in the sexes with humour and dating, and how men and women make decisions.

Chromosomal Differences

Let's begin by first taking a look at human sex differences from the time when a new human life is conceived. Humans normally have 23 pairs of chromosomes in each cell. That is, 46 chromosomes altogether. One of those pairs separates the sexes. In males, this pair is XY chromosomes, and in females, this pair is XX chromosomes. Our bodies each contain billions of cells. Each cell contains more than 20,000 genes in them. Our genes, besides many other things, are what make us look slightly different from one human being to another. For example, the colour of our eyes and hair, and our height. The only human cells that do not contain 23 pairs of chromosomes are reproductive cells. This means that instead of 46 chromosomes, the female egg will have 23 chromosomes and the male sperm will have 23 chromosomes. The female egg also has the X chromosome, and each male sperm individually may have either the X or Y chromosome. At the point of conception, when a sperm enters the egg and combines, it is the chromosome of the sperm that determines the sex of the new human.[18] At conception, the egg and the sperm unite to become a single embryo cell containing the normal 23 pairs of chromosomes, before splitting and continuously splitting again. After the chromosomal sex differences are in place at conception to make a new embryo, the respective biological sex male (XY) and female (XX) genome codes is already determined and provides the sole source of all subsequent sex differences during development in the womb and later from baby child into adulthood.[19] Irrespective of the sex of the embryo, up to around 6 weeks into the gestation period, it will develop along the lines of female genomes. Then around the 6th to 7th week of gestation, if it is a boy, a gene on the Y chromosome will induce changes that

Chapter 3: Differences Between The Sexes   49

causes the development of the testes. By the 9th week of gestation, production of testosterone begins and results in the development of the reproductive system and masculinization – the normal development of male sex characteristics – of the genitalia and the brain. By contrast, development of female sex characteristics will automatically follow its own normal path in the absence of a male Y chromosome.[20] Sometimes abnormalities can occur due to an abnormal mixture of sex chromosomes, but this is unusual.[21] [22] There are considerable overlap between the two sexes, with a suggested 95% of similarities between the genomes of males and females.

The average man is taller, larger in size and physically stronger by comparison to the average woman. Women on average have brains that are 11% smaller than men's in proportion to their body size.[23] However, a woman's hippocampus (curved-shaped structure in the temporal lobe of the brain), critical for learning and memorization, is larger than a man's.[24] Women have periods and can get pregnant, and on average live longer than men. However, they also lose their reproductive ability earlier than men. Men and women are also quite different to each other in terms of how they interact with the world around them. Research has consistently shown that men are greater risk takers, especially when women they perceive as being attractive are involved.[25] They also are more likely to exaggerate their feats and accomplishments in the workplace, which along with their inflated sense of self-importance and self-worth often manifests in causing them to be more successful in negotiating and demanding consistently higher pay rises and promotions than women.[26] [27] Ebun, already aware of this phenomenon through her MBA studies, has used this knowledge to pitch herself successfully at interviews for a higher pay band than what was originally on offer.

Brains of Each Sex Process Information Differently

Despite science research going back more than 150 years trying to prove sex differences in human brains, it turns out there is not much difference between them at all. They are effectively the same. However, researchers at the University of Pennsylvania scanned the brains of nearly 1,000 men, women and boys and girls. They found striking differences in how men and women's brains are connected and may also explain how the sexes approach tasks differently.

Male Brain

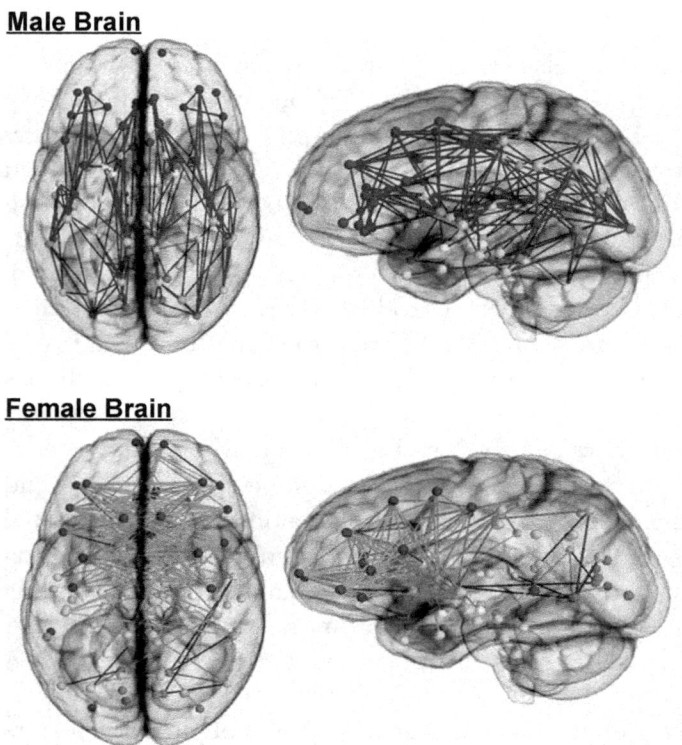

Female Brain

Images used with Permission. Credit: Ragini Verma, PhD, Professor of Radiology, Professor of Neurosurgery, Penn Medicine, University of Pennsylvania.[28]

Male brains are wired front to back, with fewer connections bridging the two hemispheres. But in females, the pathways criss-cross between left and right.[29] In practical terms, what this means is that men and women use both sides of their brains, just differently. These differences, also speculatively reinforce an already widely held perception. That is, men are single task focused, and women are more equipped to handle multitasking. While most people, including ourselves, may not have any doubts about this, there is currently no scientific evidence to back this up.

Regardless of sex, for most people, the left brain hemisphere controls language and speech, and the right brain hemisphere regulates emotions, facial recognition, non-verbal cues and tones and intonations in voice, and visuospatial processing.[30] [31] Also, the left hemisphere looks after the right side of the body's motor skills and the right hemisphere looks after the left side of the body's motor skills. However, it is also worth noting that no part of the human brain works alone, but is very much a multi-tasking computer machine that utilises both hemispheres in everything it does for us. For example, our creative thought processes use a widespread whole-brain network, not simply right or left hemisphere.[32] Similarly, solving mathematical problems uses both hemispheres of the brain.[33] This should not be a surprise, because to solve maths problems can require a combination of creative and logic skills.

Sex Hormones

Normally, the biological sex will determine which sex steroid hormone is dominant in either a man or a woman. For women this will be estrogen and for men this will be testosterone. However, both men and women have testosterone and estrogen, and both play a part for normal bodily and sexual functioning in both sexes. Men have around 15 times more testosterone in them than women.[34] The true figure can vary from one individual to another and also the time of day the sample for analysis is taken. For example, testosterone levels in men peak at around 8 am and then lower throughout the day till around 8 pm in the evening. Then testosterone levels climb during the night.[35] Testosterone regulates sex drive (libido), and is also responsible for bone mass, muscle mass and strength, and the production of sperm in men. Some of the testosterone that the body produces is converted to estrogen (estradiol).[36] Testosterone also affects a range of behavioural attributes, such as aggressiveness, competitiveness, status-seeking and social hierarchy, and willingness to take risks, as well as primary actions such as sex drive and being motivated by sexual attraction.[37][38][39]

Women produce the majority of their estrogen from their ovaries. Testing for accurate estrogen levels in women is not as straightforward as testing for testosterone levels in either sex. This is because there are three main types of estrogen, and the level will be dependent upon a woman's stage in life:
- Estrone is the primary form of estrogen after menopause.
- Estradiol is the strongest and primary form of estrogen in a woman's body during her reproductive years.
- Estriol is the primary form of estrogen during pregnancy.

Factors that can cause fluctuations and affect accuracy in readings of estrogen in premenopausal women are:
- The day on which a woman is tested in her monthly cycle as she draws near to or away from her ovulation date.
- If she is taking medications that contain a synthesised form of estrogen, such as the contraceptive pill or if she is on hormone replacement therapy.[40]

As a guide, premenopausal women (dependent upon their monthly cycle) have approximately 6-10 times more estrogen (estradiol) than men."[41][42][43][44]

Estrogen (estradial) has important health effects on skin, blood vessels, bone, muscle, coagulation, hepatic cells, adipose tissue, the kidneys, the gastrointestinal tract, brain, lung, and pancreas in both sexes.[45] Estrogen also profoundly affects memory, emotions, mood, mental state, and neurodevelopment. Neurodevelopment is a term used for how a brain will develop neurological pathways that influence performance or function. For example: social skills, intellectual functioning, reading ability, speech, coordination, attention and focus skills, etc.[46] Estrogen in men, regulates erectile responses. If the level of estrogen in men is too high or testosterone is too low, it can lead to erectile dysfunction.[47] If the estrogen level is too low in a premenopausal woman, then this can lead to vaginal dryness, mood and irritability, headaches, and hot flushes, and other common overlapping symptoms of a woman going through the menopause.

Neither estrogen nor testosterone work in isolation, but rather work in combination with a whole range of other hormones that interact with instructions throughout the brain, central nervous system and the body.

Gender Differences – Communication & Behaviour

Gender is defined by the World Health Organisation as follows:

> "Gender refers to the characteristics of women, men, girls and boys that are socially constructed. This includes norms, behaviours and roles associated with being a woman, man, girl or boy, as well as relationships with each other."[48]

Gender works differently to biological sex because it refers to normative behaviours and characteristics a society or culture anticipates to see in their males in terms of their masculinity and females in terms of their femininity. There are already many decades of research that has been carried out to describe what is regarded as either feminine or masculine communication styles. Even before the expert sociolinguist professor, Deborah Tannen in 1990 wrote her international bestselling book, *You Just Don't Understand – Women and Men in Conversation*, research studies have consistently presented a picture of the kind of communication style and behaviours that are normally expected from the two sexes.

Features of Normatively "Feminine" and "Masculine" Communication Styles

Feminine	*Masculine*
Indirectness	Directness
Facilitative	Competitive
Collaborative	Autonomous
Collegial	Confrontational
Collective sharing	One-upmanship
Talks less	Talks more
Supportive simultaneous talk	Topic changing
Supportive feedback	Disruptive interruptions
Person/process orientated	Task/outcome orientated
Relational practice	Referential practice
Status equalising	Status enhancing
Affiliative	Assertive

Table used with Permission. Credit: Susan S. Case, PhD, Assoc. Professor of Organizational Behavior, Assoc. Professor of Women and Gender Studies, Assoc. Professor Social Justice Institute, Weatherhead School of Management, Case Western Reserve University.[49]

From research carried out by Professor Susan S. Case of Case Western Reserve University, and as exemplified from her research in the table above, feminine style used by most women was found in 87% of communication observed, and masculine style in men was observed in 75% of their communication. The remainder in

Chapter 3: Differences Between The Sexes 55

both groups would use what she calls a Wide Verbal Repertoire discourse style, that is, a mixture of the two styles.[50] With regard to which of the sexes talk the most, this is widely contested. However, Professor Deborah Tannen of Georgetown University in Washington, D.C., in a 2017, *Time* article, states that women friends talk far more than men privately, but men talk far more than women in public forums, especially in meetings. Tannen, also states that women can find themselves, in what she describes as a double bind. If women talk in a way that is associated with authority then this risks them being perceived as aggressive, and subject to damning labels. If they hold back from talking then they risk being underestimated.[51] We discuss this phenomenon in more detail in Chapter 4, under the section, Gender Traits.

Nature Interacts With Nurture

It is hard to say how much of our normative behaviours and characteristics are influenced by:
- Hormones prenatally (before birth).
- Our hormones affecting our behaviour as we proactively and reactively respond to our environment.
- The gender expectations of the society and culture we were raised up in.
- Social, cultural, and religious norms, values, and traditions.

This complexity of what influences our personality and behaviour is often reflected in the so-called controversial debate of 'nature versus nurture'. However, we think that a healthier way of looking at this is from the perspective of how nature interacts with nurture (or environment). In other words, our biological sex intrinsically plays a key part in how our masculine or feminine behaviour interacts with the world around us. Professor Simon Baron-Cohen, author of, *The Essential Difference*, exemplifies this nature first position by referencing three studies conducted in his lab at Cambridge University.[52] The purpose of the studies was to determine, using one year olds and new born babies as subjects, which sex made longer eye contact with a human face. In the first study, one year old girls looked significantly more often at their parent's face than did boys.[53] In the second study, one year old girls and boys were shown short video clips, each comprising of either human faces or cars. The girls looked significantly longer at the faces and the boys looked significantly longer at the cars.[54] In the third study, involving new born babies in the Rosie Maternity Hospital in Cambridge, and who could not yet have been influenced by social and cultural factors, were tested to see if there was a difference between the sexes in looking time at a woman's smiling face (also known as a social object for the purpose of the experiment) and a 'mobile' (physical-mechanical looking object). The mobile consisted of a ball the size of a head with rearranged face-like features and material hanging from it to make it more mechanical looking. The results showed that the girl babies looked longer at the face and the boy babies looked longer at the mobile.[55] Professor Baron-Cohen, in his concluding remarks to these studies, states: "This difference at birth echoes a pattern we have seen right across the human lifespan. For example, on average, women engage in more 'consistent' social smiling and 'maintained' eye contact than does the average man. The fact that this difference is present at birth strongly suggests that biology plays a role."[56]

Our behaviours may at times be accompanied by our expressions of emotions and feelings. The basic universal emotions in all humans are: fear, anger, happiness or joy, sadness, surprise, and shame (which can be split into either guilt or disgust).[57] It is arguable that probably all other mammals (to varying degrees) have these as well. As a point of interest, love is not an emotion and has no facial expression, but is a state of being that encompasses all basic emotions.[58] How a person expresses their emotions and behaviours can reveal their character as a person to others.

Sex Differences in Academic & Work Preferences

Males and females are both equally intelligent; one is not more intelligent than the other. But their interests in which academic subjects to learn and occupations they choose to do are often different to each other. Let's start by comparing academic preferences between the sexes. In the UK, the vast majority of A Level and BTEC Extended Diploma subjects are studied by 16-18 year olds at sixth form colleges. Approximately 75% of UK A level students who choose computer science, physics, further maths, design & technology and economics are male, and approximately 75% of students who choose the arts – notably English literature, art and design, psychology and sociology are female.[59] However, both male and female students do equally well in these subjects at both GCSE and A level.[60][61] Choices in which A Level and BTEC Extended Diplomas to take are likely to influence a male or female student's choice of which undergraduate university course they do, as well as occupation choices after this. However, the choices that influence which A Level or BTEC subjects that are chosen at 16 years of age are likely to be influenced by the option GCSE subjects that are chosen when a male or female secondary school student is 14 years old. The culmination of these choices often lead to many courses at universities being dominated by one sex more than the other. For example, in subjects like physical and mathematical sciences these will consistently attract 40% enrolment among women, but in courses such as engineering and technology, and computer science this figure drops to 15%.[62] By contrast, male undergraduate enrolment on psychology courses is 21%,[63] adult nursing is 8% and mental health nursing is 23%.[64]

There is another fascinating fact that these preference choices bring out. The career guidance researcher, Dale J Prediger, in 1982 published his research work that grouped occupations according to the tasks in them into either person-centred or things-centred category type occupations.[65] Person-centred occupations are ones that either have direct interactions with people or directly impact on people such as psychologists, nursing, social work and teaching. On the other hand, things-centred occupations may involve mechanics, engineering, physics, electrical, technical, construction, technology, etc.[66][67] Later studies by American researchers Rong Su, James Rounds and Patrick Armstrong, built on Prediger's study to come up with two conclusive findings:

1. Person-centred occupations were found to be mainly done by women and things-centred occupations were mainly done by men, and
2. Also, these two categories where mainly driven by interests (preferences and choices) that were trait-like; innate in the character and personality of a person according to their respective sex.[68][69]

These feminine type person-centred and masculine type things-centred differences are also reflected consistently in research studies that show women generally do better than men at verbal fluency and recognition of facial emotional expression, and men generally do better than women at visuospatial abilities and navigation tasks.[70][71][72][73] Some of our readers may not be surprised by many of the above facts and figures, but together, they show that choice of academic subjects and careers commonly and consistently reflect differences in preferences made by the different sexes.

Empathisers and Systemisers

Professor Simon Baron-Cohen, in his book, The Essential Difference, presents alternatives to the normative feminine and masculine styles, as described above. He suggests that women are more what he calls, 'Empathisers' and men are more 'Systemisers'. He also emphasises that the word 'more' means not all. But rather, that men and women may be a combination of both.[74]

Baron-Cohen describes an Empathiser as someone who can spontaneously and naturally tune into another person's thoughts, feelings and emotions, and respond to them with an appropriate emotion. They are driven to care for or offer comfort to another person, even if they are not related to them. He also makes the point that an Empathiser does more listening than talking.[75] Hence the reason why probably less men are really good at it, because they talk more in public forums and interrupt more.[76] [77] Baron-Cohen describes a Systemiser as a type of person who likes to figure out how things work. They may use a process of logical deduction through trial and error to do this. Examples of this could be having an interest in vehicle mechanics, electrical systems, construction and engineering, and devising military or competitive sporting strategies. Baron-Cohen also includes maths, physics, computer science, engineering and economics as typical interests for a Systemiser type of person.[78] As discussed above, around 75% of students who choose to enrol in these subjects for their A Levels are male, and therefore could arguably, be described as Systemisers.[79]

The Role of Humour in Dating

Using humour as a way of attracting and signalling romantic interest is an understated aspect in dating and relationships. Studies have found that a man generally looks for a lady who will appreciate their jokes, and a lady generally look for a man who makes them laugh.[80] Researchers from Austria, Karl Grammer and Irenaus Eibl-Eibesfeldt published their studies on laughter and sex differences in human behaviour in 1990, and found when a man goes out on a date, he will commonly use humour as a way to find out if a lady is attractive for him. He will try to impress the lady with a few jokes and hope to get her to laugh. If she laughs slightly louder than him and he laughs as well, then it may indicate a sexual chemistry between them, and that he is interested in her. If the lady does not laugh vocally or she is glancing around then this may indicate lack of interest.[81] In over 30 years this research has never been challenged and is consistently authoritatively referenced in peer reviewed science papers to the present day.

Robert R Provine, Professor of Psychology and Neurobiology at the University of Maryland, analysed 3,745 personal dating ads in 8 American newspapers on the same day in 1996, and found that when humour was referred to, females were more likely (62% more) to mention laughter in their ads than males. Also that females were more than twice as likely to seek humour, than offer it, and males were a third more likely to offer it, than seek it. Provine's findings were conclusive: Women seek men who make them laugh, and men are eager and desirous to oblige.[82] Ten years later, in 2006, Psychologists Eric R. Bressler, from Westfield State University, Rod A. Martin, from University of Western Ontario and Sigal Balshine from McMaster University, published their research findings on the production of humour and appreciating it in dating. Although both men and women valued a good sense of humour in a relationship, it was clear that each sex interprets how humour should be used on a date differently. They found that although women like to produce and appreciate humour, when they are on a date they prefer much more to appreciate it. On the other hand, when a man is on a date with a lady, he prefers that she appreciates his humour.[83] Also, men generally have no sexual attraction for a funny lady on a date.[84] A man will therefore use humour in his mating behaviour for sexual mate attraction, and hope that the lady's response will be positive.

In summary, both men and women can be humorous and good at telling jokes. However on dates, men like to use humour to tell jokes so they can display their sexual attraction, and is therefore part of the chase for them. If a lady uses humour on a date more than the man, this could be perceived as friendship or banter type behaviour; funny but not sexually attractive in a dating sense to him. When a relationship is already established or a couple are having to deal with an external crisis or challenge, a lady may successfully use humour, especially to defuse or give welcome relief to a tense situation.[85] A takeaway point from this for humorous ladies, especially female comedians, is when going out on a date, to choose to let the man lead, including in the area of humour, or at least make sure they deliberately use it less than him, until the daters have had time to get to know each other. If a man reading this, feels that humour is not his strong point, then when out on a date, at least smile a lot, act positively and try your best to come across as having a light-hearted view on life.

Male & Female Decision Making

The way that women and men's brains are connected may help us in our understanding of how the different sexes make decisions and deal with risk. When men are in a highly competitive environment testosterone levels in them go high,[86] [87] and their single-minded focus can lead them to make riskier decisions when big rewards are in sight. Women are more likely to allow themselves more time for a more comprehensive reasoned decision to be made. This often means that women are accused of being risk adverse, but this is far from the truth. Instead, they generally prefer not to go for the bigger risks but for smaller and more dependable rewards they can count on.[88] However, the quality of decision making between the sexes is the same. This means that neither men nor women are better at making more effective decisions than the other.

The way that men make risk taking decisions is probably not easy to scientifically explain, but speculatively may be as a consequence of how males, being single focused, process information laterally in their brains (as described above). In practice, they appear to often quickly weigh up the known information against the possible risks and potential big rewards, and then 'voila', a decision is quickly made. If he makes the right call, he is considered a hero or a genius. If the decision is wrong, then the man is more likely to simply shrug his shoulders, forget about it and move on. To women who do not understand this male psyche phenomenon, they may look at this kind of decision making behaviour as nothing less than unsafe and reckless. But this is how people who work on the world's financial trading floors make their decisions every second of the day, and the funds for our pensions and investments depend on them getting it right, hopefully at least most of the time! Unfortunately, as of up to 2018, women generally only accounted for 12-15% of trading roles. However, banks have been moving towards correcting this imbalance by reaping the benefits of also having women traders.[89]

To summarise, men are not better at making decisions than women, they just appear to make faster ones, because generally, they may rely more on their experience and gut feeling and being driven by the bigger reward. Whereas women, generally, are more data driven in wanting to get all their facts in place first, including crossing the "t's and doting the "i's", before going for smaller but more certain rewards.

Dating: Men Are Hormonally Equipped to Make the First Move

With all this knowledge about how men's and women's brains are wired differently, and which sex often takes bigger risks, you might wonder how much this relates to dating. Quite a lot actually! Men are built to take the risks in initiating and making first contact. The testosterone, dopamine and Noradrenaline (US, Norepinephrine) in them drives them to do it. We discuss hormones further in Chapter 11: Let's Talk About SEX. Also, men's single focused minds are generally built to cope and shrug off rejection and disappointment significantly better than women. From an early age, boys learn how to deal with criticism, fighting, teasing and taunting with other boys in and out of school and experiencing winning and losing by playing and following sports teams. Girls are less likely to go through as many of these valuable lessons. For instance, schoolgirls are considerably more likely than schoolboys to quit competing in sports. This is a worldwide phenomenon, and is typified in research carried out by Canadian Women & Sport, in partnership with Canadian Tire Jumpstart Charities. They found that a sharp decline of girls in sport participation starts at around the age of 12, with girls more than three times as likely to drop out of sport in adolescence compared to boys. The dropout rate among adolescent boys is 1 in 10.[90] As a consequence, when these girls grow into young ladies, they are less equipped to handle rejection.[91] Whereas, boys growing into men have always been innately suited to deal with it. In the world of dating, it is the men that are built for taking all the risks in asking a lady out, because it is them that can take the rejection and shrug it off if the lady says, "No". In Chapter 4: Men Chase & Women Challenge, we will go into the reasons for this in more detail.

Chapter 4: Men Chase & Women Challenge

In this chapter, we will discuss the crucial role that gender plays in dating. You may recall, when we briefly discussed gender in Chapter 3: Differences Between the Sexes, that gender refers to characteristics and behaviours that are considered to be normative in respect to either a man or woman in a particular society or culture. Also, men and women generally have normative expectations of how they anticipate the other sex should communicate, act and behave in a relationship. Understanding how these normative gender expectations work will help you to not only present yourself in the most attractive and appealing way, but also positively influence how the other person sees and desires you. With this objective, we will explore in detail why men need to do the chasing, and why women need to put up a bit of a challenge to show the men they are worth the world to have.

Men Chase & Women Challenge

The question that we frequently get asked by ladies, "Can I ask a man out?" The answer, in simple terms is, "No". Not if a lady wants to increase her chances of getting married. We argue strongly, by using science research to prove that it should be men who do the chasing and women should play hard to get. Men value and prize what costs them a lot to get. When a man makes an approach to a lady, he accepts the risk of embarrassment he may feel if she rejects his advance. However, men tend to easily shrug off rejection, and simply move on to the next lady that catches their eye. If a lady puts up a bit of a challenge and plays hard to get, and eventually through the man's persistence he wins her over, he will remember the amount of time, effort and resources that went into capturing her heart. In short, he will know it cost him a lot to get her, and value her more for it. However, what happens if a lady sees and likes a man who seems to be a little shy to ask her out on a date or he hasn't noticed her, what then? In Chapter 6, there is a whole section dedicated to giving lots of effective and proven strategies that ladies can use to attract the attention of a potential male suitor without having to chase him.

Let's now take a look at some of the main reasons why women need to allow themselves to be a challenge to men.
1. Men are natural risk takers because of the male dominant hormone, testosterone. Testosterone is directly linked (along with dopamine) to risk taking behaviours in men.[92] Women also have testosterone, but men produce 15 times more than women.[93] This is why men are regarded as the ancestral warriors and hunters and take the risks in hunting big game, and why ancestral skeletons consistently show it was the male that would most often die as a result of war and other violent conflicts, with fatal injuries sustained to the head and chest.[94] Throughout the world, it is men more than women that are at higher risk to succumb to injuries or death as a result of accidents, falls, infections, firearms, car crashes, fires and war. Men also live shorter lives, and are more likely to be murdered or die from suicide than women.[95] Archaeological discoveries of ancient burial sites have also revealed some women found

to be buried with tools and weaponry used for hunting, and possibly for community self-defence and battle, but these are not as common as male ancient burial sites that also contain tools and weaponry.[96] In addition to this, ancient and modern history are full of examples of multi-millions of male warriors who fell in battle, including war graves of fallen soldiers from the First World War to the present. Men are psychologically and physiologically designed and built to be hunters and warriors, and therefore are naturally suited to be the risk taker, that is, the chasers in relationships.

2. If a woman is to be seen by a man as a person of high value and worth, she needs to let him do the chasing. Men will only chase and strive for what they believe is of value and worth to them. Consider, for example, an Old Master oil painting which is only worth what someone is willing to pay for it, and yet people pay considerable sums to possess these, because they are seen as holding great value. In the same way, if a man is not paying for the dates, or chasing the lady he is meant to be interested in, this means he does not see her as a reward worth pursuing or a prize worth winning, then he will not value her.

3. Men are visually sex driven in terms of what they find attractive. If a man sees a lady that he is sexually attracted to, he may approach her. A woman cannot know in advance what exactly a man is attracted to until he comes to her. He could be into blondes, or prefers either light or dark skinned women, or likes a particular shape of woman, etc. Statistically, men are less concerned about race than women. In our experience, this is because women generally place a higher importance than men on hoping to marry a man from the same culture or religion. Nonetheless, the vast majority of relationships consist of couples from the same racial background.[97][98]

4. Multiple research studies on female initiated dating at American university campuses, where a lady makes the first

move, found:
- Although men, appeared to welcome female initiated dates, they interpreted them as being a sexual advance, even though females are more likely to be interested in seeking friendships.[99][100]
- Women were perceived as being less attractive by men when they initiate the first date, than those that waited to be approached by men.[101]
- Sexual activity involving genital contact occurred in 63% of female-initiated dates and 56% of male-initiated dates.[102]
- Over 92% of female-initiated relationships would eventually fizzle out, (with at least 41% of these ending by the third date).[103][104] No data is available to show if any of the remainder 8% female-initiated relationships actually survived beyond university. However, from Facebook data, about 28% of married US graduates, had attended the same college/university during the same time as each other.[105] It is therefore not unreasonable to assume that the vast majority of these relationships (that progressed to marriage) were a direct consequence of male-initiated dating.

Together, what these findings illustrate is that although a man would be flattered by a lady making the first move, if he did not fancy her in a sexually attractive sense, then romance leading to marriage was considerably unlikely to happen. In short, since the chase had no value for them, then neither will the lady.

Hunter Warriors & Care-Giver Co-Breadwinners

If ancestral man was regarded as the hunter warrior; provider and protector, and ancestral woman, the gatherer nurturer; child-bearer, caregiver and protector of the young, how then do we fairly define the role that a woman plays in a 21st century marriage? This is a very reasonable and justifiable question to ask, even though there are no straightforward answers. This is because, in today's world, a woman may either be a traditional homemaker, or have to go out to work as a co-breadwinner with her husband to balance the household finances, or may even be working and providing the only source of income for the whole family. The principal hormone (with others) that drives maternal nurturing, bonding, and protection of the young is oxytocin.[106] Both men and women produce oxytocin, but women produce it approximately 3 times more than men.[107] This means that normatively speaking, women are biologically predisposed to the role of child caregiver, and oxytocin in combination with dopamine supports the pleasure and reward system which motivates them to want to do it.[108,109,110] In practice, however, this may not be so in every case, because there are many stay-at-home care-giver dads to prove otherwise (currently, in the US, 2% by choice and possibly an additional variable 12% not in employment but also stay at home and are the main caregivers to their children).[111] Putting aside for the moment, the highly creditable actions of these caregiver fathers, research studies have consistently indicated that women continue to bear the major responsibility for housework and childcare, whether or not they also do paid employment.[112] This is important to bear in mind, because the backdrop to this fact is that the figures for co-breadwinner couples, where both parents are working, is 62.3% in the US,[113] and 73.9% in the UK.[114]

Katie Newkirk, Maureen Perry-Jenkins and Aline G. Sayer from the University of Massachusetts, published in 2017, their research study on 108 working class couples' attitude to housework and childcare responsibilities. Both husbands and wives worked full-time, but the husbands worked longer and for better pay than their wives. However, if one of the couple stopped work, the consequences could reduce the income in the household to either near or at the poverty line. Therefore, husbands appreciated their wives accepting co-breadwinner responsibilities. According to the authors of this study, when wives felt that husbands were doing what they perceived was fair, with regards to the house chores and childcare responsibilities (or husbands were at least making an effort), marriages "reported fewer conflicts, suggesting that working-class mothers may hold some expectations that housework is their responsibility, and thus see a modest inequity as acceptable, but not a large inequity." Middle-class parents, having higher financial resources are more able to afford to pay for domestic and childcare services.[115] Also, Professor John M. Gottman, in his book, The Seven Principles for Making Marriage Work, states that 33% of wives are satisfied with the childcare arrangements in their marriages, thus leaving 67% that are not. He believes the marital bliss experienced by 33% of wives is due to fathers having successfully transitioned from couple-hood to accepting their responsibilities in joint parenting, rather than making mothers do all the work.[116]

What we can learn from all this is that trying to define the roles of either 21st century husband or wife by comparing them against ancestral man or woman is very problematic. What is not problematic to understand, from Gottman's findings, is that 67% of wives feel disrespected and unsupported by their husbands, because these husband-fathers are not doing their fair share of childcare and housework.[117] The solution is simple. Husbands need to discuss, agree and follow through with real appreciable action. The alternative is, if husbands do not do their fair share then this will be interpreted by their wives as a lack of commitment to the marriage, and if not dealt with, could eventually lead to its failure.[118][119][120]

Men Value Virtue, Not Lust

When it comes to male attraction for potential female marriage partners, there are two important principles that we explain to people more than any other. These are:

1. A woman of virtue is a Woman of Worth, and
2. Men fall in love with virtue, not lust.

We can illustrate this by using a very short story that Jesus gave in the Bible. It is known as the Parable of the Hidden Treasure (Matthew 13:44), and can be used to illustrate these two points in an interesting way:

> "The kingdom of heaven is like treasure hidden in a field. When a man found it, he hid it again, and then in his joy went and sold all he had and bought that field."

The meaning of the parable is about the importance of being eager to possess spiritual riches, because they have higher eternal worth attached to them, rather than trying to hold onto material wealth that does not last. In dating and relationships, we can exemplify the "treasure" to represent a woman's worth and value to a man. When she is eagerly desired by a prospective suitor, he will crazily (like the man in the parable) do anything it takes in order to have her. Steve Harvey, the well-known comedian, author, TV personality and dating coach, regularly reminds ladies that when a man is interested in a lady, he is only interested in her price. That is, to know how much it will cost him to get her. If the lady has no standards or values, then she is free, and men like things that are free, but they will not value her.[121] Let's examine what ladies and men daters can learn and apply from this parable.

Ladies: A woman should see herself as being like the treasure in the field; being of significant value and worth. So that she presents to the man as a challenge worth pursuing and having, no matter how great the cost, because she is worth much more. This is what it means to be a Woman of Worth. Men value more, what they have to pay or fight for. It is therefore, imperative, that men find dating and courting for marriage a challenge to them. If he does not value the potential reward in the chase, then he will treat the catch like discarding a sweet wrapper once he has consumed the sweet. In other words, if the woman makes it too easy for him, her value to him will be significantly diminished. If a lady reading this, refuses to accept this, she is reading the wrong book. She may be interested in having a relationship, but not marriage. If a lady has no value to a man, or she does not see value in herself, he will not marry her.

Men: Imagine if you suddenly meet the woman of your dreams. Everything about her says to you, that like the "treasure" in the parable, she is the One. But you do not feel that it is the right time for you to think about getting married and settling down. Maybe, you have yet to finish university or other further education and training. Or, you are just at the beginning of your career or profession. Even though you may not feel ready now, do you let this beautiful lady go, with the full knowledge that later in life you may never meet a similar high value lady again? As you know, some people never seem to meet the right One for them, ever in their life. But she is there, looking at you right now. Do you let her get away, just because you do not feel ready for commitment right now? Like the man who finds the treasure in a field that does not at that point belong to him, do you let the treasure go or do you do everything in your power, like the man, to acquire it? If you do not buy the field, someone else will. That is how life and relationships work. In the same way, if you let go of a beautiful woman of worth, then she will slip out of your arms, and into the arms of another. It is not surprising how many young men, once this is explained to them, all respond back saying, "Oh, I didn't see it like that before. You have got me thinking." Of course, we cannot change everyone's mind, but we hope this has got you thinking as well.

When to Have Sex

Many people like to express their intimate feelings of love with each other by including sex into their relationship before marriage. But not everyone shares this view.

We advise that a lady should wait to have sex with a man she is dating until:

(a) She has first of all got to know him, his character and behaviour,
(b) He has been able to demonstrate that he is reliable, dependable, trustworthy, and
(c) He has also very importantly demonstrated he is emotionally into her.

For this reason, we strongly advocate that ladies should wait at least 90 days before allowing a man to have sex with them. We discuss the reasons for this, in great detail, including all the scientific evidence behind this position in Chapter 11: Let's Talk about SEX. If a man cannot accept this and walks away, it means he was never a stayer and was most probably a player all along. Let him walk!

However, if you do not believe in sex before marriage, then we strongly advise that you stick solidly to your principles, because your beliefs are part of your identity, and will be one of the main things that attract the right life partner to you. Also, your beliefs speak loudly about the values that are important to you, and what your partner also values about you. Otherwise, your character and credibility will be compromised, and at some point may lead to the relationship coming to an end sooner or later.

What is a Woman of Worth?

In this book, you will see us refer a lot of times to the phrase we have coined, a "Woman of Worth", to describe the kind of woman that men would like to have as a wife. There are many descriptions from ancient and modern literature, that try to describe what a Woman of Worth is. For example, the Bible describes such a lady as, "A wife of noble character who can find? She is worth far more than rubies." (Proverbs 31:10).

Here is our own list of traits that men look for in a Woman of Worth:

1. She is confident in herself and has a strong sense of dignity about herself.
2. She is certain about her choices and knows what she wants.
3. She is purposeful and intentional in her relationships.
4. She will only accept a man who is kind and respectful to her and all others.
5. She has a high regard for her personal health, hygiene and appearance.
6. She dresses in a way that ensures the respect of others.
7. She is always considerate, polite, respectful, and never uses swear words or offensive language on a date under any circumstances.
8. On sex (a or b):
    a) She does not have sex with a man until:
        - At least 90 days into the relationship,
        - He has demonstrated and proven himself to be emotionally attached to her, and
        - Willing to be completely exclusive with her. Or,
    b) She does not believe in having sex before marriage because her beliefs and values are important to her.
9. She projects loyalty for her man, and aims to look good for both herself and him only.
10. She attracts compliments and willingly gives them.

What Is a 21st Century Gentleman?

In this book, when we refer to men, we are anticipating that they will act like gentlemen, in their conduct and behaviour towards their lady as well as family, friends and strangers. A gentleman in historical terms, may have been a man from the landed gentry, but may not have been part of the nobility and aristocracy. The codes that he followed may have been similar to the medieval knightly codes of chivalry. In other words, he would protect his lady and others, provide and be seen to be generous and courteous. His word would be his bond, and therefore he would carry out what he promised to do, because of his integrity. He was regarded as being distinguished, smartly presented, of good character and beyond reproach.

Below, is our take on how a 21st Century Gentleman should behave and conduct himself with his lady (and others as well). Some of the points from our Woman of Worth list above, are also mentioned in this list as well.

Here is our own list of traits that ladies look for in a 21st Century Gentleman:

1. He is at all times kind, polite and respectful to his lady, and also to others (including waiting staff at restaurants, etc.). He also keeps his cool at all times, and is never rude or uses swear words or offensive language when he is with his lady, under any circumstances.
2. He is a man of honour and integrity, and keeps his word, including being on time and calling his lady when he says he will.
3. He is seen to be generous and humble; not extravagant, boastful or proud.
4. He dresses appropriately for the occasion, and has a high regard for his personal health, hygiene and appearance.
5. He will always put his lady first, such as:

- Holding doors open for her.
- Pulling out her chair for her.
- Giving up his seat.
- Letting her order first.
- Offering to drop her off first before he parks far away.

6. He proves he can provide for his lady by:
   - Always paying for dates (with the possible exception of his birthday).
   - Giving her gifts (like flowers, etc.) and,
   - Constantly doing things for her

7. He is always seen to protect his lady by:
   - Standing up for her.
   - Stepping in during awkward situations.
   - Walking on the outside of the sidewalk.
   - Sharing his umbrella.
   - Offering his jacket if it is cold or wet.
   - Making sure his lady gets home after a date or sees her to her taxi cab.
   - Calls or texts her to make sure she got home safely.

8. On sex (a or b):
   a) He respects his lady's values of keeping to the minimum 90 days no sex rule. Also, consensual sex is very important to him. He therefore never forces himself on his lady, and always accepts "no" means "no". Or,
   b) He respects his lady's values of no sex before marriage as though they are his, and will never try to get her to compromise on her values.

9. He, at all times respects his lady's privacy, and regards all communication between them as being sacred and private, including texts, calls, photos, videos, and will not send them to third parties (including friends or websites) even if

the relationship ends.
10. He is quick to compliment his lady on:
    - Her appearance (dress, new hair style, etc.).
    - When she does things for him or for others.
    - Her accomplishments.

Watching Each Other

Besides the above, and this applies to both men and women, please remember that both of you are watching each other in terms of your attitudes and behaviour. Each are asking themselves whether the other will be an asset or liability around their family and friends, and whether they can be trusted around the opposite sex. Each dater is also interested to see how the other behaves maturely and responsibly, and also what and how things are said. Avoid getting drunk or doing illicit drugs. They will make a person look foolish and irresponsible and also possibly be portrayed as being high risk to be around. Such behaviour demonstrates lack of purpose in life and a turn off for those looking for a long term committed relationship leading to marriage.

'Treasured & Cherished' vs 'Admired & Respected'

If we want our partner to relate with us in the way we would like, we need to relate with them in the way they would like. Sounds a bit obvious, right? Possibly, but not necessarily, so let's explain. You may have read in some dating books or heard in some relationship discussions, a simplistic but controversial statement, that, it is a man's role to love his lady and a woman's role to respect her man. We believe both men and women should be treated equally with an abundance of kindness, love and respect for each other. However, it is how they relate with each other that is generally slightly different.

We have already discussed how men are generally higher risk takers than women. Normatively speaking, men see their role as leader, protector and provider. For example, our hunter warrior man is the one who carries the responsibility to place himself in harm's way to protect his lady and family from danger. No man in his right mind is ever going to give the job for guarding his life to his lady. Both his life and her life are his responsibility to protect, and he is always consciously aware of this. But what if a lady earns more than her man or is the one who mostly makes the financial decisions? Does that mean that she is the provider-breadwinner? In some cases, this may well be true. However, if it is not money he is directly providing then it may be services around the house, such as fixing, making and mending things. To put this all together, men have an ego, which represents their sense of self-esteem or self-importance, and needs stroking every now and then, because it tells them they are appreciated. Men's ego also makes them in relationships want to be 'Admired and Respected' by their ladies. This might sound foolish or petty to some ladies reading this, but it does not remove the truth from this fact. When a lady next sees her man (or a father figure in her life), she can test this out. She can say to him, "Please let me rest my arm inside yours." Then see how big a smile he beams out with pride. It is a testosterone and normative masculine behaviour trait thing in men, which is linked to aggression, status seeking and respect in terms of social hierarchy.[122] [123] As a husband, he craves the Admiration and Respect of his wife for being a provider (or seen to be doing his best in this) for his family, and doing what needs to be done around the house, including fixing and solving things, as well as protecting them by keeping his wife and family safe from danger.

When ladies are looking for marriage it is because they are attracted to what they perceive as the emotional security and stability that they feel marriage can offer them, including seeing the marriage relationship as a safe-haven for the couple and their family.[124] There is another side of security which women rely on, that is feeling protected. This is part of the duties of not only ancestral man but also, as stated above, our 21st Century Gentleman. Sometimes, the other attraction that marriage offers to ladies is the married status itself, and the recognition that society gives married women. But this last point, works both ways for women and men. To help men interpret what this means in practice, a lady will look for emotional supportiveness, intimacy and tenderness from her man. Irrespective of whether she is earning more money than he is, she will expect him to be seen to protect and provide (or at least, considerably contribute) for her and their children's needs. This will include the anticipation that her man will exclusively invest his financial and emotional resources into his marriage and family. A wife will also expect to see consistent attempts in career progression from her husband, in terms of promotion and salary increases, to cover higher costs associated with a growing family. A wife will use all of these things to help her determine if her husband genuinely and exclusively loves, treasurers (that is values her), and cherishes her.

To sum up, normatively, a husband wants his wife to Admire and Respect him, and a wife wants her husband to Treasure and Cherish her. But let's say, a lady is reading this and she either runs her own successful business or is successful in her career. In the workplace, she may have many men reporting and taking their instructions from her. She is therefore justified and deserves to be admired and respected by her colleagues and peers for the position she holds and what she does in her role. However, there is no comparison in this regard with a workplace and a marriage. How a husband and wife relate with each other in their marriage is entirely different to a workplace setting. For a start, in a workplace, there should not be any over familiarity between a supervisor/manager and their employee subordinate, unless there is already an established couple relationship between them. Both will expect boundaries to be respected, but in intimate relationships such as marriage, no boundaries exist, and therefore how a husband and wife will relate with each other will be different to a colleague-to-colleague relationship in a workplace setting. If a lady craves to be the Admired and Respected partner in the relationship, please see the section below: Female Led Relationships, for more information on this.

Gender Traits

As the above example of a high flying woman with a career illustrates, it can be hard for such a successful lady to switch off from being who she is in the workplace. She may not unreasonably feel this is a natural representation of who she is outside of her workplace setting as well. As the section on The Role of Humour in Dating, in Chapter 3, highlights, if a lady shows more masculine traits on her dates, it will usually be a turn off to a man. However, fortunately for ladies in this position, who also desire to be Treasured and Cherished by their man, research studies have shown that they can tone down masculine traits if it suits them and circumstances demand it. One such compelling study, published in 2011 by Olivia A. O'Neill from George Mason University and Charles A. O'Reilly from Stanford University, followed 132 business school MBA graduates over a period of 8 years. They found that those women who had strong masculine traits of assertiveness, confidence, and aggressiveness, and who were able to selectively tone this down to allow their femininity to rise, were significantly and consistently more likely to get promoted, and also more often. By contrast, women who exhibited overt masculine traits were perceived as being less socially skilled and, consequently, less likeable and less likely to be promoted.[125] Sex disparity in pay and promotion opportunities is a well-researched area going back over 50 years, a lot of workable strategies and solutions that women can adopt to overcome these disparities have been discovered.[126] For ladies who are struggling with career enhancement and also desire to be decently paid for what they do, we highly recommend Linda Babcock and Sara Laschever's self-help books, *Women Don't Ask* (2003), and its

Chapter 4: Men Chase & Women Challenge

sequel, *Ask for It* (2008). Both books are well researched and fully address the issues of femininity and masculinity in the workplace, and offer huge amounts of practical advice on how best women can effectively negotiate for pay rises and promotions, and are as relevant today as when they were first published.

What, then, is a masculine-trait lady to do if she wants to be Treasured and Cherished by a masculine driven man? We appreciate that for some ladies in this situation it can be difficult to do something that feels unnatural for them. However, just as when attending a job interview, if a candidate wants the job, they will ensure the way they present themselves, including the way they come across, meets the expectations of the interview panel. It's the same in dating. If a dater wants to stand the best possible chance of a follow up date, then they have to either meet or exceed the expectations of the other dater. Ebun is an MBA business graduate with some masculine behaviours herself. She took a hormone test out of interest, which indicated higher levels of testosterone than found in most women. However, she also knows how to tone down her masculinity to allow her femininity to rise. She also wants to be Treasured and Cherished by Stephen. She craves at times being able to lean on his shoulder when she is looking for emotional support through an emotionally challenging time. She sees this as also part of Stephen's marital job description. It would be difficult for Stephen to respond in a masculine caring and protecting way if both he and Ebun are competing for masculine roles in the relationship.

One day we randomly met and briefly chatted with Pam, aged 19, about all things dating and relationships (as we do!). She was not our client, but described herself as bi-sexual and explained to us she was already self-aware of these gender behaviour traits. She said to us that if she was attracted to a female (who was feminine driven) she would behave in a masculine ("stud" as she described it) way. If she was attracted to a man, she would behave in a feminine driven way. She explained that how she behaves would reflect how she wanted to be treated in the relationship but more importantly, for her to be seen to have an attractive character to the person she was interested in. Of course, not everyone is as fluid with their sexual orientation and gender as this. Also, we know that not every woman can as easily flick some kind of gender switch, like the above mentioned successful female MBA business graduates. However, being aware of how a lady can tone down her normative masculine traits to allow her femininity to come more to the fore can powerfully enhance her chances of success in dating and relationships.

Which One Are You?

You may have read the above section on 'Treasured and Cherished vs Admired and Respected', and feel you can already identify with one of them in terms of how you want your partner to relate with you. However, if not, try the tests below to help you. The first test is the main one, but if you are still not sure, then also please do the other two. The tests may not have any scientific value, but could be fun to do!

TEST 1: Treasured and Cherished vs Admired and Respected – You see two cards on the table facing up. One card says, 'Treasured and Cherished', and the other card says, 'Admired and Respected'. You can only pick one card. Do you want your partner to Treasure and Cherish you or to Admire and Respect you?

A: Treasured and Cherished
B: Admired and Respected

Which card are you going to pick up (A or B)? _____

TEST 2: Humour – You are using an online dating service. Of the dating profiles you have seen, you have reduced your final selection down to two people, A and B, who seem to offer the closest match to what you are looking for. However, because of commitments, you can only select one of them to go on a first date with. To help you decide, you see in each of their respective profiles, this statement:

Person A: I hope you will say funny things to me and make me laugh.
Person B: I will say funny things to you and hope to make you laugh.

Which person are you going to meet and have a first date with (A or B)? _____

<u>TEST 3: Empathiser Systemiser Trait</u> – This test is adapted from Professor Simon Baron-Cohen's book, The Essential Difference (and used with the author's permission), of the kind of magazines that a Systemiser or Empathiser type of person might pick up from a magazine seller's racks at a railway station.[127] Empathisers are people who are listeners and tuned emotionally into the thoughts, feelings and emotions of others. They are also driven to care for or offer comfort to another person.[128] Systemisers like to build, take things apart and fix them. They also like to know how things work, construct things and come up with competitive strategies.[129] We all may have a bit of both but one is usually significantly more dominant than the other. Try this test out to find out whether you are more of an Empathiser or Systemiser type of person.

You are about to make a long train journey, and you would like to pick up some magazines to read to pass the time. You see two magazine racks in front of you. You must pick 3 magazines of your choice because you will have plenty of time to read them. They can be a mix from either rack. For example, you can either pick 3 magazines from one rack or 2 from one rack and 1 from the other. Please tick which 3 magazines you wish to choose for your journey.

RACK 'A'	RACK 'B'
[ ] Glamorous Fashion	[ ] Computers
[ ] Romance	[ ] Cars
[ ] Beauty	[ ] Economics
[ ] Intimacy	[ ] Live sporting events
[ ] Emotional problems and agony-aunts/uncles	[ ] Science and technology
[ ] Counselling	[ ] Home electrical and plumbing repairs
[ ] Relationship advice	[ ] Music Equipment
[ ] Parenting	[ ] Audio sound systems
[ ] Interior and home design	[ ] Action

Which magazine rack got the most ticks (A or B)? _____

<u>RESULTS: *How Did You Do?*</u> In your answers, if you picked 2 or more 'A's then it means that you mostly prefer to be Treasured and Cherished by your partner. If you picked 2 or more 'B's then it means you mostly prefer to be Admired and Respected by your partner. In case you struggled a bit with trying to work out what was being asked. Test 1, was to find out if you are either mainly 'A' feminine driven or 'B' masculine driven. Test 2, if you picked B and like to tell jokes on the first date, then you are more likely to be masculine driven. In Test 3, Rack 'A' is for Empathisers, and Rack 'B' is for Systemisers. If you picked 2 or more magazines from Rack 'A' you are probably more feminine driven.

<u>FINDINGS:</u> *"What do my results mean?"* If the above tests identify that you want to be Treasured and Cherished by your partner, then you are the one that needs to put up a challenge and be chased. If you need your partner to Admire and Respect you, then you need

to absolutely be the one to do all the chasing.

Female Led Relationships

If you are a highly focused career woman (rather than being a woman with a career) and having done the above tests you identify more with being Admired and Respected, then it is likely that you may prefer to be in what is commonly called, a Female Led Relationship (FLR). There are not many couples that have this type of relationship. Also, research around FLRs is very weak on evidence, but if you are a lady, then we suggest you probably need a man who ideally likes to be Treasured and Cherished. In order for an FLR to be successful, both partners need to have a secure understanding of their emotional role in the relationship. This is important because research has shown that only 15% of men are naturally domestically inclined.[130] Some dads work from home and do a good job in looking after their children, but that is not what we are talking about here. We are referring to males who actually enjoy with a passion doing housework and being the primary at home caregiver parent (as opposed to merely needing to do it). To have a successful FLR, the couple need to have open and regularly reviewed discussions with each other to decide how roles in the relationship should play out. This is to avoid the risk of both partners wanting to be either the Treasured and Cherished or Admired and Respected partner at the same time as the other.

Problems with Duo Masculine/Feminine Driven Couples

In this section, we are only expressing our opinion, rather than being emphatic. If you disagree with what we are about to say, then please do not let that distract you from benefiting from the rest of the book. Just carry on with the next section.

In our view there would be a problem with having either two

masculine driven or two feminine driven partners in the same relationship, because it is likely to cause an imbalance. Let's hypothetically take a look at each of the different duo similar gender relationship scenarios:

- *Duo Feminine* – If the man is feminine driven, who will his feminine driven lady go to when she is looking for a strong emotionally detached enough shoulder to lean on in a time of crisis, despair or loss? Some women can provide this, but not as easily if they also are the one that need the emotional shoring up as well. Also, having two feminine energy people in a relationship could also present a problem in the bedroom, since it is usually more common for a masculine testosterone driven partner to initiate sex.[131] In a duo masculine driven relationship, initiating sex is less likely to be a problem for either partner, because the testosterone assertiveness levels in each of them is also likely to be high.

- *Duo Masculine* – If the woman is masculine energy then she is also likely to be competitive and strongly assertive in the same way as her man is. The high risk is that both will be looking to position themselves for hierarchy, status seeking and dominance in the relationship. For example, both may feel the need to show status by demonstrating they are earning more than the other. Eventually they are likely to grow tiresome and weary of the competitiveness between them.

We all rightly recognise that in the 21st century, expectations have changed in terms of equality. However, biology does not change the order of how men and women normatively relate with each other. If there is likely to be an issue of a couple being either duo masculine or duo feminine driven and they also believe they are still sincerely meant for each other, then discussions between them in terms of how they see their respective roles need to take place and be kept under regular review. This will allow for sufficient latitude to handle how feelings and emotions are managed and supported, and to avoid potential misunderstandings as described above.

Risks of Too Many Women

Just as in business, supply and demand affect the value that people put on things. It is the same in relationships as well. If in a particular community, cultural, religious or other social setting there are substantially more women than men then this is very unhealthy for long term relationship making. In such situations, men are considerably more likely to opt for shorter term casual sex relationships,[132] because they do not need to try so hard at attracting mates. This may also compel them to go outside of that immediate environment to get a lady life partner of what they feel is of a higher value and worth to them (even if this perception is wrong). Likewise, when there are substantially more women than men in the same community, this leads to lowering of moral standards and feelings of self-esteem and self-worth in women.[133] On the other hand, when there are less women than men, competition among men significantly increases. This leads to greater quest in men to go for monogamous marriage as a way of holding on to a woman for sexual exclusivity and having children by her that he will know are 100% his.[134] Both of these scenarios are a worldwide cross-cultural phenomenon. If a lady wants to be married and finds herself in such a place where there are substantially more women than men, and there are no purposeful and practical efforts to change this, she should consider her options to change environment where the ratios of men and women are more balanced.

STEP 2: Start Dating

Chapter 5: Getting Started

Welcome to Step 2. This is where we go straight into the topic of all things dating. The important thing to keep in mind about dating, especially when it is for marriage, is that it's a numbers game. Some people find their match straight away. For others, it takes a little while to eventually meet the One. It is not every date that will lead to you falling in love. It is not every relationship that is meant to be. It is not every person you meet that will be as marriage-minded as you. How is it possible to avoid wasting time and false hopes? That is difficult to answer. However, by following the simple principles laid out in this book, you will significantly increase your chances of meeting and building up a successful relationship with the right person, and also, crucially learn how to avoid the players and time wasters. In this chapter, we will discuss various strategies you can use to greatly increase your success in meeting the right person.

When to Start Dating

There is nothing like the present to get into dating and relationship making. However, if you have just recently come out of a long term relationship or coping with the loss of a life partner, or your previous relationship was abusive, it will make sense to take your time before starting a new relationship. This is to allow much needed time for emotional healing and mending to take place. Also, creating a big enough time gap between the ending of one relationship and the start of another, helps to avoid a 'love on the rebound' relationship situation next time. Which is highly likely to end in hurt and failure. A definition of a love on the rebound relationship is when a new relationship is started too soon before allowing enough time to get over unresolved feelings of grief, hurt, and pain from a previous relationship.

Divorced or Widowed: If you do not have children from a previous relationship then dating can begin at any time. In any case, our advice is not to begin dating until at least 6 to 12 months from the previous relationship legally ending, to allow time for painful feelings of anger, hurt or bereavement to subside. Otherwise, you may find yourself holding back from being able to fully emotionally commit to a new partner in a new relationship. If after 12 months, you are still dealing with any of these feelings, then you are still not ready to move on and it may be helpful to consider speaking to a therapist, or seeking pastoral support if you are part of a religious community. We would also encourage you to read our bonus chapter, Dating & Divorced, Widowed, or Was in a Long Term Relationship, where you will also get lots of additional help and tips to advise you on your love journey. If you have children, please also see our bonus chapter, Dating & Single Parenthood.

Ladies: If you still have strong feelings for your former partner and want to get back with him, then we suggest you wait no longer than eight weeks from the time of last contact to see if he will communicate with you again. If you have not heard from him by then, you should, emotionally draw a line, move on and begin dating again, because he has already forgotten about you and emotionally moved on. The originators of our strategy to wait up to eight weeks are Dr. Patricia Allen and Sandra Harmon, co-authors of, *Getting To "I Do"*. They compellingly reason in their book that by the fourth week of breaking up with a lady, a man can keep himself busy with working, dating others and living without her. However, if a man is really interested in her it will be around 6-8 weeks that he will miss her and then call her.[135] We have seen this with daters ourselves, and that is why we encourage lady daters to move on if they have not heard anything by the eighth week.

Avoiding Love on the Rebound Relationships

To follow on from the above section, it is important to avoid dating anyone who has recently come out of either a long term or abusive relationship. The reason is that:

- They will still be coping with emotional hurts, pain or loss from their previous relationship.
- Their emotions are going to be too raw for them to fully trust in a new relationship.
- Their keenness to jump into a new relationship so quickly after the end of a previous one, could indicate that they are emotionally needy.
- They may unfairly compare a new dater's behaviour with how their ex-partner treated them.

All of these are red flags, and if you do find yourself drawn into such a relationship then it would be better to break it off. For similar reasons, do not date a person who:

- Is still married (including those who are separated) under any circumstances. Such relationships end up with hearts getting broken and new marriages formed from them rarely, if ever, last.
- Has just recently, within the past 2 months, come out of a long term sexual relationship (of more than a year). Don't

be fooled by outside appearances. Less than 2 months is insufficient time for their emotions to be genuinely settled.
- Still has obvious unresolved hurts and feelings connected to a previous relationship. Tell them they can contact you in 6 months' time, even if they say it is not their fault. Fine, but it is not yours either.
- Has been divorced or widowed less than 6 months prior. This is because both divorce and loss of a life partner are very traumatic life experiences. If they are divorced, then you have a right to ask them what 3 things they learnt from their previous marriage that they will make sure never gets repeated.

Getting Started

Dating, like any social skill is something that is learnt by doing. Some dates may go well and others may have to be treated as a learning experience. Dating can make you feel a bit nervous at first, and this is totally normal and to be expected. The person you will be meeting will appreciate you anyway. Besides, they are also very likely to be feeling just as nervous as you, even if they manage to do a good job at hiding it.

No one learns to drive a car and pass the test on the same day. Dating, like any other social skill, is perfected by the more you practice it. As you go on dates, the better and more confident at it you will become. If you feel nervous about the idea of meeting new people, then volunteer to help at work conferences or charity events. Also, a good idea for confidence building could be to get involved in local charities like food banks, soup kitchens, hospitals or hospices. Any of these will increase your empathy skills as well.[136] Empathy is an asset for making powerful long lasting relationships. If you are already involved in charity work, consider volunteering in a role that is more people-facing. You can also increase your confidence by getting into conversations with your cab driver. Ask how their day is going, and be ready with follow up questions self-esteem. Meeting and talking to new people will turn out to be great fun as you get used to doing it. You also get to learn and find out about amazing new things from listening to the experiences of others. You may even get a date out of it as well!

When Two People Meet For the First Time

When two people meet up on a first date and all the signs are good that they seem to be getting along well with each other, very often a chemical attraction is triggered in the brain by a combination of hormones that give a desire to connect. This initial attraction feeling, may be strong enough to prompt a dater to want to meet this person again. Sexual attraction can trigger feelings of light-headedness, euphoria, sleepless nights, loss of appetite, accelerated breathing, etc. These feelings generally suspend our normal rational thinking processes that may otherwise get in the way. This is what falling in love does. It drowns out our normal critical thinking skills in our brain to make us overlook the imperfections of the person we are interested in. This creates in us a desire to want to explore more with the person; to meet them again and find out if there is any compatibility with each other. The two main hormones that are responsible for sexual desire in both men and women are testosterone and dopamine. Although, other hormones are actively involved as well. We discuss the role of hormones further, as well as the scientific reasons why we advocate a couple should wait at least 90 days first before having sex, in Chapter 11: Let's Talk About SEX.

If there is no immediate sexual attraction, but a person wants to meet their date again because they feel at ease and comfortable with them, that is normal and absolutely fine. Sometimes, sexual attraction takes time to take hold. One reason for this could be because a dater may like the other person but may not be sure how they actually feel about them. However, at some point, as the relationship progresses, if no sexual attraction is felt, then it means the two people are unlikely to be right for each other (unless both are asexual, that is, they don't experience feelings or desires of sexual attraction for anyone).

If things in the new relationship are going well, it can generally take around 3 to 6 months for these initial euphoric feelings to subside, and give way to more meaningful deeper emotional attachment feelings. By this time you both should feel sufficiently comfortable around each other to let your guard down. Also, around this time, you should both be receiving from each other strong non-verbal cues that demonstrate you both are genuinely emotionally into each other and intend to stick around. We say non-verbal cues, because love is not wholly dependent on what a person says, but about what they also do. This could be a man buying gifts for his lady, always paying for the dates, and always doing things for her. We discuss more about this in chapter 8. However, in the meantime, what we are hoping to show here is that it takes time to build a genuine and meaningful relationship. Rather than the fictitious 'love at first sight' that Hollywood sometimes portrays in their movies.

Want To Get Married In A Year?

The dating period can last anything from around 3 months before it might be able to progress to the next Step, which is courtship. Courtship is there to test the relationship, remove doubts and make sure the couple are suitable for each other for marriage. This can take around 6-9 months, but sometimes longer. It is therefore not impossible to be married in a year if the attitude by both partners towards the relationship is intentional and focused. However, in reality, if a wedding is planned to be a big and elaborate affair, the costs will rise along with the time needed to organise it.

Intentional Relationships

One of the things that sets this dating and relationship book apart from any other is its emphasis that dating needs to be intentional in the decisions concerning a relationship if marriage is the focus. Our definition of being intentional is about making decisions and taking actions that prioritise what is important to you so that you achieve a specific outcome or result in the future. The outcome in this regard is for you to get married to the right person and enjoy a happy lifelong marriage with them. The point of being intentional is not to speed up the process to marriage, but rather that when you review the relationship every few months or so, you feel that progress is being made in terms of the direction you want the relationship to go. However, the pace of the relationship should always be a natural one.

What is Intentional Dating?

- Being intentional is being open and upfront about what kind relationship you are looking for.
- Being intentional is deciding on what you want and steering the relationship it in that direction.
- If you are looking for something serious, then you are not looking for a one night hook-up. That is intentional.
- If you are looking for a relationship that could lead to marriage. That is also intentional.
- Being intentional in dating, can help filter out the time wasters and players, because their values and what they are looking for in a relationship will not line up with your own.

Here are some examples of the kind of excuses that some people may use to avoid relationship commitment towards marriage, and all these should be treated as red flags for the kind of people to avoid. They may say:

- "I am not ready." Follow this up by asking, "Please explain

what you mean by this?"
- "I am too young." Follow this up by asking, "Roughly, how old do you think you would like to be before you consider getting married?"
- "I want to focus on my career right now." Follow this up by asking, "What level do you want your career to be at and what other things do you feel you need to have achieved first before you may feel ready for marriage?"
- "I still want to live my life first before thinking about settling down."
- "I do not feel that marriage is important me."
- "Marriage is just a piece of paper."

We have all heard these excuses and many more like them. This book has been written so that you will know how to quickly dismiss these time wasters from your life, move on and focus on those that are serious about building a relationship that could potentially lead to marriage.

On the other hand, if both of you are marriage minded anyway, this does make the process of developing an intentional relationship a lot easier than if only one of you are. However, putting pressure on a partner, to have the relationship defined too soon, when they are still getting to know you, could be a big turn off and may scare them away. Obviously, if you and your dater's future plans are different, this could be a red flag because this would indicate there may be incompatibility issues between you. In which case, both of you would need to discuss this to see if any differences in the plans can be overcome through compromise or accept that you are not right for each other.

Daniel's story exemplifies many of the issues that can come up with intentional dating. Stephen was in between meetings, and met Daniel, who told him he came to London from abroad to study business management and also to work. He successfully got employment in marketing, and then saw an opportunity in the same company to do accountancy, his preferred occupation. He had been dating for around a year, a lady who was living in Glasgow, Scotland, but was also from his country of origin. He described his dating with this lady as "a bit of a long distance relationship". He told Stephen that he explained to her, he could not commit to her because he wanted to set up a business in about 2-3 years' time, and that was his number one priority. It was quite clear listening to Daniel that this lady had strong feelings for him, but that she felt they were not being reciprocated. It was at this point that Stephen interjected and explained to Daniel that he coaches people on how to get married. Stephen asked Daniel if this lady is the One for him. He said he hoped so, but that his first priority was first of all to set up a business. Stephen then said that if she was his client, after 6 months of such a relationship, he would have advised her to move on. Daniel quickly replied back that he had explained to her he was not looking for commitment right now. Then, as soon as he said this, something had dropped in him to make him realise he had contradicted himself. Stephen did not have to say anything further because it was quite clear looking at Daniel's face, he suddenly came face to face with his true feelings about this lady. Sometimes, being intentional in relationship making is not about rushing and hurrying up to get a result, but simply a matter of honestly considering what is really important and realising that doing nothing could mean losing everything, including lifelong happiness.

Men: Women are attracted to purposeful men. They see them as being mature, emotionally stable, dependable, and reliable providers and protectors. They get a feeling of security from them, because the man comes across with more confidence and sureness in where he is going. Being purposeful means:
- Strategically planning out how a vision or a goal will be achieved.
- Being focused on the realistic steps required to complete a

mission or assignment.
- Being self-driven to get to where they feel they need to be in life.
- Taking the necessary steps to achieve what they want to do in life.

If a man does not know what he wants to do with his life, he becomes unattractive and a risky option to a lady. Your purpose in life is often guided by the things you care most about doing and achieving. This could be: having a family, achieving financial freedom, being successful in a chosen career, contributing to the success of a charity's goal or mission, working towards being successful in business, gaining a university degree or professional qualification, etc.

Men: What are you doing that show you are making progress in achieving your goals? Is the lady you are currently dating in your plans? If she is, does she know it? In other words, have you told her? Do your plans match up with her own aspirations in life? Is there room to negotiate or compromise?

Defining the Relationship

You may have heard of the term, 'defining the relationship'. Defining the relationship is about understanding how significant each person is to the other. As we get to know someone, what we think and feel about them will naturally change. We may develop a closer more emotionally connected relationship with them. Or, it may feel like the relationship has not grown or progressed in the way we hoped for.

Defining a relationship can be done by asking such questions as:
- What does this relationship mean to each of us?
- What relationship status would each give the other, and how does your partner introduce you to others (such as

their friends or family)? This could be, for example: 'boyfriend/girlfriend', 'special friend', 'work colleague', 'partner', 'other half', 'fiancé', or just by your first name only. How a person introduces you to others often gives information on how important you really are to them.
- Are both partners happy with where the relationship is right now?
- Is your partner treating you with the same level of kindness and respectfulness you are giving them? If not, it is likely to indicate that you are either not in their future plans or you may be in an abusive relationship.

Defining a relationship requires each partner to make clear what they are really looking for from the relationship. For example, a man may say to his lady, "I would like us to be exclusive with each other." This should set the relationship up for the next stage, which is courtship, but not always, because marriage may be far from either daters mind. He or she may be content with a boyfriend/girlfriend type of relationship. He or she may not see themselves ever getting married or indeed having children. Therefore, the key purpose for defining the relationship is to make an honest assessment on whether or not it has a meaningful future.

If after 6 months of dating, and the man has not asked his lady about going exclusive, then it means that he just sees her as a good friend or perhaps a friend with sexual benefits only. If a relationship is 6 months old, then the lady would be justified to ask her partner to define how he sees their relationship. This is to potentially avoid wasting any further time on a relationship that may not be going anywhere. To put this into perspective, after 6 months of dating, you should definitely be in the courtship period, that is, if your focus is to get married.

Ladies: Defining a relationship also helps to define the quality of it.

For example, do you feel safe with your man? Do you feel you are valued and being treated with enough kindness and respectfulness by him? Are you emotionally in his head all the time that he can be trusted for an exclusively committed relationship? These questions, of course, can work both ways. However, if you think your partner is taking you or your feelings for granted, then you may need to reduce his access to you until he sees you as the true Woman of Worth you are.

In the first 3 months of a relationship, when you both are getting to know each other, it is advised not to get fixated with such terms as 'intentional relationships' and 'defining the relationship'. However, at some point around the 4-6 months mark into the relationship, it is appropriate to have these in mind to ensure your expectations for the relationship are reasonably on track for you.

Multiple Dating vs "Two Timing"?

A question that we often get asked, "Can I see others while I am still looking for the One, or is this 'two timing'?" We say, until you are in an exclusively committed relationship, you have no allegiance to anyone. Although, as a new relationship progresses after about one or two months, things can start to take shape that way. But until the man says to a lady, "I would like us to now to be exclusive with each other", there is nothing stopping either the man or woman seeing anyone else. Multiple dating is where a person is regularly going out on dates with different daters without any obligation to any. It is therefore not the same as "two timing" someone; that is, seeing another person behind a partner's back. In fact, we encourage multiple dating, because as we have already stated, to find the right, Mr or Miss Right, for you, is a bit of a numbers game. Therefore, it does not make sense to treat every date you go on as if you were already exclusive with them. Get to know them first. Make sure that by the time you both want to be exclusively committed to each other, that you both have attachment feelings for each other. Also, make sure the other person is compatibly right for you, and they blend well with your personality, before you agree to go exclusive with them. These are the reasons why we say that people seeking the One for their life should not restrict themselves initially to dating only one person at a time, but rather over time to filter down to one person.

There are four major benefits to multiple dating:
1. It means you avoid focusing on just one person, who may be a time waster, at the end of the day.
2. It means you are less likely to be infatuated, fixated or obsessed over just one person. Therefore dating becomes much healthier and a more enjoyable experience.
3. When a man knows he is competing with other admirers for the attention of a lady he likes, he will naturally be more competitive and therefore, try harder to win her over.
4. If you have a religious faith or values about not having sex before marriage, then going on multiple dates means that you are less likely to give in to sleeping with anyone. However, not every culture is accepting of multiple dating.

The question that often gets asked on a first date is, "Are you seeing anybody else?" To this, we advise you to reply by saying, "I am keeping my options open, because I have not met the right person yet." A similar question to this is, "Are you dating other people?" You can reply, "I have not committed to anyone, so I am happy to be meeting you." It can take many months to find out if one person over another, is the right person for you.

Special Note: If you are a part of a religious community it is not advised to do multiple dating in a place of worship. This is because, religious communities are generally socially close-knit places, and they usually have a set of dating guidelines in place for its members to follow. The reasons for this is to uphold the religious values and sacredness of the place of worship, and at the same time, ensure the pastoral care and support, as well as the spiritual, moral and emotional welfare of its members is safeguarded.

Being Kind & Respectful

There is a universal law which says, "Do unto others as you would have them do to you." In actual fact, it's from the Bible. The author of the quotation is Jesus (Matthew 7:12). In the same way that no one would disagree with the value of these wise words, in an ideal world everyone should be kind and respectful to each other. When a person persistently falls short of showing kindness and respectfulness to their partner in a relationship, this is a clear sign that it is an abusive relationship. In Duana C. Welch's book, Love Factually, she states that if a person finds a partner who is kind and respectful, then the "relationship will probably work, and if [not], it won't." Welch further asserts that if a person makes kindness and respect a must-have character trait they are looking for in a partner, they "are extremely likely to avoid partnering with an abuser".[137]

The important takeaway from this is, if you don't feel that your partner is being kind and respectful to you, then he or she is the wrong choice for you. If a person says that their partner is kind and respectful to them in his or her own way, what is really being said is that he or she shows unkind and disrespectful behaviour. There is no middle ground. Suppose a person promises to change their bad behaviour towards you, but every once in a while they still treat you badly. In that case, the wedding plans should immediately be halted. This is because, how your partner treats you before the wedding will reflect exactly how they will treat you when you are married.

Behaviour Character Tests

Here are five character suitability tests that you can use to help you

Chapter 5: Getting Started

work out if your date's character, behaviour and manner is good or not. If you cannot say their behaviour is acceptable to any of these then they are the wrong person for you.

1. Is your date kind and respectful to you and other people? Remember, there is no middle ground to this.
2. Is your date always polite and well-mannered to you and others? Do they consistently use swear words or other offensive language in their conversation? We strongly believe that if a person would not use bad or offensive language at a job interview, they should not use bad or offensive words on a date, where they should be trying to make a good character impression of themselves.
3. When you go to a restaurant or other places, is your date rude or impolite to the staff at the venue? Similarly, is your date very discreet and polite to you and everyone else regardless of whether or not the experience went well?
4. If your date has a cab booking app on their smartphone like Uber, Lyft, Bolt, etc., ask them what their rider customer rating is. This is a rating out of 5 stars that cab hire drivers have to rate their riders on their experience of them. If the person you are dating has a rating of less than 4 stars then that could be a red flag and an early warning to possible bad behaviour issues.
5. If you go out on a car trip, and your date is the one who is driving, see how they behave themselves when they are driving during a busy time on the road. Are they able to drive and behave calmly and peacefully or do they get easily angry with other road users? Do they quickly accept everyone makes mistakes or do they blame others loudly for everything that happens on the road? Do you feel safe when they are driving you?

Dealing with Time wasters

A dating time waster is someone who has no genuine intention of building a meaningful relationship towards marriage. Sometimes, even people who had no intention of marriage at the outset of a relationship can actually change their mind because they have grown strong emotional attachment feelings for their partner and do not want to risk losing them. However, ladies should be especially weary of men who pose as if they are looking for a serious relationship, when in reality they are just looking for a relationship that provides access to have sex only. They should also be weary of men who wish to waste precious years of their life trying to encourage them into having a cohabitating relationship. Such men, usually see marriage as just a piece of paper but still want to enjoy sexual benefits without making a full commitment.

Risks of Cohabitation

Some try to pitch that cohabitation can act as a compatibility test that enables a couple to find out if they are meant for each other. However, cohabitation relationships are very risky, because the majority of these end in failure,[138] and ultimately steal precious years of a woman's fertility body clock. Also, research has consistently found that marriages that had a cohabitation element to them before a couple are engaged carry a significantly higher risk of divorce than those who cohabitated after a couple were engaged.[139] [140] We think this is because engagement clearly defines the direction and purpose for a relationship, as well as demonstrating a significantly greater commitment to it. We, therefore, strongly advise against cohabitation before marriage unless a lady has been proposed to, got an engagement ring on her finger and has agreed a wedding date that is just around the corner (that is, within 3-6 months' time).

Having said all of the above, if you are already in a cohabitating relationship and plan to get married, we discuss different ways you can give your marriage the best possible chance of success, in Chapter 19: Marriage Preparation.

Actors, Musicians & Entrepreneurs

If a person is an actor, musician, or entrepreneur, and they see themselves as potentially being either the main or co-breadwinner in a marriage, then before entering into a relationship they should first of all have a proven track record of success in their chosen field. This is because in reality, very few actors, musicians and entrepreneurs are able to consistently maintain their success in the longer term. For this reason, very few of them manage to maintain long term meaningful relationships. They may even need to rely on the financial support of a partner to get them through the quiet times when work may not be regular. To understand the difference between a business person and an entrepreneur:

- A business person usually follows a path that is not likely to be original and others have already shown to be successful.
- An entrepreneur creates their own path by initiating an original product, service, brand or idea.

The entrepreneur's pathway may offer the prospect of hugely bigger rewards, but so is the higher risk of failure. We are not saying that people should avoid actors, musicians and entrepreneurs, just that readers should have their eyes wide open to the larger risks of financial instability in relationships connected with people from these professions.

Chapter 6: How to Stand Out & Get Noticed

In Chapter 1: Principles of Love Attraction, we looked at many different ways you can boost your attractiveness. For example, we mentioned when you go out on a date always dress to impress, especially if it is your first time of meeting. Not many men, these days, dress up in suits for dates any more. However, men who do wear suits succeed in making themselves stand out much more than those that do not (even if they choose not to wear a tie). This is because a suit can convey a strong message that the person wearing it is an achiever and a good provider. Dressing up, including smart casual, is highly respectful to your date, because it shows that you have made an effort to impress them. In this chapter, we will be building on the themes of love attraction, to help you get noticed and stand out among the competition. Also, we will show ladies how they can use a few simple hints, tips and strategies to get men, even the most shy, chasing after them.

Getting Noticed – How You Look

Normally, when a man is looking at a lady he is drawn to, he is immediately checking over her anatomy. This may not be a surprise for many of our readers reading this. However, it is the way that men are naturally programmed to be. Men try to hide this, but probably many times ladies have caught them out and have politely and graciously chosen to ignore it. To illustrate this, in a social gathering, a man may spot a lady that catches his attention. His immediate interest in her will be physical, because it is only based on what his eyes can see. However, if both the man and the lady work together in the same organisation, attraction for each other is likely to be based on a combination of appearance, personality and demeanour. This is because both will already have had the chance to observe what the other's character is like.

Ladies: When going out on your dates, we strongly encourage you not to wear short, tight fitting, or revealing clothing. Although wearing clothes that appear to show more skin than fabric will definitely work to capture the sexual attention of a man. The message that gets conveyed to him (regardless of whether or not a woman feels it is true), is that she is not looking for a serious relationship. When a lady dresses modestly and wears clothing that accentuates her body's shape in a respectful way, she sends a powerful message to a man that she is loyal and has a high sense of self-worth. This is the kind of dressing style that a man is looking for in a lady that he feels is true 'wife material'.

If a lady feels overly conscious about how a part of her body protrudes, she could wear darker colours and looser clothing to hang over those areas. If a lady wants to wear red lipstick and modest make-up that enhances her facial features, along with big earrings and high heels that is all fine. Also, wearing a correct fitting bra that enhances a lady's upper body shape makes sense. Many of the bigger clothing retailers that sell women's underwear often have trained female staff available to help women especially for this. Try to wear garments that hide the underwear lines. While you want your female shape to get noticed, you also need to portray yourself as a Woman of Worth.

Getting Noticed – Good Health

Looking after your health and maintaining high energy levels is very attractive. This applies to both men and women. Doing regular exercise and also eating in a healthy way will add to your overall feelings of confidence and help you feel attractive at the same time.

Getting Noticed – Good Teeth

Women, especially, look at men's teeth. This is because, if a lady likes a man, she may also imagine what a kiss from him would be like, even if she has no intention of kissing him there and then. If a person's teeth are discoloured, they should have them professionally cleaned, and also possibly consider having dental whitening treatment. Also, if teeth need to be straightened or gaps are obvious due to missing teeth, dental cosmetic treatment may assist with this. If a person has bad mouth odour problems that are persisting, then they should get a dentist to check their teeth and gums to find out if there are any medical issues that need to be treated. When you go out on a date, we advise that you take along a breath freshener spray, especially if you smoke or vape.

Ladies: How to Get a Date

To re-cap on what we have discussed before in Chapter 4: Men Chase & Women Challenge. Research has shown that if a lady does not play hard to get, that is, she makes it too easy for a man to have her, his value of her will be low. This is because men only value highly what cost them dearly to get. Sooner or later he will discard her, and instead go for someone whose heart is harder to win over, and he will treasure and cherish her much more because of it. This is why we say that a lady should make herself a bit of a challenge for a man to get her. An example of how a lady could do this is by giving the impression to the man that she has a busy diary, and that she cannot just drop everything suddenly to see him. Doing this will make him value both her and her time more.

As emphasised above, men place a high importance on physical attraction when it comes to selecting a mate. All men are different, and each man has different preferences to what is physically attractive to them. A lady will not know if a man she is interested in, is into blondes or brunettes or dark hair, or if he likes tall or short or big or small or plus-sized or slender shaped women, or prefers women who have a light or dark skin tone, or women from a particular race or mixes of races or ethnicity or anything else. In fact, a lady will have no idea until a man comes up to her and asks her out on a date. Since a lady cannot predict or know in advance what a guy thinks is attractive, it makes complete sense to always let a man make the first move. Having said all of that, there are exceptions and we will now look at seven different hints, tips and strategies that ladies can use to get noticed by a man they are interested in.

1. The Five Second Look

Psychologist, Monica M. Moore from the University of Missouri, in 1985 published her paper on how females attract the attention of males through non-verbal cues. She observed females in a social setting would commonly flirt by gazing at a man for more than 3 seconds to gain his interest.[141] In 1994, co-authors, Dr. Patricia Allen and Sandra Harmon in their book, Getting To "I Do", stated a similar strategy, where they expand the length of this female gaze to 5 seconds.[142] We believe this is exactly right, and is a powerful technique to gain a man's attention. All a lady needs to do is smile and look directly at the eyes of the man she is interested in for 5 seconds. Do not break eye contact with him and don't stop smiling at him. Otherwise, he will not know if you really like him. But 5 full seconds tells him that he definitely will not get rejected if he comes over to you. However, if he does not, don't be disappointed, because he may simply be flattered that you noticed him at all. He may not really be into you, or he may already be in a committed relationship. Remember, the point of this technique is that while you are signalling your interest to him, you still need him to come over to you, so that you maintain being a challenge for him, and he will still have to chase you. If a man asks you to come over to him, politely refuse, because the guy is 100% not interested in a serious relationship with you.

2. Swerve By and Smile

This is a similar strategy to the first one, but you still need to allow the man to make the first move. The next time you are at either a party or other type of social gathering, gently swerve past the man you like, and as you do, look and smile directly at him. Once you have passed him, briefly look back at him, and then walk on. If he follows you, great. If not, then no problem.

3. Stand or Sit Alone

When you are looking to get noticed, try to sit or stand a way from others or at a distance from your other girl-friends. Doing this will increase the confidence of a man to come up to you. But do not leave a party or other event with a stranger, or follow him into any quite areas under any circumstances. This is for your physical safety. Tell him, if he wants to talk to you, he can talk to you where you are. If you like the man, allow him to take your number to call you sometime later. However, if you either change your mind about him or think you will not be safe with him, you can just block his calls.

4. Dropping the Handkerchief

This is a well-known and effective technique that women have used since probably before the days of medieval knights and chivalry. When you see a guy you are interested in, walk past and drop a handkerchief (or other object) almost as if by accident, on the floor. The least he will do is pick it up for you and give you back your handkerchief. Once he does, you can say "thank you", smile at him, and say, "how kind", he is. Then if you have extra boldness, say to him, "My name is ..." Then wait for him to respond in kind. You will soon know if he is interested in you.

5. Networking

For networking events, conferences, conventions, or cultural gatherings, this could provide the perfect excuse to strike up a conversation. If he has a conference badge you could start your conversation with overtly noticing it and calling him by his first name. Conversation starters could be:

- "Are you here for the conference as well?"
- "Are you here to learn something in your field of interest or are you one of the exhibitors?"
- "What is your interest in this event?"
- "Did you like the presentation, what did you get out of it?"
- "How are you linked to the people running this event?"
- "Did you come far for this event?"

6. Asking for Help

If there is a man you know and like, and want to know him better, get him to do something for you. For example, ask him to carry or move something or assist you in some other way. For example, you could carry something but pretend it is a bit awkward or too heavy for you, and ask the man to open the door for you. The idea is that he will want to come to your aid by offering to carry it for you. Then as he does, get talking. We are sure you will come up with plenty of different ways you can make this work.

7. Offering a Lift

If you have got to know a man you are interested in, because you participate in the same regular activity together, offer him a lift in your car.

Once you can see that you have successfully gained a man's interest, you need to quickly revert to playing hard to get. It is the responsibility of the man to get your contact details. If he gives you his number or business card, never call him, but you can text him or write on the back of his card your number and let him know he is free to call you. A man will definitely not value you as much if you call him first, even if he strongly invites you to call him. It is only his ego talking, or at best, he is only being polite, nothing else.

Safety Warning: Whatever you do, do not risk putting yourself in danger. For example, do not give or accept lifts from strangers or follow anyone to quite areas of a building. If you are both attending the same conference, and you are staying at a hotel, do not follow him to his room and do not allow him to follow you to yours. This is for your physical safety, especially if you have had some alcohol. Remember also, if you like a man, allow him to take your number to call you sometime later. However, if you either change your mind about him or think you will not be safe with him, you can just block his calls.

Flirting

A question that is commonly asked: "Is it okay to flirt?" Whether consciously or unconsciously, all people from all cultures around the world flirt when they want to arouse the mating interest of another. When flirting is subconsciously done, a person may give off leaks through their eyes, body language and tones in our voices about their attraction feelings for someone else. However, not every society and culture finds overt flirting acceptable. For example, flirting in a place of worship, such as a church or mosque or temple, would be seen as being disrespectful.

Men: "She's Out of Your League, Mate!"

This phrase could be said to a man as banter by his friends when he may be considering pursuing a lady that they might think is either:

- Too attractive for him, or
- Economically better off than he is, or
- More educated than he is, or
- In a higher societal class than he is.

Dating apps that are heavily photo focused do not work for everyone. This is because a user is generally judged on them by how other users rate their photos for physical attractiveness and appearance. Also, other users on these apps generally pick potential dating matches based on similar attractiveness levels to themselves. However, looking at the world around you, there are plenty of examples of highly attractive ladies going out with what many might argue are not as attractive looking guys. Now clearly, beauty is in the eye of the beholder and to such a lady, she may not view her guy as being unattractive at all. After all, we are all different in what we may view as being attractive or unattractive. Certainly, after a couple have been dating for a while, a lady may no longer look at the physical surface level, but be more interested in what she feels about him, his character and what she is looking for from the relationship. This obviously includes how much she feels safe, secure and loved by him. Let's take a look at a few real-life stories that illustrate when one person seems be out of the league of another. Can you work out what it was that attracted the lady to her man?

- Sarah, 34, is a former model and divorced mum with two young children. Although she knows she is very attractive, she also wants to be realistic and recognises that not many men around her age range may be willing to share in the commitment to raise another man's children. She therefore needs a man to accept a ready-made family. In order to significantly increase her chances of getting a reliable, mature and financially stable husband, she has decided to forgo her usual upper age limit of no older than 5-7 years. Sarah was introduced to Josh, 55, through a mutual acquaintance at a party they both attended. He is divorced and has two adult children from his previous marriage, but they no longer live at home. Josh took her number and they agreed to meet for lunch. By appearance alone, they certainly did not look like a perfectly matched couple. Also, given her age and good looks, he would need to have something really special to compensate for his bulging belly and receding hair line. Fortunately, he does. He has an established career, owns his own home and has a successful side line business that he wants to continue to do when he retires. To their surprise, they also have lots of things in common. They both like current affairs, political biographies, and visiting stately homes and castles. They also enjoy cooking and trying out different foods from different cultures together. Sarah likes to help out at a local charity shop for the homeless every week and Josh volunteers at a local hospice. Sarah is also passionate about going to the gym 2-3 times a week, and although Josh can't promise to stick with that one, he did enjoy going for long walks with a local walking club up to a few years ago, which he wants to take up again. Sarah thinks that's a great idea, and says, "Let me know when you renew your membership of the walking club and I'll come along."

- Marco, 28, works in the construction trade as an electrical sub-contractor, but hopes to build up his business to be a main contractor one day, and then have a team of others working for him. He used to be in the military where he also qualified as an electrician, but he was medically discharged owing to suffering a wound in his left leg, and means he has a slight limp, but fortunately, can still get around unaided. At the moment, he rents his accommodation. Lily, 27, is a master's degree holder and has a successful career working in a bank. She earns considerably more than Marco, and already has a property she has a mortgage on. Her faith is very important to her and wants to marry someone who also shares the same faith and values as she does. Both Marco and Lily go to the same place of worship, where he also volunteers helping out with any electrical problems they have. One Sunday, after service, they somehow found themselves talking to each other in the church lobby. While they talked, they realised they seemed to share similar things in common with each other, and agreed to meet up the following Saturday for a brief lunch and a game of crazy golf at the local park. That came about because, randomly, in their conversation, Lily said that she always wanted to give golf a try. Although Marco also didn't have a clue how to play, had always been quick to see an opportunity when it presented itself.

- Anthony, a professional artist, met Tara, a self-employed advertising copywriter, in their local park one day, while she was taking Rusty, her dog for walk. Both are 34 years old. He goes there when the weather is good, but has to use a wheelchair owing to a disability. They got talking when she sat down on a park bench close to where he was. Anthony, who loves dogs, asked Tara about hers, and from there on, just got talking and talking. They agreed to meet up again. They also found they both have a strong interest in philosophy and poetry that stemmed from their respective university days. During their dating they also discovered they liked history and joined the local historical society and also decided to give some of their time volunteering together at a local museum. After a year,

Anthony popped the question and they agreed to set a date for marriage six months later.

In the light of the above life stories, being attracted to a lady that seems on the surface to be out of a man's normal league is not as strange as it sounds. Most of the while the thing that stops men from approaching ladies who are viewed as being too attractive for them is fear. However, fear can be viewed as False Evidence Appearing Real. Put simply, you don't know until you try.

Some people may have said that Ebun was out of Stephen's league. She had been privately educated. By contrast, Stephen went to a normal state school. Their ethnicity and cultural backgrounds are also very different. What was it that assisted Stephen to get Ebun hooked on him and agree to be his wife? That is very easy to explain in one word, "compatibility". We have many things in common. We are both university degree holders, although Ebun also has one better, a Master in Business Administration. We also share the same religious beliefs and values, as well as many other social interests as well. It was through church that we met. We nearly always found ourselves working on similar church projects, and it was through that our friendship developed.

If a man is looking for a lady who is out of his normal physical attractiveness range, he is very unlikely to get her through a dating app (except through niche apps, such as those that specifically target for example religion, ethnicity or similar). For a man to stand a chance to get a lady who has a higher attractiveness level than he does, they ideally should have similar compatibility interests. This could be like Marco and Lily being members of a local place of worship or like Anthony and Tara, having things in common like being active members of a local interest group. We discussed the importance of compatibility in Chapter 2: How to Get Your Most Compatible Date Match.

Persistence Pays

Sometimes, a lady can be difficult to get close to. She may guard her heart for the faithful man she thinks will deserve and treasure it most. The only way to break through this seemingly tough exterior is by regularly going out on dates together to build up her feelings of emotional attachment and trust for him. Also, the man needs to always be available to fix, solve and do things for her. This could include picking her up and dropping her off, as well as possibly regularly buying her small gifts. To get such a lady may require a lot of patience. If the lady is not saying "no" and not giving clear signs of disinterest, a man should not give up because persistence may lead her to eventually trust the man and give her heart to him. By contrast, if a man is always doing things for a lady and she does not agree to go on a date with him, then it is very likely that she does not want a relationship with him, and prefers to possibly keep him in her friend zone instead. More about being in the Friend Zone below.

The Friend Zone

A basic description of the friend zone is when two people know each other reasonably well, because they share the same circle of friends or work together. However, one of them has strong romantic feelings of attraction for the other but these feelings are not reciprocated. In such situations, it may be impossible to escape this zone. If you feel you are in this position and the person you are interested in is always acting calm, rational and matter-of-factly around you, then it means they definitely do not have any feelings of attraction for you. They just see you as a good friend, or perhaps even, more like a brother or sister to them. The bottom line is that they do not see you as mating material for them. In either case, you should not take it personally. If you are in this situation, then it would be more emotionally profitable for you to cast your fishing line for romance somewhere else. The reason for this is, the chances of turning a friend zone relationship into something romantic has a very low chance of success. Notwithstanding, here are our strategies to get out of the friend zone:

Ladies: If you feel that a man may have put you in his friend zone, the easiest way to test what his feelings are about you is to offer to take him out for a sandwich lunch somewhere. Make sure that when he sees you at the meeting, you are dressed up in something that is feminine smart casual but is different to what he has seen you wear before. Also, consider going for a different hairstyle look as well. If at the end of your lunch he insists on paying, then that could be a very good sign. However, if he feels responsible for you somehow, as if you were his younger sister, then he may pay anyway, and no progress will have been made. If he lets you pay or he offers to go halves only, then that means friendship is all he has in mind for you. If he responds positively, then tell him you look forward to doing it again. You will then have opened the door for him, but he needs to still walk through it. He still has to chase you at the end of the day.

Men: You have to be seen to be taking the lead. This is because ancestral man was a hunter warrior. It is your job therefore, to chase, and your job also to lead. Leading means being proactive. If you are normally calm and rational about life all the time and you can't sense any rush of excitement feelings going through your body as a result of taking a risk, it means that you are romantically dull. Also, always being relaxed and feeling content can be signs of low testosterone levels. That means it is time to eat healthy and do regular exercise such as going to the gym or running to raise your testosterone levels. The idea is to move from the friendly vibe to the lover vibe. This means that it is time to change from being dull to being proactive, fun and interesting to be around. This is the time to really exploit all you have learnt about the lady you are interested in. She told you that she likes men who are dressed in a particular way. She may have told you about a particular perfume for men she likes. She may have also told you about the character of the kind of guy she generally falls for. Implement your learnings, which means you may have to change your look and style. This may include changing your wardrobe for sharper newer clothing. Also practise good hygiene and regular grooming of your head hair and eye brows and getting rid of over grown hair in the nose and ears region. You should also ensure that if you have a beard and moustache they are regularly trimmed or consider having a fresh clean shaven look instead. All of these help to break the pattern of familiarity. Treat her to a light lunch or play crazy golf or indoor bowling or doing a walking sightseeing tour together. The point is to be doing something that is fun and active that will involve constantly smiling and looking into each other's eyes. The bottom line is that you have to take the relationship from the fun level to the attraction level.

Both: Take careful note of the above points. Also:
- Ask a trusted friend for an objective opinion on what they think about your dressing style and your personality, behaviour and demeanour with other people. Ask them what they think is either attractive or could be off-putting to someone of the opposite sex.
- Try taking a break of 3-6 months away from your group of friends, if you share the same circle of friends. It will break the pattern of over familiarity that exists between you. Come back with a fresh new image and makeover. For example, a new hair style, and trendy looking clothing and shoes.
- When you are alone with the person you would like to strike up a relationship with, make positive comments, like, "You look really awesome in that outfit". Or, "I liked very much what you said about…" Making statements like this are highly affirming and have the power to make the person you are interested in, think and feel differently

about you.

To do any of these successfully, you need to change yourself before you can expect other people to change how they think or feel about you.

Chapter 7: Where to Meet People

In recent years, one of the more common ways daters are using to meet others is through online dating apps. You may already have had previous experience of using these. We will look at online dating in closer detail in Chapter 9. In this chapter we will focus on different strategies for meeting new people offline, in the real world. Let's take a look at the many different ways that people currently meet.

Friends & Family

One of the most common ways people meet their marriage partners is through an introduction by either friends or family. Friends are a good option because they will know you very well, and maybe able to recommend someone they know to you. Also, it is very common for couples to have first met each other through a friend's party or other type of social gathering. Likewise, family networks can be a very good source for introductions, particularly if you have an ethnic background and want to meet someone with the same heritage, values and beliefs as you have. Ask your friends and family to be on the lookout for you. Also, when you get to hear of a party or other type of social gathering, accept the invitation. However, before you go, make sure you take note and follow the hints, tips and suggestions in Chapter 1: Principles for Love Attraction.

Making New Relationships

If you feel that the options for meeting new people seem to be a bit limited where you are, then this could be a good time to think about moving to somewhere new. Also, finding a new activity to take part in, can be a great way of meeting new people and having fun at the same time. We advise people to look for new group activities and interests they know they would enjoy trying and having a go at. Also, most importantly, make sure that the organisation or activity you want to join has a good balance of the sexes represented in it. For example, if you are a man, but always thought of taking up golf that may be a good fit if you are looking for exercise, but not if you are also looking for love, because around 75% of golfers are men.[143] On the other hand, if you are a lady, this could be a very good and wise option for you! However, for the man, it may be better, in this case, if he takes up tennis instead, where participation of the sexes are a little more balanced at 41% female and 59% male.[144] On the other hand, women make up over 80% of the recreational level Scrabble players, but men appear to consistently outperform women at higher levels of tournament playing.[145] Whatever new activity you wish to try, when looking for love, you can see that it may be worthwhile to do a little research beforehand.

Meeting people who share the same interests, activities and beliefs that you like to do means that you will already have something in common to build a relationship with. Examples of special interest groups worth exploring are:
- Political parties.
- Places of worship.

- Local activism groups, such as conservation and archaeology.
- Historical re-enactment societies.
- Local repertoire companies for amateur acting.
- Community welfare action and support groups.

Also, an excellent resource well worth checking out is the website Meetup.com. They are a portal to help groups advertise and encourage others to join them. A group that mainly targets people who are aged 50 plus, is the University of the Third Age for higher education (u3a.org.uk). They have local groups across the UK, and provide a wide range of opportunities for people to come together, learn and explore new ideas, skills and activities in a fun and relaxed environment.

Other places we know where people have met and found love:
- On a train to work.
- At a bar or club.
- A family or friend's party.
- Social or cultural events, such as weddings.
- Conferences, exhibitions, conventions and other special events.

The internet is an amazing source of information. Try putting into a search, 'conference' or 'exhibition' or 'convention' and then your area of interest, such as 'sci-fi', and see what comes up. If you decide to go to an event that is out of town, try to get one of your friends to go along with you for fun.

Getting Out of Your Comfort Zone

Remaining in a comfort zone can keep us from doing new things and meeting new people. A comfort zone is where a person feels mentally safe and at ease. By a person not coming out of their comfort zone to meet new people, they are guaranteed not to risk their feelings getting hurt. However, they also risk not getting married either. Making progress in life, including with relationships, sometimes carries with it a little risk and uncertainty. That is what makes falling in love such an exhilarating experience. Along the way, some people may let us down, but that does not mean everybody will. When you date someone new and form a close relationship with them, there is no guarantee you will not get emotionally hurt. If they do, and it is something you can overlook, then forgive them. If the problem is too great for you to overlook, wish them well, move on, go back to the dating pool and start again. As we said before, dating is a numbers game. It requires coming out of your comfort zone to meet with new people, until you eventually find the right One for you. That person is out there. It could be number 1, it could be number 100, but he or she is out there, and you will have to keep coming out of your comfort zone for as many times as is necessary until you meet that right One.

Leaving your comfort zone to meet new people might require you to:

- Go out to different places for dates and trying out new experiences.
- Move to a different part of town or a new city, to expand your opportunities to meet new people.
- Ask your employer for a location transfer to move to a different branch or part of the company.
- Find new hobbies, interests, or educational courses or join new clubs and societies.
- Consider dating a person of a different race or ethnicity to yourself. For more information, please see our bonus chapter on Interracial & Interethnic Relationships.
- Consider expanding your dating age range. For more information, please see our bonus chapter on Age Differences.

All these are powerful ways for leaving a comfort zone to meet new people. Sometimes, it may be good to take a break from environments that are over familiar to you, like existing friends or work colleagues. When you come back after a time, they will appear different to you and you will appear different to them.

Our Story

Before coming to the UK, Ebun never imagined that she would fall in love with a white Englishman. To say that Ebun, felt like she had stepped out of her comfort zone was probably a gross understatement. Also, Ebun's father always wanted her to marry someone who was from the same ethnic background and who could speak the same language. There were no end of eligible suitors who were both qualified and met his approval. However, Ebun was not convinced in her heart about any of them. At first, Ebun's father refused to consider Stephen, but as time went on, he eventually relented and gave his blessing for the marriage to proceed. The message in this story is very simple. Don't limit yourself, and never allow a comfort zone to stop you from connecting to the right God-sent man or woman of your dreams.

Conversation Starters

How to get a conversation started from scratch can be quite a daunting task. The suggestions below can be used by either sex. However, it is the responsibility of the man to take the lady's number and call her. If he says, "Let me give you my number". She should politely offer hers instead. If all else fails, the lady can give the man a miss call or better still a text with her name on it for him to call her back later. But it is always the man's duty to call the lady. If she breaks this principle, there is a high risk that he will not see her as a Woman of Worth. If he does not call her, it means that he never was really interested in her in the first place. Many men take phone numbers from ladies but end up never calling them. For them, it is simply an ego thing. If a man is sincerely interested in a lady then he will definitely call her. If he doesn't, a lady should not lose any sleep over it. Just move on.

Everyday things can be great to use to get a conversation started. This could also make an excellent random ice breaker. Using an item that someone else is holding is like an actor using a prop on stage. Here are some conversation starter suggestions using different prop items:

- *Books* – "Are you a fan of that author? "Are you into sci-fi too?", or "Are you studying that subject?", or "What are your initial thoughts about the book?"
- *Dogs* – "That is a lovely dog. What's its name?" "Is it an easy breed to take care of? … Any advice?"
- *Cafe* – "That sandwich looks really nice. Which bread and filler do you think makes a tasty sandwich?
- *Coffee* – "Does that coffee come with good conversation?"

You can just about use anything as a prop to get a conversation going, even the weather! Always be polite, courteous and considerate. Remember to watch that you do not intrude into another person's personal space. If you notice they have a ring on their left ring finger then leave them alone. Avoid harassing anyone. If they seem to be giving short shrift answers then this emphatically means that they are not interested in you, but maybe too polite to tell you. Besides using props, there are countless other conversation starter suggestions and ideas you can try from the internet.

Workplace: Dating

Your workplace is an excellent place to get a date. People sometimes think that workplace romances are either not allowed or are heavily discouraged. However, there is no law that says you cannot meet your future spouse this way. Some companies are even open to the idea of employees dating. However, it may be worthwhile to find out about your employer's policy on romantic relationships in your workplace, if they have one. In Stephanie Losee and Helanie Olen's book, Office Mate (2007), they state:

- Between 20% and 40% of those who have been in office relationships ended up in a 'committed long-term relationship'
- According to a British study in 2005, it found that over 70% of workers have had a relationship with a person they met through work.
- The American Management Association, in 2003 found that 30% of bosses admitted to having an office romance, with 44% of these couples getting married.[146]

Admittedly, the above studies on workplace dating behaviour were done while the internet was still in its early years, and quite some time before online dating apps became explosively popular through smartphone technology. But what they do reveal is that for people who do not work from home, the workplace still offers a huge opportunity to meet and form new relationships.

Finding your mate in your workplace does have distinct advantages, as Losee and Olen advocate: "Colleagues are a group of people with shared interests, whose backgrounds have been vetted by Human Resources (the workplace version of the Admissions Office), and whose passions have drawn them to the same company."[147] Another positive advantage of workplace dating is that there is no blind dating required, because you get to see what the personality and character of the person you are interested in is really like from simply observing them in their everyday workplace setting.

Workplace: How to Strike up Interest

Don't let fear get in your way or put you off. However, don't rush things, be patient, and wait for the right moment. Remember that it is a workplace and work-based relationships should always be treated discreetly in the beginning. This applies to both men and women. You can invite the person you are interested in, to a working lunch or just to buy them lunch as a celebration or team achievement or birthday gift. After all, it's your work colleague! Lunch can simply be something low cost like a sandwich wrap and a hot drink. It doesn't have to be more elaborate than that.

Other ways you could get a date in your workplace, is through slowly building up a friendship with a colleague or going out for social activities with your work mates outside of work. Also, the next time your boss suggests you be the one to attend that business convention you used to dread, say "yes" with enthusiasm. You never know who through networking you might meet.

Ladies: If you choose to take a male work colleague out for lunch, do not discourage him from paying if he insists. Also, it is definitely okay to say to the man afterwards that you would love to do it again sometime. Though, you will have to wait for him after that to ask you out. That is the price of being a Woman of Worth. If he lets you pay or wants to go 'Dutch' (that is, each paying half), then he is unlikely to be interested in you. Forget about him and move on. On the other hand, if he asks you to go out with him again, ask him with a smile, "Is this treat on you?" If after this, he expects you to pay or go half next time, you will need to let him know plainly, "I feel, if a lady and a man go out [to eat] on their own, the man should be a gentleman and pay. I am a traditional girl and that is how I was brought up." If the lady does not do this, then there is high risk that he will keep her in his friend zone.

Men: A man asking a lady work colleague for a date is not likely to be considered as sexual harassment but persisting when she has already said "no" will be very unwelcomed and disrespectful.

Both: Do not to use office communications such as company

emails or company mobile phones for private calls and text messages. This could be viewed as an abuse of company property.

Dating at University

University is not only about studying and providing a gateway into well paid employment, it also has a very powerful side benefit of networking and making new friendships and relationships that can last for decades. Many married couples first met at university.[1-8] Universities are therefore a highly fertile ground for meeting your future life partner. University life, like the workplace, allows you to see people for who they are. University campuses are generally very big places, which means that you are very likely to meet and mix with people that already have similar passions, values and interests as your own.

Ladies: If you do find love at university and the man has still not made clear after 6 months his intentions to you in terms of where he sees the relationship going, you should ask him. Also, when discussing with him about his plans for the future, make sure his career expectations are realistic and achievable. If he is studying acting, music or wants to be an entrepreneur, then please be warned, and as mentioned in Chapter 6, these career paths are precarious and often fraught with years of financial instability.

University Romances – Warning to Female Students

Many happy lifelong marriages started by a couple meeting at university. However, along with the good times of university life, are the temptations and pressures (to have sex) from young men who are always on the look out to test their sexual prowess. Parties, night clubs, pubs, and late night drinking are very commonplace as part of the university experience for many. Also it is not uncommon for illicit drug taking and getting drunk, along with the risks to women of having drinks spiked or being needle spiked with a date rape drug. All of which compromise the safety of women. Added to these risks is the prevalence of Sexually Transmitted Infections (STI) recorded among young people between ages 15 to 24. This age group accounts for 35% of all males with a new STI and 59% of all females with a new STI. Oral sex also carries very high risks of contracting various STIs, such as gonorrhoea, genital herpes, syphilis and human papillomavirus (HPV).[149] Infertility in women is strongly linked to Gonorrhoea and chlamydia, especially in the case of chlamydia, where the damage to the fallopian tubes without treatment over time are non-reversible.[150]

If a lady engages in a sexual relationship at university, she should make sure she takes precautions. This is to avoid getting either a sexually transmitted disease or becoming pregnant. She should insist her partner wears a condom. If she accidentally gets pregnant, it will most likely lead to her having to drop out of her course entirely or at the very least have to take a year out. Also, her family may have no choice but to step in as a support system for her to carry on with her education after the baby is born. The man responsible for the pregnancy, will very likely leave her, at some point. Either leading up to or soon after the baby is born. This is because he will be focused on his own studies at university along with wanting to guard his future career prospects. He will not welcome the responsibilities that come with raising a new family. He may blame her for not taking necessary precautions or even encourage her to have an abortion. However, in most cases, he will not marry her, and she will end up being a single parent to the child. Added to this, many men will not marry a single parent mother and use their financial resources to bring up another man's child.[151] That is the reality. Please do not be naive and think it cannot happen to you.

Chapter 8: Where to Go On Dates & What to Do

In this chapter, we will look at where to go on dates, and how to get the best out of them.

When Agreeing to Meet

This section is mostly meant for ladies, but men can also learn some things here as well.

Ladies: Whether you met the man online or in real-life, you have agreed to go on a first date. Now, all you need to do is decide when. If you agree to meet up too soon, it can convey to him that you are too eager or too desperate. Instead, you need to project to him that you are truly a Woman of Worth. In fact, he should be honoured and privileged that you have agreed to see him. If not, that is a problem. He also needs to understand that you are a busy lady and that he cannot take either you or your time for granted. He therefore needs to compete for your attention. Whether a man has read this book before or not, he will not be able to guess how busy you really are. If he is respectful, he should not even try to challenge you. Because of your busy schedule, it makes sense to delay meeting your date by at least 2 or 3 days. For example, if he contacts you on Friday, you should not agree to meet before at least Sunday. If he contacts you on Tuesday, you should not agree to meet him before at least Thursday. Let's see how this works in practice with an example scenario.

Samantha had been approached earlier in the day by Arthur, who had taken her number. They had met up quite randomly in a queue at a shopping mall cafeteria, and seemed to have got a really good conversation going. They were on their lunch break, but worked at different companies. He called her as he promised, and after going through preliminaries like, "It was great to meet you today", "How are you?" etc., he then raised the idea of meeting for a date. He thinks to himself, there is nothing like the present and says, "I am free tonight, if you are." But she doesn't want to come across as being too easy or desperate, because she wants him to value her. She has the option of responding in a number of different ways. For example:

- "Sorry, I cannot do tonight because I need to meet a deadline for work. ..." Or,
- "I am meeting a girl-friend for drinks. ..." Or,
- "This is my gym class night. I can do Saturday, if that's okay with you?"

If after Samantha has given any one of these responses, and Arthur is still being pushy and insisting on a date the same day, it could be a red flag and suggest that Arthur is just a player. Dates need to be paced out, if they are to succeed in getting to courtship. If the man says that he cannot wait 2 or 3 days, because of his own commitments then agree a day further away. Otherwise, your whole dating experience will revolve around how busy he is and not you, and you will never be his priority in the relationship.

Avoid long phone calls when you have not even met each other.

When you are talking to each other on the phone, it is always better for the lady to be the one to end the call. This puts her more in control and will help to convey the message that she is a busy lady. Also, a lady, should not respond to calls or texts after midnight. Neither should she do video calls after 10 pm (or early in the morning). The ONLY reason a man would be doing this is because he wants to try to catch a lady when she is in her PJs or nightie. Under no circumstances should a lady send explicit or revealing photos of herself. It is highly disrespectful to a lady if a man asks for nude or semi-nude photos. Ladies who have obliged such requests from male partners when the relationship was going well, not uncommonly find their nude photos or videos on 'revenge' pornographic websites after a breakup.

Men Should Always Pay on Dates

A man should always pay for dates because it demonstrates he can protect and provide for his lady when they are married. To emphasise, even if his plan is that they should both be co-breadwinners, he still needs to be the one paying for the dates. A man should still pay, even if his lady earns more. The only rare exception to this principle is if either the date is a birthday treat for him or if he is in a genuine Female Led Relationship. Ladies, if a man wants to either 'go Dutch' by splitting the bill with you, or get you to pay, you are dating a time waster. There is no harm in ladies offering to pay or contribute to the bill, but this should only be done to test the man. (However, be ready to pay just in case he absurdly agrees.) In our view, men should always pay for dates all the way, leading up to and even after the couple are married.

Men: If finances are a problem then take more walks in the park or go to lower priced venues or restaurants. Don't take a lady out on dates that are going to get you into debt with your credit card. Manage your finances well throughout the whole dating and courtship experience. Go to places that are fun and are going to be sustainable for your finances to manage. Don't try to rush and pack in as many dating experiences as possible. Less really is more. So pace out your dates. Taking a lady for a walk in the park or simply going cycling and having a picnic or packed lunch are fun and great things to do. If a lady consistently expects to be taken out to places that are going to be too much of a strain on your finances, then she is simply unlikely to be the right person for you. Let her go and move on.

Allow the Man to Lead

Men should usually take responsibility to lead in choosing the dates. If you are the man, and you would like help with knowing where to go on a date, give your lady two options to pick from. You can say, "I was thinking of 'A' or 'B'. Which one would you prefer?" If she says neither, then ask her what she may have in mind. It is always better for a date to be something that both of you can look forward to and enjoy together. Sometimes, deciding on where to go on a date can require a little light negotiation. That is part of relationship building.

Where to Go On a Date

The amount of places you can go for dates is really limited by your imagination. A good fun date is where there are lots of opportunities to keep up good eye to eye contact with lots of smiles throughout. Let's take a look at a list of exciting ideas for what could make fun dates to go on:

1. Bars, cafes, simple eateries.
2. Food festivals.
3. Zoos.
4. Art galleries and museums.
5. Castles and historic houses.

Chapter 8: Where to Go On Dates & What to Do

6. Gardens and mazes.
7. Cathedrals.
8. Cycling.
9. Escape rooms.
10. Virtual reality immersive gaming experiences.
11. Indoor bowling.
12. Tourist attractions.
13. Walking tours.
14. A walk at the beach or in a public park.
15. Fly a kite.
16. Dancing classes – maybe try different genres.
17. Boat rowing at a park lake.
18. Theatres and concerts – you can sometimes get good deals on tickets for afternoon shows.
19. Comedy clubs – however, some comedy acts can be regarded as being a bit too edgy for some people.
20. Short half day courses – learn a skill like: cake baking or cooking, painting, pottery, etc.
21. Special subject talks.
22. Indoor rock climbing.
23. Dinner (see below).
24. Cinema (see below).
25. Picnics (see below).

The above are just some random ideas we thought up ourselves, but we are sure you will be able to come up with some really great ideas yourself. Also, the internet can be a great source to come up with more dating ideas if you ever get stuck. We do not generally advise going to either dinner, the cinema or picnic in the first 1 to 3 dates, unless you knew each other reasonably well before you started dating. The reasons for this is that:

- *Dinner dates* – Can be unreasonably expensive choices for dates 1 to 3, especially if the daters choose not to take their dating any further.

- *Cinema dates* – Do not give much of an opportunity for positive interaction, such as maintaining eye contact and getting to know each other properly. We, therefore, advise you avoid the cinema until after at least the third date, unless you are planning to do something else afterwards.
- *Picnics* – Are also not suitable for the first one or two dates because they can make a lady feel trapped and a bit embarrassed to leave early or slip away if she feels the date is not going well. However, having a sandwich and a drink on a park bench is a great alternative.

Hot Drinks

Science has found that when a person is carrying a hot drink, their level of attraction goes up. This is because the person who is holding the hot drink is perceived to being a warm person. The opposite affect happens with cold drinks.[152] A light-hearted takeaway from this is for daters to avoid having cold drinks on a date unless the weather is already very hot!

Mobile Phone Etiquette

When on a date, put the mobile phone either on silent or turn it off, and then put it away. Looking at mobile phones while you are meant to be enjoying the moment with your date is a turn off. If you are expecting a very important phone call or you are on call because of work, then inform your date beforehand, so that they understand why if your phone does ring, the call is important. If you have to take a call, make sure it is very brief.

First Date Conversations

Everyone gets nervous on a first date. If a dater does not, that would be unusual. Feeling nervous is perfectly natural, and the other person probably feels just as nervous as you.

Try to keep your conversations as simple and light as possible. There are lots of things that you can talk about. Such as: family, work and career, educational experiences and goals, hobbies and interests. We know that other dating coaches advise to steer clear of potentially controversial subjects like sport, religion and politics on a first date. However, these can also be compatibility areas for some people. We advise not go too deep on any subject at a first date, but also to be highly respectful and open to the opinions of others. Also, we suggest you pace yourself, and open up about yourself slowly, giving room for more things to say on the next date. Try to ask open questions like, "How do you feel/think about ..." Avoid talking about bad experiences in your past, especially previous relationships. The following are just random suggestions to get you started.

- "What interested you about my online profile, and what did you think about the choice of photos I used?"
- "What kind of things do you like to do that make you happy?"
- "Tell me more about your hobbies and interests. How did you get into them?"
- "What do you like most about your job?"
- "What would your dream job be or are you already doing it?"
- "What did you study at university, and was it the right decision for you?"
- "How many siblings do you have, and what do they do?

Try to keep your first date short to about 1-3 hours. It is not about how long the date lasts but the quality of the experience and how memorably fun it was for both of you.

Enjoying Your Date

Having light-hearted type of conversations throughout the date is the best way of ensuring a positive, relaxing and enjoyable experience. This will increase the chance of a follow up date. Even if a date experience did not go to plan, because for example, you wanted to go to a funfair in the park, but it rained all day, the important thing is to lighten up and see the funny side of things. If your date is interested in you, even if the food is terrible and the service is poor, but you managed to keep cool and calm throughout, they will be fine and will probably laugh along with you. If a date does turn out to be a disaster and the person you are with are giving lots of negative criticisms, then that could be a warning sign of their true unpleasant character.

Pace Out Your Dates

It is very important that you pace yourself when building a new relationship. It takes time to get to know someone. It also takes time for true emotional feelings of attachment to be formed. Being in a rush to get to know each other will not quicken this natural process. In fact, it could suggest that one of the daters are emotionally desperate and needy.

Ladies: In the initial stages of the relationship, we advise you not go out with a man for more than 2 times in a week. This will make the times together more enjoyable because you will have fresh things to say to each other. Then, after three or four weeks this can be increased to 3 times a week. If the man wants to see his lady more than 4 or 5 times a week and has been seeing her for at least 9 months, he would normally know by then if she is the One. However, a man will usually delay proposing until he is absolutely certain in his mind that his lady is the One for him. Hence the reason why there is no point in rushing things.

Pacing the relationship allows you both to get to know each other over a longer period of time. This will help to avoid the risk of whirlwind romances. It takes at least 6-9 months to get to know someone enough to know if they are the right person for you to marry. Therefore, it makes sense to pace your relationship, so that it will grow naturally as both of you develop deeper feelings of love for each other.

Gifts & Presents

A man may give his lady a gift as a sign of his deep affection for her. Ladies should accept gifts from men as romantic gestures, because it is one of the ways a man will demonstrate to his lady that he is emotionally into her. Different men show 'gift giving' in different ways. Some men are romantic with gifts. Others are romantic with their time and labour. Others are a combination of both. A lady should never buy gifts for her man unless it is his birthday or other very special occasion. One or three or six month anniversary from first date of meeting does not merit the kind of special occasion we are discussing here. If a lady feels she needs to buy her man a gift, even if she can easily afford it, she should ensure that it will be of a significantly less value than anything he would buy for her. To ignore this could make him feel like he is being undermined in his role as protector and provider. If a lady wants to buy her man an expensive gift, she should wait until they are married.

Gift Ideas for a Lady

Romantic gifts are given to express thoughts of affection and love for someone. Most romantic gifts need not be expensive and can include: chocolates, flowers, pendants or other fashion jewellery items, etc. A man can get lots of good ideas for romantic gifts through an internet search.

If a man wants to buy his lady a perfume it helps to know what fragrances she likes. If he is not sure what to buy her, he can take a look at reviews for various perfume brands and products on Amazon or the internet, to see how a particular perfume is rated by others. Try to buy a brand name. Not all of them are expensive, and many are modest in price. Also try to buy eau de parfum and not eau de toilette. Eau de parfum contains around 15-20 percent pure perfume essence and lasts for about 5-8 hours. Whereas, eau de toilette contains about 5-15 percent pure perfume essence and usually lasts for about 3 hours. Whatever you buy, she will appreciate the thought. Avoid buying gifts that you cannot afford, or quickly pay off from your next salary. This includes special occasions like your lady's birthday.

"Should I Kiss at the End of the Date?"

Some societies and cultures accept kissing as being a normal part of the dating process (including first dates), and some do not. Also, some women do not want to hold hands or kiss on the first date. Men should therefore be mindful and respectful of personal space boundaries and not take anything for granted. All kissing should be consensual at all times. It is a lady's personal choice if she wants to allow a kiss on the lips at the conclusion of the date. However, even consensual kissing on the lips can be quite intense and trigger a rush of oxytocin and other hormones in a lady that can take her off her guard. Alternatively, a lady may prefer to settle for either a kiss on the cheek or a light peck on the lips.

Ladies: How to Get the Guy to Be Really Into You

One of the fastest ways for a lady to get her man to develop deep emotional feelings for her is if she shares similar interests and passions in things he likes to do. When men do things together it brings out a strong sense of loyalty and camaraderie between them. When a couple do things together, it can replicate in a man similar feelings of camaraderie. As an example, if a man likes soccer, a lady could consider going to a soccer game with him. If he likes golf, she could give it a try, and may end up enjoying it.

Ladies: Safety on Dates

Just a few safety tips for ladies, which we are sure you have heard before but for the sake of completeness, are given as a healthy reminder:

- Do not have too much to drink. Alcohol reduces inhibitions. Therefore, for your own safety and welfare and also to ensure that you do not say or do something you may later regret, drink slower and drink less. If you do drink less, it is likely your date will as well. If he strongly insists that you drink more, then treat that as a red flag.
- During the date, a lady should try to be alert to ensure her drink is not tampered with. That is, spiked with a drug to incapacitate her free will and judgment.
- We advise that if you do not know your date before first meeting them, you should go home by cab after the first or second date. After this, you can agree for your date to either pick you up or drop you off. Otherwise, the man can walk you to your bus stop or train station.
- Lastly, for your own safety, make sure you keep at least someone in the loop where you are, at all times.

Recognising a Player

If during the date, the man is stroking the lady's palms, inside wrists, upper arms, shoulder, neck, ears or her back, or touches any sexual parts of her body it means that he wants to get her into bed. He is deliberately trying to manipulate the lady's oxytocin levels to sharply rise, and at the same time, reduce her inhibitions so she might sleep with him. Such a man is disrespectful and has no interest in long term relationships. In short, he is a player. Men who are respectful and kind on dates, touch sparingly and only with consent. When they do, this is likely to be limited to holding hands (again with the lady's consent) or guiding her with his arm into an entrance. A player has no concept of a woman's right to her personal space.

How to Decline Further Contact

Ladies: Below are some suggested ways to politely say to a man you are not interested in a relationship.

- "I enjoyed meeting you, but I don't feel a connection."
- "I have liked our times together, but I do not feel we are compatible with each other."
- "I feel that there is insufficient things in common between us to make it work."
- "It was good to meet you, but I feel that we are too different to make a relationship work."
- "I had a lovely time with you, but I don't think we are a good match or into the same things."
- "I like you as a friend, but I don't feel anything more than that for you."
- "I don't see you as anything other than a very good friend."

Men: Please take note. If a man continues to pursue a lady that is not interested in him, this is harassment. He should desist. Stalking and harassment are criminal offences. In short, if the man is not getting anywhere in trying to build a relationship, then he should move on, because there are plenty of other fishes in the sea. The oceans of the world are full of them.

Being 'Ghosted' - When the Man Does Not Call or Text Back the Lady

'Ghosting' is the phenomenon in dating when a person ends a relationship with someone by suddenly cutting off communication with them, for example, by no longer responding to calls or text messages. Sometimes, it does happen that after initial dates have seemingly gone so well, suddenly one of the daters without warning, breaks off contact with the other. If you are a lady, and this happens to you, we advise that you do not wait any longer than 8 weeks. If you do not hear anything from the man after this time, it means he has moved on, and so should you.[153]

If a lady has not heard anything after two or three weeks and she needs closure, then she can send him a very brief text message, such as, "Hi [Name], hope you are keeping well. Take care." Do not put, "love from" or "xxx". If he responds, he may reply, "I am good, how are you?" You can respond in the same way and just add, "Just checking on you." After that, you need to let him make the next move. In short, he has to call you. The truth is, if he has not called or texted you, then it means he is simply not interested in you. Again, time to move on!

When to Disclose Sensitive Things about Yourself

We all have sensitive and embarrassing aspects of our lives that we would only share with those we feel we can completely trust. Trust is not only earned, it is absolutely vital to any relationship. Keeping back sensitive information from your partner is likely to be treated as a betrayal of trust later on if the information is not disclosed in a timely manner. The time to disclose sensitive information with each other will be dependent upon what the information is. Our advice is to pace out sensitive information gradually, especially if there is a lot to disclose (to avoid information overload).

Information that should be disclosed before having sex:

- Sexually transmitted infections.
- Fertility issues.
- Sexual dysfunction issues (such as vaginal dryness or other pain, or erectile dysfunction, or fear of sexual intimacy, etc.)
- Gender identity dysphoria (identifying with a different gender to one a person is born with).
- Same sex attraction.
- Asexual (has no sexual feelings, desires or attraction to anyone).
- Previous marriages.
- Children that you have ever had, regardless of age or circumstances.
- Illnesses and diseases (including heart conditions, cancer, diabetes, or heredity, like sickle-cell and other blood disorders).
- Mental health problems or disorders, including psychiatric diagnosis or treatment that has not been signed off as being cured. Some of these can be genetic. Please also see our bonus chapter on Mental Health.
- Tattoos or piercings in places that are not easily seen.
- Any disability (physical or mental) whether obvious or not. For more information, please also see our bonus chapter on Dating & Disabilities
- Criminal convictions for sexual or violent offences (including spent convictions).

Information that must be disclosed between courtship and engagement:
- All of the above if you have not had sex by this time.
- Salary and other income (including pensions).

- Property and assets.
- Debts, bankruptcies, financial obligations (including spousal and child maintenance payments)
- All criminal convictions including those spent.
- Anything else that could either jeopardise a marriage relationship or might be reasonably viewed as a cause of concern by the other person.

Relationships Take Time to Build

It takes time to get to know someone and build a meaningful relationship with them. The only way you can truly know each other is when you have successfully gone through a few storms and crisis together. It is during such challenging times that feelings of emotional attachment, dependency, trust and confidence in each other get tested, grow and deepen. Going through challenging times together can help to show if you are truly meant for each other. The dating and courtship period can take at least 6 to 9 months. There are no short cuts. This is because the dating and courtship process vitally prepares you for your marriage.

Chapter 9: Online Dating

Finding Love Before the Internet

Before the 1940s, the traditional way that people met their life partners was through introductions made by family and friends, or meeting up through social gatherings or other cultural activities that happened in their local community. They may have even known each other beforehand, through living in the same vicinity or neighbourhood, perhaps living no more than 2 or 3 streets away from each other. Now-a-days, with more and more people migrating from local towns and villages to metropolitan cities, as well as from city to city, and one country to another, two people meeting each other and falling in love from the same neighbourhood is considerably less likely. Most people who live in high rise apartments do not even know their next door neighbours, never mind who else lives on the same street as they do. Before the days of the internet, some people looking for love, used personal ads in dating columns of newspapers, and replies would be made by writing to a box number in the personal ad. People also used professional introduction agencies. This was followed by premium rate phone numbers in personal ads that offered near immediate contact by people leaving their details in voicemail inboxes. From the early days of the internet in the

1990s, dating then started to go online through social media and dating websites. As a result of mobile and smartphone technology, more people than ever before can now meet new people by contacting each other instantly through social media and online dating apps that can be downloaded onto their phones. The old local neighbourhood ways of meeting have now given way to a newer kind of cyber worldwide neighbourhood that is almost accessible by anyone from nearly anywhere in the world, with a smartphone. The positive thing about online dating is that you get to meet a huge range of new people that you are unlikely to have met any other way. A possible downside is that the people you meet online may be less likely to share a similar social and cultural background experience as yourself. This may be problematic for compatibility reasons, because compatibility is important for a relationship to be sustainable. To get round this, many niche dating sites have emerged to offer people a way of meeting others, based on ethnicity, age, disability, religion, and even political party affiliation, etc. The internet has successfully introduced new ways of meeting people, but traditional ways still apply in building relationships that can go the distance for marriage.

Finding Love Online

There are many dating apps to choose from to meet people from many different cultures and societies. As a result of the internet and the ease of worldwide air travel, the world has become a smaller place. From research conducted by The Knot in 2021, 1 in 4 of engaged couples met online.[154] This is a huge leap, because only 7% of marriages in 2015 were the result of online dating.[155] Also, Stanford University Professor Michael Rosenfeld, drawing from a nationally representative survey of American adults that was conducted in 2017, found that about 39 percent of heterosexual couples reported meeting their partner online, compared to 22 percent in 2009. The same study points out that in 1995, 48% of people would meet through friends and family,

Chapter 9: Online Dating 153

but by 2017 this figure had dropped to 27%.[156] By comparison, the UK has followed a similar upward trajectory in the popularity of dating apps. Research by dating platform, eHarmony, and the Imperial College Business School, found that 32% of relationships between 2015 and 2019, started online, compared to only 19% between 2005 and 2014. By 2035, it is predicted that 50% of relationships would have begun online.[157]

In our conversation with, Clare, aged 26, about her experience with using dating apps. She told us that she met her fiancé through Tinder, and was getting married in two months' time. She also said that 4 out of 5 of her other friends who were getting married had also met their partners online. Over the years, we have heard of similar success stories of where Tinder can be a go to place for serious relationships leading to marriage. Tinder and similarly, Badoo, are widely reported to be the most popular of the photo-heavy dating apps available.[158] For many people of Clare's age, what makes these apps appealing is that users can swipe through lots of profile pictures quickly, and then simply select who they find most attractive. They work on a superficial level for both men and women, but in different ways. Both men and women will pick what looks attractive to them. However, on the science level, men mainly go for sexual attraction. With women, this is slightly less so, because, without realising it, subtly women may also lookout for good mating quality in regards to good genes. They do this by comparing left and right facial features for symmetry. If a user likes what they see, they can then go a bit deeper and look at the basic information provided in a user's profile. The problem with this is that while someone may be subjectively judged to have a really good looking appearance, they may have a very unattractive personality and character. The reverse can also be true. Someone who is judged to be below average in looks, may actually have a really warm and beautiful personality, which may ultimately get overlooked. It therefore, should not be a surprise to learn that these kind of apps appeal to those under the age of 45. In fact, over 96% of users on Tinder, are reported to fit in this category.[159] As a warning, our readers should also be aware that it is also reported that a significant number of the users on these photo heavy dating apps, are already married or in some other long term relationship.[160]

Dating App Suggestions

The following suggested dating apps are available for download on Android or iPhone. Registration on these apps is free, but some of them may require the user to pay a monthly subscription fee to access premium services, such as sending and receiving messages. Although we cannot make any specific recommendations, ultimately, the only way to find out which app may work best for you is to try some of them and see how you get on.

- Eharmony – good for serious relationships.
- Match – largest user database.
- OkCupid – tries to match users with those who are regarded as being most compatible.
- Hinge – very good for under 35s.
- Tinder – very large user database, better for under 35s.
- Badoo – very large user database for either serious or casual daters.
- Bumble – women make the first move with this app.
- Plenty of Fish – free, with very large database for all ages, race and culture.
- Happn – marketed for busy people.
- Parship – for long-term commitment, plus 52 per cent of users are graduates.
- EliteSingles – for high level earners.
- InnerCircle – elitist entry system, with application process to be approved to join it.
- SilverSingles – good for meeting older people.

- Frolo – for single parents.
- Facebook Dating – available through their main social media app and is free, and with a very large database for all ages, races and cultures.

It is widely reported that there are over a thousand dating sites to choose from on the internet. Many of which appeal to specific niche interest groups, such as religion, ethnicity, age, etc. They are relatively easy to locate, by making an internet search. For example, try typing in '[name of religion]' and then 'dating apps', or try the keywords, 'interracial dating', etc. If you like what a particular dating app or website is offering, we suggest before paying for any of their services, that you first of all check them out through making an internet search, to see if you can find independent positive reviews about them.

Creating a Username

When registering on a dating app, the first thing you need to do is create a username. When picking a username for your profile, try to pick one that sounds pleasant and upbeat, for example, Sunnyflower937 or Gallantknight223. Avoid usernames that contain sexual references or are suggestive, for example, Hotgirl123 or Superrider134. Do not use your actual name otherwise, it may be possible to find you through either an internet search or social media by linking your name and what you write in your profile. Though, this last point may be a bit muted because Tinder already allows its users to link their Instagram accounts to their profile.

Photos for your profile:
1. It is absolutely essential that you upload more than one photo (minimum of 3) on your profile, but around 6 photos are ideal.
2. Main profile photo – a photo of you alone. Dress to

impress. Dress as if you are on your first date. Women should wear something that accentuates their body shape, but not tight fitting. Men should be smart casually dressed.
3. Other photos – These can show you doing something you like to do, or holiday photos that show you enjoying yourself, or simply relaxing.
4. This is only optional: use a single group (family or friends) photo at the end. The photo should not have you standing next to anyone of a different gender to your own. Otherwise, a prospective dater, will wonder if it is your girlfriend or boyfriend next to you. Using a group photo also demonstrates you are sociable, but you must be easily distinguishable from the other people in the group. Group photos can also be used to show your true height if you do not want to mention it in the information section about yourself.
5. A photo with a pet is very good because, currently, half of the UK are pet owners.

Photo Dos and Don'ts tips:
- Do try to get a trusted friend who is good at taking photos. If you want to get a professional photographer to take your photos that is fine, but we suggest not in a studio, and make sure the photos represent things you like to do. The risk with professional photography is that the photos can end up making you look clichéd, model like or self-absorbed. Rather, you need photos that capture your personality, uniqueness, openness and show the real you.
- Do make sure the photos you have are of very high quality (no blurring, grainy looking or bad lighting) and you must be easy to spot in them. Try to use outside photos with natural lighting or inside with daylight lighting.
- Do have some photos of yourself in different scenes with about 3 different outfits. The clothing does not have to be

brand names, however they should look neat, ironed and tidy. Avoid overhanging clothing that hide your body shape. Women should not wear bikinis, revealing or tight fitting clothes because it will make them look sexually easy, and not really wanting a serious relationship. Men should be decently dressed, no shirts off, no sagging trousers, or naked poses.

- Do remember to look relaxed and smile in all your photos – this is very important! If your teeth look discoloured, then consider getting dental whitening treatment before having your photos taken. Absolutely, no sunglasses!
- Do include full body shots where the entire body – head to toe – is visible.
- Do use photos of you, doing your hobbies and interests because they make great talking points.
- Do make sure the photos are current (taken within the last 12 months of you uploading them).
- Don't use cut off body images of photos with you and someone of the opposite sex (because they can give the impression the person may be either you're your current or ex-boyfriend or girlfriend).
- Don't use photos with children or babies in them, otherwise it will be assumed they are yours. Even if they are yours, it is not advised to place their photos on a dating site.
- Don't use social media filters in your photos, because they will make you look immature and silly.

Creating Your Profile

When creating your profile, quality really does matter over quantity. Therefore, keep your profile wording short, fun and engaging. Your profile needs to reflect your positive personality.

Take your time in writing your profile. Prepare beforehand by seeing what others have written about themselves on their profiles. For example, was the style of wording attractive or off putting? You will quickly learn what sounds and looks good, when you do this. Also, you can get some good ideas on what to write by doing an internet search for sample online dating profiles.

One of the highest ranking qualities that ladies look for in a man is a genuine sense of humour. If you feel you are not the humorous type, then at least make your profile sound positive, light-hearted, hopeful and fun. Also, if you include in your profile the things you like to do, you are more likely to attract a similar kind of person. For example, you might say, "I love traveling to new places". "I love to explore castles and learn about their history". "I enjoy going to Zumba dance classes/camping/hiking, etc. …" The list of things you can say here are almost endless, but they need to be things you already do. If you are stuck on what to write about yourself, ask a friend who knows you very well to help you.

Be sincere with what you write. Do not exaggerate. Do not use swear words or other offensive language. We suggest you do not say how much you earn or where you work, but you can say what you do. Consider ending your profile by asking a question that invites anyone interested to contact you. For example, "I like to explore new places, what do you like to do?"

What Are You Looking For?

Some dating coaches argue that ladies should never state they are "Marriage Minded" because it will give the game away of why they are on the dating site in the first place. We don't think it matters one way or the other. However, if you feel this is an issue for you, there is nothing stopping you picking the option to indicate you are seeking a 'Long Term/Serious Relationship'. In this instance, if a person sends you a message through the dating app asking you what you are really looking for, you can simply respond, "I am looking to meet new people and happy to see if something develops later on from there." This is, after all, stating the obvious.

Who You Are Looking For?

When describing the kind of person you are looking for, try to be as simple and brief as possible. If you are too specific, then it may reduce the number of responses you get.

When writing your profile, you could say things like, "I am looking for someone who doesn't take life too seriously. I love going for walks and visiting places of interest. I also have an interest in current affairs. I have a small pet dog, and hope you are okay with that?" Alternatively, you could say, "Looking for someone to have fun and explore [museums/art galleries/new travel destinations, etc.] with." The important thing is not to get bogged down with details and keep it light.

If you are looking for a person who believes in God, saying, "Must be God fearing" is okay. However, if your religious faith is important to you, then it would be better to say, "My Christian [or other religion] faith is important to me, I hope it is important to you too?"

Do not use negatives, such as, "Cheats and liars keep away." Do not say things like, "Must be open and honest". It is the same thing as saying, 'All liars keep away'. The fact is that while some people are not open and honest, these are the minority. At the end of the day, trust is earnt, and it takes time to trust anyone in a new relationship.

Sticking to What Is Important to You

Everybody has values, beliefs, aspirations, principles and preferences that are important to them. Deciding the non-negotiable items is very important. You may recall that we treated this in Chapter 2, in the section called: Making a Needs Wish List. As you work on your profile, you can use the list you completed there to help you.

Checking Out Profiles

When looking at profiles you are interested in, check if there are any obvious compatibility areas you share with them. Avoid profiles that have negative statements, such as:

- "I am not looking for…"
- "He must be financially stable/solvent…"
- "No drama queens …"
- "No high maintenance …"
- "Not into playing games …"
- "No gold diggers/cheaters/liars …"
- "Knows how to treat a lady …"

Obviously, this is not an exhaustive list. Profiles that contain negative statements generally reveal bad past relationship experiences that have not been satisfactorily dealt with.

What is a High-Maintenance Lady?

When men think of a lady as 'high-maintenance', they often feel she is not worth the trouble. A stereotypical view of a high-maintenance lady is someone who has higher than normal expectations and therefore may come across as demanding, difficult to please or deal with. The vast majority of ladies are not like this. However, if a lady sees on a man's profile, "No high-maintenance ladies please". It is better that she passes over them, because the man may well be either a lazy romantic or still dealing with negative emotions arising from a previous relationship.

Also, despite how people on social media at times look and pose in their photos and videos as if they are living the dream, very few are really like that in real-life. They are just ordinary human beings, working or studying, and trying to make ends meet, like everyone else. We have come across many people in meaningful relationships who met through their respective social media platforms. In reality, there are very few genuine high maintenance people, and they are unlikely to last in long term relationships. Most people want to date someone who has a good nature and manners, knows how to hygienically take care of themselves, and dresses well and appropriate for special occasions.

Making First Contact

When a man wants to make contact with a lady, he should avoid using single word sentence greetings like, "Hey!" Because, it doesn't say anything, and often makes a lady want to ignore the message. Instead, he should ask her about something on her profile that either sounds interesting or better still that you both have in common. You could say, for example, "I notice on your profile that you like to travel. I do as well. Which countries have you been to, and which is your favourite?" Or, you could say, "Hope your day has been good. From your photo, I can see that you like to drink wine. Which do you prefer, red or white?" If you are really stuck, then go through the person's photos. You could say, "The landscape in the background looks awesome! Is that one of your holiday pics?" Or, "I love your dog, what's their name? How old is it?" Or, how about, "That is a great photo of you doing gardening (or rock climbing). Is that your passion?" Or, "Lovely photo of you holding the glass of wine. If I invite you to go for a drinks somewhere, would you accept?" These are just icebreaker type questions that may hopefully get a positive response and a conversation going.

Ladies: If a man offers his number, and you like him, just send him a text saying, "This is [your name], from [name of dating app]. You can call me on this number." If you are comfortable sending him your number, through the dating app, then that is fine. As we have discussed before, he needs to be the one asking you out on a date. Avoid long conversations on the phone until you get to meet each other. Similarly, avoid pro-longed texting back and forth to each other. If he is not offering a meet up after the 6th or 7th text, then delay responding to him longer and longer each time until he gets the message. Remember that it is the man's responsibility to chase you. You need to be a challenge to him. This also shows him that you are a true Woman of Worth.

Men: Try to make your conversation light hearted. Do not use sexual references or suggestive language, because both are a huge turn off. When text messaging, always try to use correct spelling and good grammar, because many ladies actually look at this. Always be polite, and show good manners and behaviour. Once you have got a good flowing conversation going, then ask for a meet up.

Safety

Ladies: Don't go on a date with a man without first telling someone else who you are meeting with, and where you are going. Give regular updates to that person on your location, whilst on the date. You can also use your smartphone to share your location with a trusted friend or family member.

Also, if you are not confident about giving out your personal number, there is nothing stopping you getting a cheap phone and a pay as you go sim card. That way, you can keep your dating life separate to your everyday life.

Beware - Online Dating Scams

Romance fraud, in the UK alone, increased by 20% in 2020 (compared with 2019) with victims losing around £68 million pounds,[161] and 63% of victims being women.[162] Dating scammers use online dating apps and websites pretending to be genuine daters. The vast majority of them steal profile pictures of real people from their social media profiles. They always give excuses for not being able to meet you and always ask for money once a sufficient rapport has been established.

Why do these scammers succeed in duping people who may otherwise feel they are too smart to be scammed? When a person is sincerely searching for love and romance, it is only natural to hope that the other person is trustworthy to at least begin a relationship with. Falling in love, by its very nature, makes us vulnerable. It also causes the normal rational and critical thinking areas of the brain to be clouded. Dating scammers use this to build a false relationship, which the victim genuinely believes is real. When people are being duped in this way, they may not know it until it is too late. This is why dating scammers sound so convincing and why so many people get scammed by them.

Always be on your guard and refuse requests for money. Treat these requests as red flags and alarm bells. These scammers will give many reasons why they need you to desperately send money to them. Here are some examples:

- Hospital fees for either themselves or a supposed sick relative.
- Money for visa and flights to visit you.
- Investment money for a business.
- Help towards paying for accommodation or university fees.

- Paying for online gift cards.

If anyone asks you for money, just ask a friend or family member or other trusted person what they think. Or imagine it is you giving the advice if the situation were reversed. What would you tell them? The reason why banks now flood customers with warnings asking them to check who they are sending money to is because of the thousands of people who get duped into sending their hard earned life savings to these online fraudsters.

Catfishing – What is it?

Catfishing is luring a person into an online relationship with no interest of meeting them in real-life. You can see many examples of it by watching episode clips from MTV's series Catfish, on Youtube. Catfishing is done by people who are too scared or cowardly to show who they really are. Many times the catfisher knows their victim in real-life. They will keep up an online relationship for many months (sometimes longer) by hiding behind a false profile. Their purpose is to enjoy a fantasy relationship. We are sharing this so that you do not waste time with people who try to keep their victim online but refuse to meet in real-life. This is not normal behaviour for people who want a genuine relationship. A normal person, who is genuinely interested in wanting a real relationship, will want to get off the dating app as quickly as possible to arrange to meet with you as soon as possible. If this is not happening, then move on!

Checking for Fake Profile Photos

If you want to find out if a profile you suspect has a fake photo on it, you can use Google Images search facility for this. Please follow these instructions.

Laptop or a desktop computer:

Chapter 9: Online Dating 165

1. Go to the Google search page.
2. Click on the camera icon in the search bar to the right.
3. Either drag and drop a photo into the box or upload a file of the photo or copy and paste the link to where the photo is on the Internet.

Android smartphone
1. Open up your web browser.
2. Tap the three dots icon in the top right hand corner of the screen.
3. Tap the 'Desktop site' option to enable it.
4. Go to the Google search page. If you do not see the desktop version, then type in the search bar 'Google search', and then do a search.
5. Tap on camera icon in the search bar to the right.
6. Either drag and drop a photo into the box or upload a file of the photo from your phone or copy and paste the link to where the photo is on the Internet.

iPhone
1. Open the Safari browser.
2. For:
    - iPhone iOS 13 and above, click on the 'aA' button next to the address bar, and then select 'Request Desktop Website' from the options.
    - iPhone iOS 12 and earlier versions, tap and hold on the "Refresh" button next to the address bar, and then select 'Request Desktop Website' from the options.
3. Go to the Google search page. If you do not see the desktop version, then type in the search bar 'Google search', and then do a search.
4. Either drag and drop a photo into the box or upload a file of the photo from your phone or copy and paste the link to where the photo is on the Internet.

Chapter Recap

Ladies: If you choose to use an online dating app, once a man has contacted you and, you think you like him, the object is to get offline as quickly as possible. So that you can meet up in the real world. Unfortunately, there are many time wasters out there that do not want to meet up in real-life. You can discourage such men, by taking longer and longer to respond their messages. Always give short but positive answers. Despite the initial excitement of having been picked out by someone, he should not be able to take your time for granted. Also, never agree to a same day or next day meet up. Your time is important to you and, it is not unreasonable for a prospective dater to understand that. Irrespective of how empowering for women that online dating is, you need to ensure that you remain a challenge for a man. So that they will be the one chasing you and value you more for it!

Men: Online dating provides people with a great opportunity to meet someone for a relationship that could lead to marriage. Whether online or offline, throughout the dating and relationship building process, it is your job as the man to do the chasing. Online dating does not change this. Therefore, once you feel you are interested in a lady, then secure a date and meet up with her as quickly as possible so that she does not think you are not a serious person. Ensure, you are always polite, courteous, well-mannered and well-behaved. If she turns you down at any time, then accept it because she may not feel a connection or perhaps believes there isn't enough in common between you two to take things further. Be a gentleman and wish her well with her own love search and, then move on.

Chapter 10: Long Distance Relationships

Engaging in a Long Distance Relationship

Long distance relationships face particular challenges and difficulties that are unique and different to ordinary relationships. For the purpose of this chapter, our definition of a long distance relationship is when each dater lives in a different city or country to the other, and the distance between them is more than a 2 to 3 hours' drive. In practice, this means that the frequency of being able to meet up for dates will be significantly less compared with normal dating.

Pitfalls of Long Distance Relationships

Let's take a look at some of the pitfalls of long distance relationships, and why it is often very difficult to make them work.

1. Long distance relationships can last a very long time, even going into years before a couple may feel ready to get married and then live together as husband and wife. If you are considering embarking on such a relationship, we

strongly advise that you first of all check out the visa requirements for the country you both wish to reside in.
2. If you did not know each other beforehand, communication can be very difficult, especially when trying to think of things to say to each other. This is because, although you can talk about your family, work and what things you got up to during the day, it can be very difficult to sustain these type of discussions in the longer term.
3. Communicating when you are in different time zones to each other could mean that it is very easy to miss the exact time you are meant to call each other if things such as work or other activities get in the way. Also, making a phone call to a person in a different country can be expensive, even if you can make your calls using an international phone calling app on your smartphone. If the internet signal is not reliable or strong enough, then it will be hard to make video calls to see each other.
4. Feelings of jealousy or insecurity about the relationship may be hard to deal with. Genuine trust is earnt in a relationship by being around someone and seeing how they behave. It is difficult to do this in a long distance relationship, because you only have the word of the person you are dating to rely on.
5. Compatibility is essential for building a long lasting marriage. Actively making compatibility a bedrock of the relationship will be very difficult to do in a long distance relationship. For more information on compatibility, please see Chapter 2.
6. There may be a time that you could end up getting 'ghosted' by your long distance dater. He or she may not return your text or calls for days or weeks because they are exploring other dating options locally to them. Also, they may give up with the relationship because they might feel it was not going anywhere. How long will you give it before you lose faith in the relationship and decide to move on?

7. Your long distance relationship dater may ask you for money. Unless a proposal has been made and accepted through a face to face meeting in the real world, and your marriage date is no more than 3-6 months away, we strongly advise that you do not do this under any circumstances. For more information on reasons why you should not send money to a dater, please see Chapter 9, at the section called, 'Beware - Online Dating Scams'.

Before going ahead with a long distance relationship you need to be sincere with yourself about whether or not it truly makes sense for you to try it. We have come across people here in the UK with spouses abroad and in limbo because they cannot prove they earn enough to meet the minimum annual income requirement of £18,600. We recommend that you do your research regarding the spouse visa requirements for the relevant country you may both wish to reside in, but ideally before emotional attachment feelings begin to form.

How Far Away Is Too Far Away?

If it is not practical for the two daters to be able to meet up at least once a week, it will be difficult for them to get to know each other properly. This is why long distance relationships are rarely successful, unless the couple already knew each other reasonably well in real-life to begin with. Long distance relationships also carry sexual fidelity issues. We know of many women who were in a long distance relationship and would choose to take a pragmatic view and say, "At the end of the day, men are men. What he does away from me is fine as long as I don't get to hear about it." To us, this is not a healthy view to have for a relationship. Also, relationships that were the result of a holiday abroad are often founded on feelings based on lust, and therefore can be very difficult to sustain in the longer term.

Becoming emotionally invested and bonded in a relationship almost solely through making phone calls, text messages or video calls but not actually meeting in real-life is a false relationship. It is not possible to know someone enough for a marriage to work unless there is regular contact in real-life. Also, despite how a person may come across in either a phone or video call, a dater will have absolutely no way of being able to check to know if what the other person is saying to them is true. This is how romance scammers work. They first of all try to build up an emotional attachment bond from a distance, and then convince a person that the relationship is real, before asking for money.

Making Long Distance Relationships Work

Long distance relationships should be treated in the same way as if both daters were living in the same city. For instance, it is the man's duty to go to the lady's city. Even if he offers to pay for the lady's ticket to come to him, she should politely decline, because his motives for paying for her flight and hotel can only be because he wants to have sex with her and nothing else. When the man visits the lady in her city, he should stay at a hotel. We strongly advise that she should not follow him to his room. If the lady wants to successfully demonstrate that she is a Woman of Worth, she should not sleep with the man until she fully knows that he is emotionally attached and committed to her. Normally, this takes around 2-3 months, but it is likely to take much longer if visits are not frequent enough to get to know each other properly. Once sex comes into the relationship, it can be very difficult (if not impossible) to separate lust from genuine emotions and feelings. If a lady chooses to ignore this advice of refraining from sex before a proper emotional commitment has been established, then she should at least make sure the man is wearing a condom to protect against unwanted pregnancy and sexually transmitted infections. With long distance relationships, people can say and lie about anything and it will be difficult to prove otherwise.

If after the man has visited his lady in her city for the first 2 or 3 times and she wants to go to his city, then again, we suggest she books a hotel or she stays at one of her family's or friend's home, but not his. Don't invite him back to your hotel room or go to his place for at least the first 2 visits. Don't be in a rush to hurry the relationship forward. It normally takes quite a few months to get to know someone properly, to see as many sides of their character as possible. A long distance relationship that is rushed is likely to lead to conflicts and unhappiness in marriage. Therefore, don't try to fit several months of dating and relationship making into only a few days.

Unfortunately, given the nature of long distance relationships, fidelity is not guaranteed when you are away from each other. Giving a man sex, even after waiting for 3 months does not guarantee he will be faithful behind his lady's back. If he takes his religious faith seriously or he has high moral values then, that may reduce the likelihood of unfaithfulness, but it is no guarantee. Trust has to work both ways, but it takes time to build up trust in the first place. Therefore, our advice is very simple, despite the limited time constraints on when daters and couples can see each other for short intermittent periods at a time, don't hurry love, but instead take your time. Let the relationship grow naturally. Your marriage, when the time comes, is more likely to be happier as a result.

Our Story

Stephen and Ebun's dating and courtship journey was approximately three and half years, although we knew about each other before then. We originally met each other through attending the same church, and found ourselves constantly working together on the same church projects. During this time, Ebun was also studying for her MBA in the UK, and then once this was completed she returned to Nigeria. However, we still kept in touch with each other every day. Ebun did not want to get married in the UK because it was important for her to be married with her family around her. A year and a half later, in 2016, Stephen travelled to Nigeria to get married to Ebun. Throughout that time, they kept in daily contact by phone. The internet reception was not reliable where she was living. Because of this, we could not make video calls easily, but we still could send photos and very brief videos through Whatsapp. In Ebun's spouse visa application to the UK Home Office, she submitted our marriage certificate, international phone call logs, Whatsapp message correspondence, plenty of photos of Stephen and Ebun, and our families, as well as testimonial letters from those who knew about us in the UK. All of which were used to prove there was a genuine love story to back up her application. Our story may sound a bit matter-of-factly the way it is presented. However, behind the scenes was a lot of emotional highs and lows. Most of which was around maintaining a long distance relationship, organising the marriage, and dealing with the expensive and stressful process of making the UK spouse visa application. Which, with God's help we successfully did.

Chapter 11: Let's Talk About SEX

Emotional Intimacy & Sexual Intimacy

Everyone who aspires to have a deep, meaningful and passionate relationship will want to put emotional intimacy at the heart of it. Emotional intimacy, is when a couple trust each other enough to exclusively share their deepest personal thoughts, feelings, experiences and secrets with each other. Emotional intimacy begins to happen when two people have grown deep emotional attachment feelings for each other. By contrast, sexual intimacy is where a couple engage in sexual activities but the relationship does not necessarily require an emotional connection with each other. The main difference between the two is that emotional intimacy does not mean that sex is also taking place. Neither does sexual intimacy assume that a couple are in an emotionally meaningful long term relationship. If a couple are having sex before they have grown enough emotional attachment feelings for each other, then the relationship is based on lust. The problem with lust is that it clouds the emotions to prevent a couple from being able to truly understand what each genuinely feels about the other.

For a relationship to be emotionally satisfying and rewarding for both partners, it's important for them to first develop their emotional intimacy for each other as much as possible before sex takes place. Therefore, the primary purpose of this chapter is to help couples, through the use of science research, decide at what point to introduce sexual intimacy into the relationship. If a lady wants to have sex before marriage, then like other dating and relationship coaches, we advise she adopts the 90 day no sex rule. We also recognise that not everyone believes in sex before marriage. For example, because of our Christian religious beliefs and values, we did not have sex before we got married. We have, therefore, included advice for people in this category in both this chapter and previously, in Chapter 4. In this chapter, we discuss fully both the scientific evidence and the practical merits to support why a lady should wait at least 90 days into her relationship before having sex.

The 90 Day Rule

You may have heard of the 90 day rule before or read about it in other dating books. The original concept for it came from Steve Harvey, the well-known US TV and media personality. He introduced it in his book, Act Like a Lady, Think Like a Man.[163] The purpose of the 90 day rule is for a man to prove himself worthy to a lady before giving him sex, as a 'benefit' of the relationship. His thinking in coming up with the rule is that if a person works for, (he examples,) the US Post Office, Fedex or Ford Motor Company, they would have to complete a 90 day probationary period first to prove themselves as a satisfactory and trust worthy worker before their employment would be confirmed and they would be entitled also to the full package of company benefits (such as healthcare, etc.). His argument is that there is sufficient justifiable comparativeness between a company needing to get to know a new employee and a lady also needing to get to know a new man in a new relationship. Therefore, having at least a 90 day probationary period where the man needs to prove himself that he is actively and emotionally committed to his lady in the new relationship is very reasonable before he should expect the benefits of sex. Steve Harvey also believes it would take at least 90 days for a lady to get to know a man sufficiently well to find out if he is genuine or not. That is, whether he is a stayer or a player.[164] As a result of Steve Harvey's book becoming a best seller, it brought his 90 day rule into wider public prominence, and has also become a standard form of advice among many dating and relationship coaches. Also, since the publication of Steve Harvey's book in 2009, science has both caught up and confirmed that the 90 day rule has very strong merits attached to it, in explaining the amount of time it generally takes for a man to fall in love and emotionally commit to a lady. Although, there are some people out there that had sex early on in a relationship and are still with their partner till today, as Steve Harvey also asserts, that is rare.[165]

Obviously, some men will fall in love and genuinely desire to commit exclusively earlier than 90 days, and some will take longer than this. But the problem with having sex before 90 days, is that it still takes time to sufficiently know a person's character properly. There is no short cut to this.

One day, we met up with a young lady, called Tamara. She was with her friend, Stacey, and we were talking about dating and relationships (as we do!). Stacey asked for some advice and tips. Stephen then raised about the 90 day no sex rule. Tamara then said that she met her partner at university, and as a result of reading Steve Harvey's book she implemented the 90 day rule, which she strongly credits as to the reason why they were still happily together.

If a man is a stayer, he will accept the 90 day no sex rule just to be with his lady. He will stay, not because he likes it, but because he likes her. If he does not stay, then he is either a player or simply doesn't see her in his future. If he needs sex to either make sure he loves her or to find out if it is worthwhile investing his time and resources on her, then he is automatically the wrong man for her, because eventually, he will leave her. If he does stay in the relationship beyond 90 days without having sex, then she will know he is considerably less likely to be a player and a time waster. If you want a relationship to last long and have the best possible chance of happiness and success, you have to allow time get to know the other person before sex takes place. 90 days to wait for sex in that respect appears to be a small price to pay. As the title of the 1966 Motown hit song by The Supremes (and many others since) says, "You Can't Hurry Love".

Jasmine, came to us to ask for some relationship advice, because she did not think her partner was taking her seriously. Unfortunately, the relationship she was in, reflected the cost of not waiting 90 days to get to know him and find out more about his character first. Jasmine and her boyfriend had just moved into an apartment together. She recounted to us an incident, where she had come home in a cab from the supermarket with some shopping bags. She said that her boyfriend was waiting for her to help her with the bags, as they had arranged. As the cab pulled up, her boyfriend, was talking to someone on the phone. Jasmine then heard her boyfriend say to the other person on the phone, "I have got to go now because I have to help 'someone' with their shopping." Jasmine then asked us what we thought about this. We said, that while her boyfriend may have felt he was being honourable by helping her with the shopping bags, we would question whether it was honourable to reduce her status from girlfriend or partner to just a "someone". This story illustrates the importance of ensuring there is mutually strong emotional attachment feelings first before having sex. If the man fails to prove to his lady that he is genuinely emotionally committed to her within the first 90 days of a relationship, then the probationary period will have to be extended. An easy maxim for ladies to remember and follow here is: **If you are not in his head, then**

Chapter 11: Let's Talk About SEX 177

don't get in his bed!

Let's now go a bit deeper in understanding the science behind why ladies should wait 90 days before having sex.

The Science That Supports the 90 Days Rule

In 2011, a research study was carried out to compare the cultural differences of how long it took for US and Eastern Europeans to fall in love. It was found that 90% of Lithuanians surveyed fell in love within a month of meeting someone new. By comparison, 58% of Americans who were surveyed take much longer to fall in love, from between two months to a year.[166] Similar findings was confirmed in 2013, when research conducted by YouGov for Eharmony found that on average, men take around three months to say, "I love you".[167] Together, these findings show that it takes time for emotional attachment feelings to grow as a couple get to know each other. This raises an important question: How do you define in a couple relationship, the stages for growing in love? We break these stages into three:

Stage 1 – Romantic/Falling in love: Is a love attraction for another person, brought about by sexual chemistry, and can include feelings of exhilaration, euphoria, and happiness.[168] All of these sensations are typical experiences of a person embarking on a new relationship. These feelings are brought on through a release of the hormones dopamine, noradrenaline and testosterone.[169] Testosterone is central to sexual desire in both men and women.[170] However, women require a combination of both testosterone and estrogen for their sex drive (libido). Romantic feelings and sexual arousal de-activates critical thinking and normal rational judgment.[171][172] This aids a dater to fall in love by not seeing the imperfections of their dating partner. Instead, they are totally captivated and fall head over heels in love with their new love interest. Another way to put this is, when we fall in love, we lose sight of our senses. As a result, we become crazy in love.[173] As the daters grow in their love for each other, they begin to emotionally bond with each other. However, genuine emotional attachment feelings take time to develop. Notwithstanding, it is important to also point out that not everyone will grow in their relationship to develop genuine feelings of bonding and attachment, not even after 90 days. This could be for any number of reasons. For example:

1. A dater simply does not wish to commit to the relationship because the person they are dating is not in their future plans, or
2. A dater pretends they are committed in the hope of getting sexual access, or
3. A dater's heart is not really in the relationship, or
4. A dater has trust or hurt issues with the person they are dating, or
5. Because of previously being in an abusive relationship, it is hindering a dater from fully emotionally trusting the other person in a new relationship.

If any of the above reasons apply to you, particularly ladies, we advise that you delay in agreeing to have sex. Also, in later sections of this chapter, we have included our Emotional Attachment Test and Character Match Test to help you to know if you are ready to introduce sex into your relationship.

We have put romantic love and falling in love together in the same stage. Although they are slightly different, they eventually behave in the same way. The main difference between the two is that romantic love is often based on instant sexual attraction. Whereas falling in love is delayed or slower to take effect. An example of this could be, two people who work in the same workplace. They may have known each other from a distance, but never properly related with each other before. However, circumstances, such as working on the same project together got them talking with each other, and from there, they began to unexpectedly fall in love and experience a strong chemical attraction for each other.

Stage 2 – Being in love: The couple will know they are in this stage, because the initial feelings of romantic attraction and falling in love have already waned, and have been replaced with feelings of emotional attachment and exclusive commitment. The relationship continues to grow, because, dopamine continues to be released and gives the couple the irresistible and addictive urge to want to keep seeing each other. This is where the hormones, oxytocin and vasopressin come in. They influence pair bonding and emotional attachment. Together, these hormones can make a couple appear almost inseparable, because they simply love the feeling of being around each other. The couple may also experience feelings for the need for 'togetherness'. That is, the feeling of wanting to do things and be seen together. They may also refer themselves as, "we", in conversations with others.

Whereas, at the beginning of the relationship, each dater would normally be on their guard to ensure they present the best impression of themselves to the other, by now their guard will be down and as a result, they will be more authentic and relaxed around each other. This also means that the couple will notice each other's faults and imperfections, and at the same time, learn to adjust to sharing more of their lives together. Therefore, the being in love stage is also an adjustment period of getting to know each other better, and most importantly, to find out if the couple are suited for each other. Lastly, in this stage, a couple should begin to experience feelings of being emotionally interdependent upon each other. The being in love stage is reflective of what is normally experienced in courtship onwards, which we discuss fully in Chapter 12: Courtship – Assessing Suitability for Each Other.

Stage 3 – Compassionate love: This marks the stage when feelings of emotional attachment have fully taken hold. Compassionate love in a couple relationship is an enduring kind of intimate love that also involves deep feelings of mutual respect, trust, sacrifice and affection. Compassionate love is focused on emotional interdependence, intimacy and long lasting commitment. When a couple is in this stage, they are either ready for marriage, that is, engagement, or are already married.

There are no clear timelines between the three stages. However, the stage between romantically falling in love and being in love can begin to happen between 2 to 4 months, but could take longer, before an exclusive commitment is made. Also, men generally get a strong knowing that they are with the One for them, within 6 to 12 months, but again, sometimes this feeling can take longer. Most times, men may either delay or refuse to act on making a full commitment towards marriage because they may feel that not enough things are in place, such as a sense that their career needs to be more advanced or their financial position needs to be stronger. There may, of course, be many other reasons why a man does not fully commit to marriage. If a lady is not careful, she may end up in a long-term relationship that eventually leads nowhere, and wasting several years of her life in the process. This is a very common problem that can easily disadvantage a lady, because she has to consider her biological body clock, if she wishes to have children one day. This is significantly less of a problem for men, who can potentially have children, even at 90 years old. We discuss in greater detail the broad topic of fertility issues in Chapter 20: Sexuality & Fertility. But for now, let's turn our attention to explore in greater detail the role that hormones play in the game of love.

The Hormones of Love

Hormones influence every aspect of our relationships in terms of our interactions, physiological responses, thoughts, feelings and behaviours. From the love perspective, without them, nobody would mate with anyone, and the human race, along with every other species on the planet would have never have existed. In this

Chapter 11: Let's Talk About SEX

section we will take a look at the major hormones that are implicated in the feelings of love and desire. Before we begin, it is worth bearing in mind that hormones do not work independently of each other. Rather they work together with other hormones, like an ensemble of musicians performing together.

Testosterone – Men, primarily release testosterone from their testes, and women mainly release testosterone from their ovaries. Testosterone is also released from the adrenal glands in both men and women. These are small, triangular-shaped glands located on top of both kidneys. In males, a huge release of testosterone takes place around puberty. This causes sperm creation, strengthening of muscles and bones, bodily hair growth, deeper vocal pitch, as well as the masculinisation of the brain and the way it processes information. Male testosterone production peaks at around age 17-19, this high level is maintained until age 30, and then it goes into a slow steady decline, along with lower sex drive and longer recovery times after each ejaculation. Also, when men are single, their testosterone levels increase. However, when they are married, their testosterone levels decrease (but oxytocin in them supplements this to maintain a healthy fulfilling monogamous sex life in the marriage). Testosterone also regulates the sex drive (libido) of both men and women. Testosterone is also implicated in behaviour, such as aggression, risk-taking and competitiveness,[174] as well as status-seeking and social hierarchy.[175] [176] Often times, when we think of aggression, we may picture in our mind, a person acting in a hostile or violent way towards another, but there is another type of common aggression that psychologists define as 'instrumental'. This type of aggression is not necessarily emotionally driven, but a means to an end. In other words, it is predominantly, goal-driven, and is also mainly regulated by testosterone.[177] Examples of this could be financial market traders, competitive sports people, entrepreneurs, and politicians vying for power and influence, particularly at election time. In dating, we might see instrumental aggression with two men trying to compete and outdo each other to win the heart of a lady.

Estrogen – In women, estrogen is primarily released in their ovaries. Men produce estrogen, but they do this by converting some of their testosterone in to this hormone. In women, it helps to develop and maintain their reproductive system. At the time of puberty, a surge of estrogen is released and causes the female development characteristics, such as breasts, curvier body and more weight gain in the hips area to become more noticeable. Estrogen promotes vaginal lubrication for sex, it is also implicated in memory, mood and mental wellness, and coordination.[178]

Dopamine – Is a chemical hormone that uses the brain's neurological pathways to stimulate the pleasure and reward system in the brain. In other words, dopamine gives a person the anticipation of reward and pleasure, not happiness; to want more, and never be satisfied. It can help you pick up good habits, but also reinforce bad ones. Dopamine can arouse desire in a person for a long term relationship or simply for casual sex because of the pursuit of lust alone. Dopamine, oxytocin, and vasopressin are all produced in the hypothalamus, which is located in the lower area of the brain. When romantic feelings and sexual arousal happens, regions around the hypothalamus area of the brain are activated.[179] When we are attracted to someone new or the relationship is still fresh, dopamine is released. Dopamine can make us feel happy and light-headed, giving us exhilarating and all-consuming thoughts about the person we want to date. Dopamine gets released when we crave for a particular new experience or see and meet someone new (or when we reconnect with someone we haven't seen in a long time). Dopamine can also cause addictive behaviour. For example, with eating disorders, drugs, alcohol, gambling, pornography, as well as cravings for new sexual experiences. In 1965, when Mick Jagger sang, "I Can't Get No Satisfaction", it appeared he really meant it. It's been widely reported that he has slept with around 4,000 women.[180][181] When players go through numerous sexual partners it is the dopamine at work, driving their addiction. Therefore, if a person has sex too early in a relationship, without having built up enough feelings of emotional attachment, then lust is very likely to be confused with genuine feelings, with no real way to tell them apart.

Noradrenaline (or US, Norepinephrine) – The general function of noradrenaline is to mobilize the brain and body for action during situations of stress or danger, in what is commonly termed the 'fight-or-flight' response. Noradrenaline is also produced in the hypothalamus region. Noradrenaline along with dopamine, gives you heightened feelings of happiness and euphoria when in love. Noradrenaline also sends messages to your adrenal glands, which are situated above your kidneys, to release adrenaline. This causes your heart to beat faster and sends your blood rushing faster around your body.[182] In love attraction situations, this is what causes the heightened feelings of excitement, sweaty palms and nervousness.[183] It compels a person, especially men, to actively connect. Helen Fisher, bestselling author, anthropologist and human behaviour researcher, makes a compelling comparison between daters and explorers. She argues that they both share similar traits, because both experience the typical sensation feelings of boundless energy and excitement rush in the pursuit of discovery in a new adventure or attraction. Fisher puts this down to the key hormones implicated in this being dopamine and noradrenaline.[184] Daters, just like explorers, are each on their own adventure of risk and excitement, but for daters, this is about seeking adventure for new love.

Serotonin – is known as a 'happy' or calming hormone. Normally, it is the serotonin hormone that is meant to keep our emotions and feelings calm when we get excited. But when dealing with feelings of love, this hormone significantly reduces, as dopamine levels rise, hence the feelings of obsession and infatuation in the early stages of romantic love.[185] After sexual activity, especially when orgasm is achieved, the body releases serotonin for feelings of good mood and relaxation (hence the feeling of drowsiness and desire to sleep after sex). Serotonin is mainly stored in the gut area, and helps regulate mood, body temperature, and appetite. It helps to counter the effects of dopamine, but low levels of serotonin can lead to feelings of depression. When depression is diagnosed, antidepressants are often prescribed, but these can cause serotonin levels to increase and can delay or inhibit ejaculation in men. A healthy balanced diet and regular exercise are very good for general well-being and help to keep serotonin levels balanced.

Oxytocin – otherwise called the "love" bonding hormone. Oxytocin aids mother-infant bonding and plays a pivotal role in breastfeeding. Both men and women produce oxytocin, but women produce it approximately 3 times more than men.[186] When a woman has sex with a man, this can create in her an intense feeling and desire to want to bond with him. This feeling maybe strong enough in some cases to falsely convince her that he is the One. This is because when oxytocin is released in the brain, it binds to receptors that can cause her to have deep emotional attachment. This is simply oxytocin doing its job. Both oxytocin and vasopressin are known in psychology as 'social hormones'. When a man is in a long-term exclusive relationship with a lady he cares deeply about, his testosterone levels reduce, and this allows oxytocin's bonding influence, along with the hormone vasopressin, to take effect for exclusive monogamous mate pairing and bonding.[187] If a man has sex with a woman and he is not emotionally into her, then his testosterone levels will remain high and as a result, in a matter of time, he will move on to the next sexual conquest.[188][189] Ladies beware! It can sometimes take up to a year or longer for a man's testosterone levels to eventually reduce as a result of being in an emotionally attached and committed relationship.[190] There is no timeline for how long it can take for a man's feelings to become strong enough for him to want to exclusively commit to his lady. This is the reason why we say a lady should wait at least 90 days before having sex.

Vasopressin – both males and females produce this hormone. The respective receptors in the brain for oxytocin and vasopressin are responsive to either hormone. This is because they are structurally similar, but influence human behaviour differently.[191] The hormones responsible for bonding in an exclusive (monogamous) relationship are primarily oxytocin in females and oxytocin and vasopressin in males.[192] All mammals have oxytocin and vasopressin hormones for mating,[193] but very few, such as humans and prairie voles (hamster sized rodents) have the vasopressin and oxytocin brain connectors to encourage monogamy and mate-guarding behaviour.[194] Prairie voles are therefore preferred for use in research to understand the hormonal affects to do with the neuroscience behind love. They have been extensively used to study monogamy by contrasting them with meadow or montane voles, which are very promiscuous.[195] The attraction to using voles is that their breeding and lifespans are very short, and the experiments required for this type of bioscience research is exceptionally invasive.[196] Meaning, it cannot be done on humans. However, humans have also participated in some of this research when it has been safe to do so. Much of the neuroscience of what we know about social monogamy (that is, the science behind how humans make and maintain lifelong relationships), is fundamentally as a result of the research carried out on voles, and other similar species. At the simplified and basic level, prairie voles compare well with humans, because they share similarities in brain behaviour connections. This makes them scientifically useful, as a working comparison to understand what also goes on in the human brain, especially when it comes to human mate bonding.[197] [198]

Finally, vasopressin is the principle hormone that is implicated to influence a man's behaviour of aggression for mate guarding; to prevent other males having access to his lady.[199] [200] The ultimate sign of mate guarding is when a man proposes to his lady and gives her an engagement ring (and later a wedding ring). To show that she is officially spoken for and taken, and to ward off other males. A man, also, commonly will wear and display a wedding ring for the same reason; to communicate to other ladies that he too is taken.

Beware of Love Rascals

There is another reason to wait at least 90 days. Research done by Hasse Walum and colleagues at the Karolinska Institute in Stockholm, Sweden, suggests there is a single gene linked to vasopressin's subtype receptor (V1aR) called, RS3 334, which is associated to how men bond. In the study, 552 men who were surveyed, had been in a relationship for five or more years. Men who had two copies of RS3 334 were more likely to be unmarried, and if they were married, they were twice as likely to have a marital crisis.[201] In other words, these men had serious commitment issues. Going back to the prairie voles, research was carried out to establish how the males bonded and which ones didn't. The males that did bond were described as "residents". The males that would not bond were aptly called "wanderers". The vasopressin receptors in the resident male prairie voles make them very territorial and monogamously guard access to their mates in their territory. Whereas, the wanderers were more likely to be promiscuous because the vasopressin receptor was not stable to influence their behaviour.[202] The consequence of this is they have no respect for anyone's territory and have no interest in providing and protecting for any baby voles they sire. We have men like that in every society. They refuse to commit, but will sire children from different women and don't want to accept any responsibility for any of them.[203]

Unfortunately, for ladies, there are no pathology tests available out there to test in advance a partner's attitudes to commitment and faithfulness. However, there is a guide that women can follow. According to research, it appears that if a man reacts in an out of proportion or uncontrolled aggressive manner to people or things, it could indicate that he has a significantly higher than normal level of testosterone. Having too much testosterone in the system may be great for male fertility, but not always good for stability in relationships. If a man has significantly higher levels of testosterone than normal, it may also indicate that he could be prone to more aggressive and abusive behaviour, and less likely to marry, and if he does marry it is likely to end up in divorce.[204] Also, in a study carried out by Manchester Metropolitan University, they analysed over 300 domestic homicide reviews in England and Wales, between 2012 and 2018. They found that in cases where victims had been killed by their current or ex-partner, more than half had experienced coercive and controlling behaviour in the relationship.[205]

The only real test to tell if a man or a lady is suitable for marriage, which has been used for thousands of years, is to watch their character; not by what they say, but by what they do. In quoting the wise words of Jesus in Matthew 7:16-20:

> "By their fruit you will recognise them. Do people pick grapes from thorn bushes, or figs from thistles? Likewise, every good tree bears good fruit, but a bad tree bears bad fruit. A good tree cannot bear bad fruit, and a bad tree cannot bear good fruit. Every tree that does not bear good fruit is cut down and thrown into the fire. Thus, by their fruit you will recognize them."

The 'fruit' that Jesus is referring to is a person's character. It takes time for fruit on a tree to grow. Likewise, it takes time to get to know a person, and it can take time for their full character to be revealed. Love in a relationship is not something that can be hurried, and is therefore a good reason not to rush into the trap of having sex too early. This is why we advise strongly, that you should get to know the personality and character of the dater first.

90 Day Rule: Conclusion

In a new relationship, it takes time to get to know a person's genuine character. It is not something that can be done in only one or two months. If a lady consents to sex without ensuring her man has genuine emotional attachment feelings for her, then he is less likely to cherish her and give her the love and commitment she is looking for in the longer term. This is because, as we stated in Chapter 4, men fall in love with virtue, not lust. Also, the scientific evidence highlights the fact that not all men are as trustworthy and sincere as they may present themselves to be. In other words, just because a man has promised his lady he will be good to her, does not mean he will. Research clearly shows that it takes men time to fall in love. This is why we strongly advocate Steve Harvey's 90 day rule as both wise and reliable advice. In other words, before a lady allows a man to have sex with her, she should first of all make sure he is really emotionally into her and highly values her. Also, she should watch and pay careful attention to his character and how he treats her and others. This sets the relationship on the right track towards being intentional for marriage. If the man is a commitment type of guy, then making him wait for 90 days will only increase his desire to stay with his lady. If he does not want to wait, then break off the relationship, and move on, because he is either just a player or a timewaster. Alternatively, breaking off the relationship, may give time and space for a man to fully evaluate his true feelings towards the lady.

Emotional Attachment Test for Ladies: How to Know If a Man Is Really Emotionally Into a Lady

It can be very easy for a man to say that he wants to exclusively commit to his lady, when doing so may enhance his chances of getting sexual access to her. But how does a lady really know that her man is genuine about his feelings for her, especially if they are approaching the 90 day point in the relationship? The answer is

Chapter 11: Let's Talk About SEX

that she needs to review the relationship before considering sex with him. If you are at this point in your relationship, you can do this by asking yourself some basic questions. Can you tick all of these boxes?

- [ ] Does your man buy you gifts and always does things for you?
- [ ] Does he call and text you every day to ask how your day went? And give you an account of what happened to him?
- [ ] Does he tell others that you are his girlfriend or partner or the special one in his life?
- [ ] Do you feel that your man genuinely sees you in his future plans?
- [ ] Has he introduced you to his friends and family?
- [ ] Do you feel he can be trusted?
- [ ] Do you feel safe with him?
- [ ] Do you feel comfortable with the thought of having sex with him? Also, is this something you genuinely want to do and are ready for?
- [ ] Do you believe him and have absolutely no doubts when he says he is exclusive with you?

If a man tries to plead with you for sex before you are ready for it, then we suggest you reply with any of these:

- "I don't have sex until I am certain that we are in a serious committed relationship. That is just how I feel about it for now."
- "I need to be in a long term relationship before I can commit to having sex. Before then, I wouldn't enjoy it because I need to feel emotional intimacy. Otherwise it will not feel right."
- "I don't believe in sex before marriage. I hope you understand."

The important thing to understand is that having sex must not simply be to satisfy a man's sexual desires, or because the lady is fearful that if she doesn't, he might leave her. If it does not feel right to have sex, then it is not the right time to do it. In that case, wait. Wait, until you are convinced it is the right time, so that it can be special for both of you.

Men: The clear fact is, if the lady you are dating is worth a lot to you, and you highly value and respect her, you will definitely not mind being patient for her, so that she can get to know you first, and be sure that she is convinced of your feelings for her. 90 days separates the players from the stayers, and your lady needs to be rightly convinced that you are in this relationship for the long haul.

Character Match Test: Are You A Good Match For Each Other?

After emotionally bonding, there may be a natural desire to want to physically bond as well. However, as pointed out earlier, it takes time to get to know the character of a person. Also, we strongly advise not to have sex unless there is evidence of a good compatibility match between you. Before committing to having sex with your partner, are you able to tick the boxes in our character match test?

- [ ] You both have shared interests, beliefs and values in common with each other.
- [ ] There is no doubt in your mind that your partner, is always kind, loving and respectful to you.
- [ ] The man is forward thinking, ambitious, driven and realistic enough in where he sees himself (in terms of achieving his life goals) in 2, 5 or 10 years' time. In other words, he has a plan and his lady is in it.
- [ ] Do you trust him or her sufficiently well by now to know that they will not betray your love by having sex with someone else behind your back?
- [ ] Have you waited at least 90 days for genuine

emotional attachment to grow in both of you?
[ ] Are you and your partner ready to be exclusively (monogamously) committed to each other?

All of these are essential keys, necessary for progressing the relationship towards having a successful marriage. If you cannot tick against these basic points then you are rushing into sex, with insufficient evidence that the relationship will have a chance to last.

"When Should I Reveal My Past?"

To take out insurance for your vehicle, home or life, etc., you usually have to answer the insurer's questions on their application form so that they can assess the risk. As part of this, they will ask you if there is any other material information that needs to be disclosed so that the company can set the right insurance fees applicable to you. In the same way, it is absolutely appropriate to disclose anything to each other that could adversely affect the relationship, especially in the area of health, financial status or personal safety. Because it may influence whether or not a person would be reasonably comfortable to remain in a relationship once they learn of it. Disclosing sensitive information and taking a chance on how a partner may react is an essential part of the process to building a relationship based on mutual respect, love and trust. When to do this is key but at the same time, may take wisdom. The guidance we advise people to follow is give out deeply personal information in stages, especially if there is a lot of it to take in. In other words, do not overload. At the same time, do not have sex until you are certain that your partner will be comfortable with you after knowing what it is you need to share with them. Otherwise, it is likely they may feel you betrayed their trust in you. To see a full list of what to disclose and when to do so, please see Chapter 8, at the section: When to Disclose Sensitive Things About Yourself.

Sexually Transmitted Infections (STI)

Before having sex with each other, including oral sex, make sure you both get yourselves tested for STIs. If you have had an STI, then make sure you are completely symptom free of the disease before engaging in any kind of sexual activity. Also, if you have an STI that is non-treatable or non-curable then do not have sex with your partner unless you have told them first about the disease, so that they can then give you their full informed consent. STIs can affect you and your partner's health and the health of any children you may have in the future. STIs can also cause fertility problems. Therefore, it is essential to get treatment as soon as possible. If you have an STI, seek medical advice on how to avoid transmission to your partner. Some STIs are curable and some are not. Some may require medication for many years, and in some cases for the remainder of a patient's life, to help manage and stabilise their health and wellbeing. For example, there are presently no cures for HIV, herpes and some gonorrhoea infections. Though in some cases, they may be able to be managed with medication. Some sexually transmitted infections lead to cancer or infertility if not spotted early enough. This is why it is very important for the couple to get themselves tested for STIs and also to disclose any STIs that are known. While some people who learn about an STI in their partner will run away, others may be willing to stay. But everyone must be allowed to make that informed choice for themselves. Not disclosing that you have an STI would be morally unethical, illegal and a huge breach of trust.

Blood Disorders

Before having sexual intercourse, both partners should consider getting themselves tested for sickle cell and thalassaemia, to make sure that both partners are not carriers. Not everyone is a carrier of a haemoglobin disorder. But it's more common among people with heritage from Africa, the Caribbean, the Mediterranean, South and Southeast Asia, and the Middle East. If both of you are carriers then your child has a 1 in 4 chance of getting a haemoglobin disease and a 1 in 2 chance of also being a carrier.

Revealing My Past – Conclusion

Revealing any details about a person's past carries risk of breaking up the relationship, but carries greater risk if this is not done. Other health related issues that should be revealed before having sex are any health problems or difficulties, genetic heredity or mental health problems. Also, if there are any convictions for sexual or violent offences (irrespective of how long ago), these need to be revealed as well. To re-iterate, anything that ultimately could impact on the viability and integrity of the relationship must be disclosed, for the sake of trust, before sex takes place, and certainly before a marriage proposal is likely to be made. Again, to see a full list of what to disclose and when to do so, please see Chapter 8, at the section: When to Disclose Sensitive Things About Yourself.

Avoid Getting Pregnant Before You Are Married

Ladies, before having sex, ensure your man wears a condom. Taking a contraceptive pill may help a lady to avoid getting pregnant, but it cannot protect her (or him) from getting a sexually transmitted disease. If the man says that he cannot either enjoy sex or even have sex if he uses a condom then it means he simply cannot be trusted and he does not have genuine respect for his lady. Finally, it is important to also bear in mind that occasionally condoms tear, and therefore, even using condoms is not entirely risk free.

Ladies should take precautions to avoid becoming pregnant outside of marriage. Few men will hang around after a lady has given birth. Those couples that do get married as a consequence of having a baby, commonly experience marriage failure. This is because the relationship is not based on happy memories. When there is insufficient love, trust and happy memories in a relationship, before marriage, then the marriage itself, will be potentially doomed from the start. Unfortunately, no amount of love and promises from a man is going to change that. We know this to be true from experience of coming across this countless times, and seeing such relationships inevitably collapse in failure. **<u>This is because men are most irresponsible when they never planned for responsibility in the first place.</u>**

If a lady gets pregnant, then she also risks the high likelihood of 18+ years of money to be spent on child rearing, plus co-parenting negotiations and challenges of being a single mother. The consequences of unplanned pregnancy and single parenthood have life changing implications. The lady may need to make compromises if she wants to find love in the future. As a result, getting into meaningful relationships that could lead to marriage will be significantly harder as well. This is because the majority of men will not consider putting their own financial resources into bringing up another man's child. For lots of positive and helpful advice on single parenthood and finding love, please see our bonus chapter on Dating and Single Parenthood.

"What If I Do Not Believe In Sex Before Marriage?"

If you do not believe in sex before marriage, then we strongly advise you not to compromise on your beliefs. Because, if you do, you will undermine your personal values which form part of the many things that attracted your partner to you in the first place. If your partner cannot respect your values and beliefs, then he or she does not genuinely respect you, and you should treat that as a red flag.

Also, believing in not having sex before marriage does not prevent a couple from having a healthy and open discussion around the topic of sex. For example, in our experience, a question that ladies often ask at church singles fellowship events is, "I understand that I should wait until after marriage before having sex, but how can I be sure that he will be able to perform on the wedding night?" This is quite easy to answer. On average, a healthy man has 3-5 erections in the night. Therefore, a lady can simply ask her partner to confirm whether or not he sometimes wakes up in the morning with an erect penis.[206] Therefore, a lady can simply ask her partner to confirm whether or not he sometimes wakes up in the morning with an erect penis. If the answer is yes, then it means that his equipment down below should be in good working order and you have nothing to worry about. If he says no, then there is likely to be either a physical health or psychological problem involved.

Risks of Casual Sex

When people break off from long term relationships, they may turn to casual sex as a way of wanting to feel loved. Research has shown that women are more likely to come off emotionally worse from casual sex because they often experience feelings of loneliness, unhappiness, and low self-esteem. This is because casual sex is meant to be just physical and therefore lacks the emotional connection that most people, especially women, crave for in a relationship.[207] don't tend to have these negative feelings. Casual sex cannot substitute for a meaningful, trusting and satisfying life long relationship. At best, it works only as a temporary stimulant with potentially harmful side effects. By contrast, the health and well being benefits of an emotionally meaningful relationship causes a decline in feelings of depression, reduction in health complaints and leads to increased self-esteem.[208]

Sexting & Sex Videos

Sexting is when using a smartphone to send messages, photos (images) or a video of a sexual nature. Our strong advice should be obvious: Don't send anything you would not want your partner to have if you broke up with them. Do not send any photo or video of yourself in a nude, semi-nude or other revealing pose to ANYONE, even if you are engaged or married to them. Never agree to do a sexually explicit or revealing photo or video having sex with anyone. Otherwise, if you break up with them there is a very high chance that those explicit photos and videos will end up on a porn site or going viral on social media. Never agree to getting undressed or revealing any part of your body on a video call, because it is very easy to video record it without you even knowing anything about it. In short, no matter how much you trust and love your partner and you think they too have the same trust values you do, do not trust them with any of the above under any circumstances!

Conclusion

Having sex is an intimate act of itself. When it is with that special someone, it can make it extra special and emotionally affirming and satisfying. If the relationship lacks enough emotional attachment and commitment feelings between you before sex, then having sex will not make it any more emotionally committed afterwards. If the feelings you have for each other are not deep enough for exclusive commitment before sex, then it is lust and not real love, and at some point, the relationship will inevitably break up. Whatever your priorities and goals are for the relationship, you should discuss them before having sex, otherwise at least one of you may end up getting hurt or even feel betrayed.

STEP 3: The Courtship Stage

Chapter 12: Courtship – Assessing Suitability for Each Other

What Is Courtship?

Many people probably regard the term 'courtship' as a little strange these days. Prior to the 20th century, courtship and marriage may have involved an element of upward social mobility or to ensure that money remains in family hands as much as possible. This was typical of the middle to upper classes. In these types of situations, introductions would have been made through family or trusted matchmakers, or attending special celebratory events, such as balls or other social events. Also, before courting or marriage unions could take place, approval must have been sought from a prospective bride's family. When approval was either refused or unlikely, it was not uncommon for a couple in love to end up eloping instead. For the working class, courtship would involve people meeting through either an introduction from family and friends or living in the same neighbourhood. Approval or blessing for these unions was largely still required from the prospective bride's family. Up to the Second World War, because of working commitments, people of the opposite sex would meet mostly on Saturdays and Sundays. They would attend dances, restaurants, cinemas, theatres, or other social events, and in time determine if a relationship is suitable for marriage. In those days, sex outside of marriage was highly discouraged, because pregnancy would have carried a huge amount of public shame for both the lady and her family. Regardless of the social class that people came from, courtship would still follow a similar pattern. Men approach women, take the lead, and pay for the outings. The point of courtship, therefore, was for the man to woo the lady! Another important aspect of courtship, which remains true to this day, is determining a couple's suitability for each other. In other words, how well they seem to get along with each other and whether they would make a suitable marriage match for each other.

Courtship shifted to dating at some point towards the end of the 19th century and the beginning of the 20th century, due to industrialisation and migration from rural areas to cities for work. Also, for women, greater access to higher education and voting rights, as well as significantly increased work opportunities, gave them greater social mobility and financial independence in their own right. At this point, dating as a means of meeting and finding love began to overtake courtship. Dating and having fun then started to become fashionable for meeting new people. If a dating relationship grew serious with feelings of love and emotional attachment, this could lead to a long-term relationship or even marriage. Also, the same as in courtship, men were expected to be the ones to ask women out, take control of the planning and paying for dates, and giving of gifts, such as flowers. Doing these things increased their standing and attractiveness as a suitable match.[209] Thus, the responsibility for wooing a lady still firmly rested with the man.

The difference between courtship and dating is that courtship is seen as socially restrictive and generally had a greater focus on

Chapter 12: Courtship – Assessing Suitability for Each Other

marriage suitability. Whereas, dating is a way to get to know someone while having fun (in the process), but not necessarily with the intentionality of marriage attached to it. In this book, we blend the two. Starting with dating and then seamlessly moving the new relationship into the courtship stage once the couple have agreed to be exclusively committed and emotionally attached to each other. The fun element does not stop: the relationship just becomes more intentional in terms of how the couple define their relationship.

Our own 21st century definition of courtship is: The period of time when two people have agreed to be exclusively committed to each other so that they can then assess their suitability for marriage. As described at the beginning of this chapter, suitability can be defined on either economic or social grounds. However, while a degree of economic and social elements may play a part in love marriages, love and companionship often play a more significant role. For example, Stephen came across a couple who had been married for 16 years. Clare was a successful banking consultant at an established consultancy practice, but when she first met Phil, he was a security guard in the same building where she worked. Their common interest at the time was they were both avid novel readers, and he had aspirations to become a writer. They fell in love, got married and two children later, are still in love and happily married. However, more than a hundred and fifty years ago, this couple would have struggled to get their relationship accepted. They would have very likely ended up eloping together. Fortunately, this is not the case any more.

A Courtship period can generally take at least 6 to 9 months for a couple to get to know each other well enough to be sure they are right for each other. But this could be sooner if a couple knew each other beforehand. For example, if they grew up in the same neighbourhood, went to the same school, worked together, or knew each other over time in another way.

Getting To Know Your Partner

During the courtship stage, you will see more of each other, and your emotional guard will naturally begin to come down. Things will also begin to settle down a bit as you become more relaxed around each other. This is only natural and makes perfect sense because you are now in a committed relationship where both of you are experiencing deep feelings for each other and are also learning to trust each other more. As your guard comes down and you begin to be more relaxed around each other, you will start to see aspects of each other's character, habits, and behaviour that you did not notice before. As the new relationship grows and is tested with problems and crises, you will learn different ways of overcoming them.

When your emotional guard is down, you will become emotionally vulnerable and sensitive to being hurt. For example, if your partner says something to you that you find offensive or off-putting, this is the time when you are more likely to pay attention and react to it. Beforehand, you may have treated comments of sarcasm, cynicism, put down kind of remarks, negative name calling, or negative criticisms as banter or just decided to let it go for other reasons. However, such remarks may no longer be as easy to overlook any more. If you feel your partner has offended or disrespected you, it is better to deal with things privately, away from the gazing eyes of others, so that your partner can explain their actions and say sorry without feeling publicly embarrassed or humiliated. If they continue to offend you, then this is a red flag, and the relationship will need to end. If a person refuses to take you or your feelings seriously before marriage, they will not take you or your feelings seriously after marriage.

The courtship period of the relationship-building process is vitally important because, you will learn to trust each other much more, as you also learn to become emotionally and mentally interdependent upon each other. Trust is earned, but can quickly

Chapter 12: Courtship – Assessing Suitability for Each Other

be lost because of infidelity or a partner not keeping to their word, or they are unreliable in some other way. People can also easily fall out of love if the relationship is taken for granted. One way to avoid that is to ensure that both of you are polite, courteous, kind, and respectful to each other at all times. You should also be quick to apologise and say sorry when a wrong has been committed. Whether you believe in God or not, the Bible has a lot of wise things to say about love in relationships:

> "Love is patient, love is kind. It does not envy, it does not boast, it is not proud. It does not dishonour others, it is not self-seeking, it is not easily angered and it keeps no record of wrongs. Love does not delight in evil but rejoices with the truth. It always protects, always trusts, always hopes, always perseveres" (1 Corinthians 13:4-7).

Love can blind us at times from seeing each other's personality and character flaws because, naturally, we may only want to see the good in a person. However, you should immediately end the relationship if you see patterns of controlling, violent and abusive behaviour. Also, if there is evidence of unfaithfulness, or secretive, or addictive behaviour, such as gambling, drinking, or drug abuse problems, then it will be wise to consider whether it is worthwhile continuing with the relationship. If such behaviour does not stop before getting married, it certainly will not stop in the marriage, despite how many promises are given. If you know that your partner is engaged in criminal activities and behaviour, would you be happy to still stay with them when they eventually get caught and go to prison?

Also, if you or your partner has mental health problems, this should be discussed, and there should be an agreement on managing behaviour on not-so-good days. For more information on this subject, please see our bonus chapter on Dating and Mental Health.

Another area in courtship you will get to know about is how well your partner can handle money. We have a chapter dedicated to this topic, in Chapter 17: Let's Talk About MONEY.

Learning How to be a Couple

As discussed in other chapters, for a happy lifelong committed relationship, it is vital to have similar interests and activities that you both can actively share and be interested in together. It is also vitally important to keep up the romance between you. Not just in terms of spending quality time alone but also to keep going on dates with each other. Keeping up with going on dates is just as important before marriage as it is afterward. Regularly setting aside dedicated romance time will help keep the fire burning in the relationship. The more you do things together; the more your emotional interdependency and reliance upon each other will grow.

Furthermore, to allow trust to grow between both of you takes being open, transparent, and accountable to each other. Being open and transparent means being honest and not keeping secrets from each other. Being accountable is not just about being a person of integrity but being true to your word. It also means taking responsibility by owning and admitting to mistakes and failures, including saying sorry, and fully making amends when the other partner has been hurt or offended by them.

Chapter 14, is dedicated to sharing with you the proven secrets of how to have a happy marriage. The best way to see your goal of having a happy marriage become a reality is for both of you to fully embrace all the points made in that chapter and ensure they become regular habits by putting them into practice at every opportunity. The secret to their success lies in the understanding that you can never do enough of them. Be polite. Look for more opportunities to be even more polite. If you are already going on dates. Go on even more dates. If you are already showing affection. Show even more. Having and maintaining a happy marriage is about keeping the love fire logs continuously burning between you, even when you least feel like it, while at the same time being sensitive and considerate of each other's needs and feelings.

Getting to Know Each Other's Family & Friends

Courtship is the time to get to know each other's family (if you have not met them already). It is not always easy to get on with a partner's family for any number of reasons. When this does happen, it can lead to friction between the couple if they don't come up with an agreeable solution to manage this. Even though, after marriage, you are expected to put each other first, each of you will still have a close relationship bond with your respective family. It is, therefore, in both your interests to be on good relationship terms with each other's family. This includes attending and participating in wider family gatherings and events. Suppose both of you have a different religion or come from entirely different cultural backgrounds. In that case, you will need to discuss what religious practices or cultural traditions are important to each of you and which ones you will agree to join with your partner and their family in commemorating. This includes deciding on which religion to raise up your children in. Always be respectful and considerate of each other's beliefs and traditions, even if you will not personally take part in them. For more information on this, please see our bonus chapter on Faith & Beliefs.

Friends, like family, can give you an insight from an objective perspective of what they think of your dating partner, but without the possible feelings of judgment. They may also be able to see some red flags that you had not previously noticed. There is no set time when it is right to be introduced to each other's friends or family, except the time that feels right for both of you. However, if this has not happened within 6 months of the relationship starting, that could be a warning sign that something is not quite right. This could be because either one of the partners is not being sincere in what they genuinely feel about the relationship, or there is a genuine feeling that one partner will not be accepted by the other's friends or family. Whatever the reason, if it is not addressed before getting married, the problem will certainly follow into the marriage, and will definitely lead to feelings of tension between you both.

Meeting Each Other's Families

If you have children, please also read the section on Consulting With Your Children in our bonus chapter on Dating and Single Parenthood. The time to meet each other's family should ideally be after you both are exclusively committed to each other. This is because meeting the family is a big step for both of you and your respective families. Your family will interpret you introducing your partner to them to mean that you are very serious about your relationship. If you have been seeing each other for at least six months, but your partner refuses to meet with your family or allow you to meet theirs that could be a red flag. You need to establish the reason, because your partner may not be as serious about the relationship as you are, or they may feel that the relationship is going too fast for them. For example, if they are a single parent, they will have to consider the feelings of their children. Alternatively, they may not actually want to get married.

Meeting the Parents

When meeting your partner's parents for the first time, it is always good etiquette to take a gift along with you. The gift is just a token of respect and appreciation, and therefore does not need to be expensive. For example, this could be, a bottle of wine, or flowers, or something sweet. If you are stuck for ideas, try the

Chapter 12: Courtship – Assessing Suitability for Each Other

internet and you will get a lot of ideas there.

When you do meet your partner's family, in the same way as dating, do not use swear words or any other offensive language, even if your partner's family does. Doing this will increase their respect of you. When you meet your partner's parents, besides them wondering and hoping they will be able to get along with you, they will also be sizing you up and wondering whether you will make a suitable spouse for their son or daughter. They will also naturally judge you in terms of what kind of parent they think you might be to any grandchildren you give them. These things may seem irrelevant at first, but that is how parents who have invested their lives and hard-earned resources into their children usually think. Above all, they will be discussing between themselves: "Do we want this stranger coming into our family, and will our son or daughter be safe with them?"

When Stephen first met Ebun's family in Nigeria, he was on a business trip, but he also took the opportunity to be able to meet them. Ebun did not travel with him because she was studying for her MBA in the UK. It was agreed to meet halfway, at a restaurant, because of the distances involved, and was an initial informal greeting kind of meeting, which they graciously allowed. Because he did not have any relatives with him (as would normally be custom for such meetings), two of his friends went with him instead. It was his first meeting with them. They were naturally suspicious of who this white man from the UK was, that was interested in their daughter. Despite Stephen's warm and open personality and embracing smiles, it was no surprise that they did not immediately take to him. However, in time, all fears were alleviated as they got to know him, and gave their blessing for us to get married two years later.

Do You Like the Look of Your Partner's Parents?

None of us can avoid getting older. Do you want to know what your partner will look like in 20 or 30 years from now? Then look no further than your partner's parents. You may have heard the sayings, "Like father, like son" or, "Like mother, like daughter." There are elements of truth in these statements. Genetically, parents pass on many of their physical features on to their children, such as facial features, body shape, hair colour, etc. Health issues can also be passed on genetically. Interestingly, many behaviours, gestures, and mannerisms can also be passed on due to direct environmental influences from parents and others. If there is anything that worries you, then you should discuss these with your partner.

Discussing Sensitive Family Issues

If there is a history of abuse in either of your families (emotional, controlling, violent, sexual, drug or alcohol dependency, or other addictive behaviours), then it is better to openly discuss these issues with each other. Having discussions around histories of abuse in families is not going to be easy, but at the same time cannot be avoided either. This kind of discussion should be treated as disclosure to each other. Openness and integrity are essential for building trust in relationships. If your partner walks away upon learning about something, let them go. They may come back once they have thought through everything. But if they do not, move on because the relationship is unlikely to work anyway, even if you had never told them.

Watch Out For Jealousy

Any man or woman in a relationship can easily develop feelings of jealousy if they believe that their partner is giving untoward attention to a person of the opposite sex. However, some

Chapter 12: Courtship – Assessing Suitability for Each Other

measure of jealousy, in moderation, can be healthy. For example, mate guarding, that is letting others know that a partner is already taken. This can subtly be done by standing close next to them in a social gathering, or if necessary to politely ward off the advances of another. That said, jealousy can be very unhealthy when expressed in controlling, violent or other abusive behaviour. Which would be a red flag warning sign to get out of the relationship as quickly as possible. If a partner in a relationship has close friends of the opposite sex, this may cause problems for the relationship. Even if he or she may argue that they prefer close friends of the opposite sex. This may prove too difficult for the relationship to cope with and could end up being a deal breaker. It makes sense, therefore, to be sensitive in trying to see how outside relationships can be viewed from your partner's perspective, and not give a chance for feelings of jealousy to take root in your relationship. Therefore, be wise about how you manage your relationships with friends of the opposite sex. Ways to prevent jealousy from being an issue are by being accountable to each other. For example, being aware of each other's movements. If the relationship is already exclusive and is more than 9 months old, and one of the partners cannot manage this kind of accountability, then it may be a sign that all is not well in other areas of the relationship.

Future Plans

Future plans is a major compatibility area, and having discussions about them is vitally important. For example, by 9 months into a relationship, a lady will want the assurance from her man that his future plans include her. Of course, this goes both ways. Having regular discussions about each other's future plans and life goals, and being able to understand them are essential. Discussions can be about:

- Where do each partner see themselves in 3, 5, and 10 years from now?

- What age would be ideal for each partner to be before they will consider getting married? What needs to be accomplished first in the life of each partner before they would consider marriage?
- How many children would each partner like?
- Career plans.
- Business aspirations.
- Educational aspirations.
- Buying a property together.
- Location – urban or rural: where you both may like to live.

Can compromise be agreed, or are any responses from a couple's discussions considered as deal breakers for the relationship? For more information about compatibility, please see Chapter 2: How to Get Your Most Compatible Date Match

Communication

One key area where courtship, and indeed, your marriage, will be tested in is the area of communication. For instance, if you were asked, what the most essential skill in communication is, you would be correct to say, "listening." Listening is a key communication skill that needs to be continuously practised to be any good at it. For your relationship to be successful each of you need to develop the habit of being a good listener to the other. In practice, this may involve listening and repeating back to your partner what you have heard them say. This is important, because it powerfully validates and affirms your partner's feelings. It also demonstrates key empathy skills in action, and is perfect for difficult negotiations and resolving conflicts. In fact, you can practice this skill in your workplace. When you do this you will find that your confidence and creativity levels will suddenly rise. The reason for this is by listening and then repeating back it actually gives the brain time to recover from being subjected to higher levels of emotional stress. At the same time, it will give yourself a chance to calm down and gather new thoughts and ideas, which may also carry a workable solution or compromise. When you try this, you will be amazed by the results you get.

A vital but often overlooked area in relationship communication is being open and approachable to give, receive, share, and seek each other's advice, thoughts, and opinions. If this goes, this is a sign that the relationship is already quickly growing apart, and needs urgent action to remedy the situation.

If a couple regularly argue before getting married, it is 100% certain, this pattern will continue afterwards. However, it is not how often a couple argue, but more importantly they are able to find ways that work for them to resolve their disagreements. Chapter 14: Let's Talk About COMMUNICATION, gives lots of practical advice and proven strategies to help a couple to effectively communicate in their relationship.

Being a Winning Team Together

We all love being part of a winning team. Being loyal in team relationship means sticking together through thick and thin, in both the good times and bad times. Therefore, true team minded people love the feelings of commitment, companionship and camaraderie they get from each other. Camaraderie speaks of a close friendship, common understanding and trust in a relationship. Also, a genuinely close friendship will put love, trust, and loyalty to each other at the heart of it because these are the sort of things that make you work harder for the good of the relationship. It is equally important to always look out for each other and ensure you have each other's back covered. An external threat against one of you should therefore be perceived as a threat against both of you. Likewise, praises from other people about one of you should be taken as praise for both of you.

In marriage, even if one brings in more money than the other, the accumulation of wealth is jointly owned and the rewards are enjoyed together. Also, as a team, when you work together, you are clearly better and stronger at being able to handle problems and dealing with crisis, than when you are alone. You can do and achieve more together. As the saying goes, "If you want to go fast, go alone. If you want to go far, go together." Team marriage is about being faithful and loyal to each other, building a home of your own together, making decisions together, and looking out for each other. Doing all of these things together means that one person is not acting alone in shouldering all of the responsibilities. Courtship allows you to practice at how well you function together as one. You can also learn to think as one, because you are not just a team, but in training to be a winning marriage team!

Cheating

Why men (and women) cheat is treated in a comprehensive section in Chapter 16: Safeguarding Your Marriage. If your partner cheats on you before marriage, then treat that as a huge red flag, because you may need to reassess the relationship. Forgiving is very good, but if you still want to stay together after an act of infidelity has been committed, then trust will also need to be restored before a marriage can take place. The reasons for the betrayal will need to be identified and measures put in place to ensure there will not be a repeat incident. You cannot marry someone who you either have low regard or trust for. Also, if a cheating partner gets either a sexually transmitted infection or a pregnancy is involved, then the repercussions can last for decades. If a person cheats before they are married they are likely to repeat their bad behaviour after they are married. In such a case, it may at least be advisable to delay engagement or wedding plans until there is definite evidence of contrition and character change, and also that the non-offending partner's heart has sufficiently healed as well.

Breaking Up

Ladies: If the man breaks up with you, let him go and move on. If you feel you cannot easily move on, wait for about eight weeks. If he has not contacted you by then, he has forgotten about you and moved on, and so should you. If before you broke up, you were having sex with him, you should delay having sex with him again until you are sure that he can demonstrate that he is willing to be committed and exclusive. If he breaks up with you a second time or cheats on you, then it is clear he never was into you in the first place or is completely unstable in relationship making. Either way, you should treat this as a serious red flag, and time for you to move on.

Courtship – Conclusion

In this chapter we begun by understanding that after the initial romantic attraction feelings of euphoria have subsided, your emotional guard will begin to come down and you will be more relaxed and vulnerable around each other. This is because you have crossed over (or in the process of crossing over) from falling in love to being in love with each other. In short, you have entered into the courtship Step in the relationship building process. Courtship is about testing the suitability for each other and at the same time learning to love and trust each other. Courtship is also the time where you learn and practice how to think and act as a team. That is, learning to be of one mind and learning how to plan things together.

If there are no areas of compatibility between you and your partner, this should be treated as a serious area of concern. This is because if there is not enough compatibility between you, there is a significantly higher likelihood that you will eventually grow apart in your relationship, and this could ultimately end in marriage failure. It is possible to create compatibility, but that requires a huge amount of hard work and effort to find the same passionate interests and activities you would both like to do together. If you are both emotionally committed to each other, then your chances of success in finding things you would enjoy doing together is very high.

Trust is also of fundamental importance in a relationship. Once lost, it is very difficult, in some cases, impossible, to get back. Trust should therefore be treated as a chest full of treasure that should be guarded no matter what, and certainly not worth gambling away on a dalliance of any description. Trust also speaks deeply about respect, loyalty and faithfulness to each other.

Apart from suitability, a couple will learn how to deal with storms and crises in the relationship. If a couple feel like they have not had to deal with any real storms or crisis yet, and the next stage seems to be for a proposal to be made, it simply means that the courtship has probably not been long enough. Likewise, if one partner idealises the other, they will not see if there are real problems within the relationship. Storms and crises have a way of bringing couples in a relationship down to earth from the clouds very quickly. They also powerfully bring couples even closer by giving good memories to hold on to of how they got through and overcame the challenges together. Also, storms and crises are very good at revealing the character of each person for who they really are. In short, don't rush courtship. In any event, we also strongly recommend pre-marital counselling for couples before they make their wedding vows to each other. This book gives you a huge head start in this.

Finally, we encourage you to use this period to really get to know each other, to build up love, trust and loyalty for each other. If both partners have an open, positive and approachable personality, they are more likely to resolve problems quicker and more effectively together.

Chapter 13: How to Have a Happy Marriage

In this chapter, we have outlined the many things that mark out a happy marriage. The reason for putting this chapter here in the Courtship Step, rather than later in Step 5, as part of marriage preparation, is so that you can begin immediately to put into practice all the positive habits and behaviours that you will need for making your own marriage to be happy and successful.

Investing in Your Marriage

Marriage is a lifelong maintenance and growth project. You add value to a house by ensuring it is well maintained and kept in good condition, including keeping up with the painting and decorating inside, and looking after your garden outside. If you put an extension on the house, it can add more to the property's value and also give more living space for the family. In the same way, for a marriage to be happy, it requires constant attention, maintenance, and personal investment in terms of time and resources. All these things add value to it and help keep your relationship healthy, vibrant, and satisfying long after your children have flown the nest.

Avoid Complacency

To keep your marriage happy, you should consider complacency as your number one enemy. Complacency happens when either one or both partners begin to take their relationship for granted. When this happens, politeness (saying pleases and thank yous to each other) can quickly become a casualty. Complacency can also be found when there is no longer an interest in keeping up attractive appearances and looking good for each other. Therefore, watch out for the almost inevitable additional 'marriage (body) weight' that is likely to be gained in just a few years of being married. This can be a good sign of feeling contented in your marriage relationship. But being overweight may not be healthy for you or attractive for your spouse to look at either. Make sure you still regularly have your hair done (and if you are a man, your facial and head hair should be kept neat, clean, and groomed). Also, continue to maintain good hygiene and dress well for each other. Ladies should especially ensure they keep and maintain their youthfulness in appearance because it reduces the risk of your man developing wandering eyes for another woman. Youthfulness has no age limit but is a state of mind.

Love, Respect & Sacrifice

In marriage, mutual love, kindness and respect for each other are vital to contributing to a peaceful, loving home. Giving each other the love, kindness, and respect each deserves also ensures that disagreements are more likely to be resolved amicably. People will only make a sacrifice for what they genuinely believe in. When both spouses believe in the success of their marriage, they will willingly do what is required to make it work. In reality, if both spouses treat each other with love, kindness, and respect, they will agree to compromise more easily with each other for what is fair and acceptable to them both. Selfishness is the exact opposite of sacrifice and is a huge barrier to creating the feeling of being one and in unity with each other. Therefore, if a partner is selfish and consistently unwilling to put their partner's needs above their own, then the marriage is not likely to last.

Agreeing Decisions Together

Making decisions between you in a relationship is all about negotiating and compromising for what is fair for both of you. This is how win-win outcomes from negotiations are achieved. Trying to get one-upmanship is the opposite of this and will ultimately lead to one person feeling resentful of the other. Regardless of whether the stronger negotiator is either a man or woman, they should always be more conciliatory to the other. Otherwise, the risk is that the disadvantaged one is more likely to close up and end up being emotionally withdrawn, especially if they do not feel like they have been sufficiently listened to. Therefore, each should be patient with the other. As the Holy Bible puts it, "Everyone should be quick to listen, slow to speak and slow to become angry" (James 1:19). When you are patient and understanding with each other, the reward for your relationship is that your love and trust for each other will deepen. This will lead to more effective and balanced decision-making overall. Jessica and Alan exemplify this point in the way they make their decisions. Before, they would always end up arguing when Alan bought something without consulting with Jessica first. To resolve this, they agreed that if a purchase of more than £100 was about to be made, they would speak to each other first to agree on whether a purchase was justified. However, when it came to summer holidays, Alan agreed that Jessica could decide where they should go, but before booking it, she would consult with him first to ensure that he was happy with the holiday plan.

Think Team – The Two Become One

Marriage is about two people uniting together to become one

team. Others outside of your marriage will also relate and treat you as one person. When they see one of you, it will be like seeing both of you. That is why most of your single friends will reduce hanging around you any more, or they may drop out of the picture altogether, as you make new friends that know you as Mr and Mrs. Also, putting the exclusivity of your marriage first is refusing to let others divide you by coming in between you. Therefore, spouses may need to remind their respective parents to keep out of their marriage (unless it is a matter of abuse). When a couple see themselves as one in purpose, they will be more motivated to resolve disagreements than risk allowing them to fester. It is for this reason that, the Bible says, "Do not let the sun go down while you are still angry" (Ephesians 4:26). If the couple have disagreements that cannot be resolved immediately, they should agree between themselves a mutually convenient time when issues can be discussed. For useful advice, tips, and strategies on ways to handle relationship conflicts, please see Chapter 14: Let's Talk About COMMUNICATION.

Holding onto Happy Memories

Having happy memories is an essential resource for a long-lasting relationship because you can look back on them to remind you of the happiness and joy you experienced at the time. They also provide an excellent resource when going through tough times. This is because happy and celebratory memories help to remind you that as you overcame previous challenges and crises, you will also get through future ones as well. Many couples will be pleasantly surprised at how many happy memories they have built over the years.

Examples of happy memories you may have already collected right now are:

- How you first met each other.

- How your first date went, and what it was that caused you to like them so much that you agreed to see them again and again.
- What it was that attracted you to your partner.
- When and how you knew your partner was the One for you.
- How you resolved your first big argument and made up.
- Wedding day and honeymoon memories.
- Spending your first Christmas together.
- Anniversary and birthday celebrations together.
- Other fun memorable dates and special occasions you experienced together before and since your wedding.
- The funniest and happiest experiences you have had together.
- The goals and achievements that have been completed and gained together.
- New baby arriving.

Write and record your own list and document it with a photo album if you can because taking photos is a powerful way to record your happy memories to look back on. These memories and experiences will be the stories of what you will be passing on to your children or grandchildren. If you feel you do not have enough happy memories, then you need to urgently begin creating more of them. Constantly doing things together and also going out on regular fun dates together are all excellent ways of making happy memories for you both to look back on in the future.

Compliments Are Powerfully Affirming

Always look for opportunities to say compliments and thank yous to each other, because these are highly affirmative and validating to hear. For example:

- "You look beautiful."
- "Thank you for dropping me off at the shops."
- "It was good the way you handled that person."
- "Thank you for the gift."
- Remember to constantly say and also text to each other, "I love you" and "xxx".

Having a Sexually Satisfying Marriage

The secret to having a long-lasting sex life in your marriage is to prioritise sex in your relationship and continually have open and honest discussions with each other about it. A research study on couples with young children led by American psychologist, John Gottman, found that couples who put their relationship first and make the enjoyment of sex a priority, even though they may have the stress of young children and work commitments to cope with, are more likely to enjoy a sexually satisfying long-term relationship built on higher levels of trust and friendship for each other.[210]

Honour Your Marriage Vows

Marriage, like any other contract, involves commitment from both parties to uphold their responsibility to fulfil all their obligations. This includes honouring your marriage vows. When trust is lost because of infidelity, it may not be easy to get it back, if at all. If one spouse feels the other is not as emotionally committed to the relationship as they are, then love, trust and respect will be quickly eroded. Love builds a marriage, whereas negative thoughts and emotions about your spouse will tear it down, and if care is not taken, it may lead to a couple emotionally growing apart and possibly lead to marriage failure. If a couple cannot agree on how to resolve their difficulties, it may need either pastoral or couple therapy intervention.

Secrets for a Happy Marriage

What are the secrets to a happy marriage? We can pretty well figure out what can bring sadness into a relationship. However, having a happy marriage does not require everything to be perfect. It is no secret to anyone that all marrieds have to work hard to make their marriage to be successful, long-lasting, and happy. John M Gottman, in his book, The Seven Principles for Making Marriage Work, cites the findings of a survey on divorce carried out by Lynn Gigy and Joan Kelly from the Divorce Mediation Project in Corte Madera, California. They found that "80% of divorced men and women said their marriage broke up because they gradually grew apart and lost a sense of closeness or did not feel loved and appreciated. Only 20 to 27% of couples said an extramarital affair was even partially to blame."[211]

Below is a list of traits that are necessary for a happy marriage. This is to help you to develop the effective habits and behaviours required for a successful and happy marriage. We also hope that you will regularly review this list together as a couple when you are married.

1. Empathy

Using empathy is demonstrating an understanding of how someone else feels by putting yourself in their shoes and seeing things from their perspective. Empathy powerfully validates another person's feelings. Examples of statements that express empathy:

- "I understand how you feel."
- "I feel your frustration when you talk about this."
- "When you told me how upset you were, it made me feel upset as well."

Some people seem to be more natural with empathy than others. If you believe that you are not good at empathy, don't worry, because not everyone is. However, it is a social skill that can be learnt. Try this method to help you to show empathy to your spouse:

   a) Listen carefully to what your spouse is saying. If it helps, do not be afraid to make notes. That is absolutely okay and your spouse is likely to appreciate that, because they will not want you to either misinterpret or forget anything they say.
   b) After your spouse has finished, repeat back to them what you heard and what you think it means they were trying to say to you. For example, "I have listened to you, and this is how I understand what you have just said."

Doing this will show that you care about what they said and at the same time validates and affirms their feelings.

2. Having a Positive and Hopeful Attitude

Happy marriages require lots of positivity in them. It is optimism without being unrealistic. Sometimes realism can be interpreted as being critically negative. The way to avoid coming across as being negative is to ask open questions, such as, "That sounds like a great idea. Why do you feel that this idea will work?" Or, "Sounds good. How did you arrive at that?" Or, "That is an interesting way of looking at things. Can you please explain further what you mean by...?" Imagine a relationship is like a hot air balloon. There is air on the outside of the balloon, and most importantly, air inside of it that is used to make it leave the ground and fly. The heating of the air inside makes the balloon lift and rise from the ground. This is what happens when there is positivity in the relationship. It causes the relationship to soar upwards. The balloon cannot rise if the relationship is hot and cold. The balloon will remain flat on the ground if there is negativity throughout. For a relationship to flourish, it is essential to have a reasonable amount of positivity, hopefulness, and some realism mixed in from both partners. Otherwise, the marriage will not go anywhere and is likely to fail. To put this into more practical language, Gottman found through his research that a marriage needs a 5:1 ratio of positivity to have a reasonable chance of being happy. This can include: touching, smiling, paying compliments to each other, laughing, etc. In other words, there must be at least five times as many positive feelings for each negative feeling between a husband and wife.[212]

3. Affection

Showing affection by kissing and cuddling each other at least twice a day is vitally important, because kissing and cuddling, holding hands, putting arms around each other, etc., all release oxytocin, the bonding hormone in both men and women. When a couple displays affection to each other, it is a powerful affirmation of their love for each other.

4. Welfare

Asking how each other's day went is very important. It demonstrates care and concern for each other. It is very good to deal with concerns as they arise. However, if an issue cannot be dealt with quickly, consider agreeing to deal with it at a regular weekly "board" meeting. This type of meeting can be used to resolve outstanding problems, and also to discuss family plans and other matters.

5. Regular dates

Going on regular weekly (or at the very least once a month) dates keeps the fire alive in the marriage.

6. Politeness

Get into the habit of always saying "please" and "thank you" to each other. This is the best way to show sincere and positive appreciation to each other. Whoever cooks, always say, "thank you" to them. When you have finished eating, this is another opportunity to say, "thank you." When your partner who cooked for you asks if you enjoyed it, always look for something positive to say, even if it was a bit difficult to eat at the time. This respects them for the effort they put into preparing it for you. A lack of "pleases" and "thank yous" is a clear warning sign that the relationship is being taken for granted.[213] If you have not already got into the habit of always saying "pleases" and "thank yous", there is nothing like the immediate present to get started. Politeness is not an option but a compulsory requirement for a happy marriage. To guarantee you will not lapse with this habit, the best thing to do is to be courteous and say "please" and "thank you" all the time to everyone, not just your spouse, family, and friends, but also with strangers like restaurant waiting staff and even with people who you may not like very much at all.

7. Saying Sorry

Apologising and saying sorry when you have offended your spouse or got things wrong is mature, respectful and validates your spouse's feelings. This is because when a person sincerely says, "sorry", they accept personal responsibility for their actions or behaviour. In fact, it is impossible for a marriage to be happy and successful if one spouse is consistently unwilling to say sorry to the other when things go wrong.

8. Use Praising, Affirming & Validating Language

These are positively powerful for demonstrating how much you appreciate and value your spouse, as well as understanding how they feel. Also, when communication problems occur, they can help to remove feelings of resentment and bitterness. Being always polite and courteous to each other, including saying an abundance of "pleases" and "thank yous", have written into them a special kind of praising, affirming and validating language.

  a) *Praising*: (also complimenting) is about making your partner feel good about a particular achievement or something they did well. For example: "I loved the dinner you prepared tonight." Or, "I am so proud of you for achieving the promotion/pay rise from work." Or, "Well done. I am so proud of you for passing your exams and graduating." Or, "Thank you for taking me out for my birthday." Or, "Your hair/dress looks gorgeous/fabulous."

  b) *Affirming*: works in a similar way to praising. Affirming takes place when you encourage your partner about something. For example: "I know you have the ability to complete your goals/pass your exam." Or, "I like the way you can stand up for what you believe in." Of, "I have complete confidence that you have what it takes to turn your business idea into a success."

  c) *Validating*: is recognising and accepting someone else's feelings and emotional experience. For example, "You said that lately the pressure from work has been getting more stressful. How would you like me to support you with this?" Or, "You have said that our new baby is keeping you up during the night to feed her. Can I help by taking turns with you? I can feed her using the bottle." Or, acknowledging, "You have a right to feel that way."

9. Keep Healthy Boundaries with In-laws

Do not allow in-laws on either side into the decisions of the marriage. Otherwise their presence will quickly be resented. Listen carefully to their advice, but do not be either obligated or feel bound by it. The final decision in marriage always rests exclusively with the couple involved. If you end up living with your parents/in-laws they should be politely reminded as many times as is necessary that their input will only be required if specifically sought in the first place. Otherwise, while living in their home, always be courteous and respectful to them, and do your best to keep your disagreements as private as possible between the both of you.

10. Honour & Respect
- a) Your marriage vows.
- b) The exclusivity of your marriage.
- c) Your marital bed.
- d) Your spouse, and look for ways to constantly show love and affection to them.

Further Reading

For further reading to learn more about effective habits to keep your marriage healthy and vibrant, we recommend, *The Seven Principles for Making Marriage Work* (John M Gottman and Nan Silver) and *For Better For Worse – The Science of a Good Marriage* (Tara Parker-Pope).

Chapter 14: Let's Talk About COMMUNICATION

Communication is vitally essential for every part of our lives, and helps us to express our thoughts, feelings, opinions and ideas to others. However, communication is not a one way street, and therefore, possessing effective listening skills is also very important. If a couple wish to aspire to having a peaceful, stable, happy and successful marriage, then they will prioritise putting effective communication skills at the heart of it. All animal species communicate, but as humans we have superior and sophisticated language, speech and emotion regions in our brains that set us apart from all other creatures. We communicate:

- By using thousands of spoken and written words in hundreds of different languages.
- Through our body language, with many overt and subtle gestures. For example, positioning and movement of our body, arms and hands, as well as facial expressions including movements of our lips and eyes.
- Through our voice pitch and tones. These carry the sounds of our words to express different emotions and feelings, such as romance, humour, aggression, joy, sadness, etc.

In relationships we use communication to let our partner know how we feel about them. This could be to express romantic words of love and affection. Or, using comforting words to show we understand and empathise with what our partner is going through. It could also be to let them know how we feel when we are disappointed with them. Which brings us to the major subject of this chapter. How to manage conflicts in a relationship.

Possibly the most common reasons for dissatisfaction in marriage are:
- Husbands complaining that their wives do not give them enough sex, and
- Wives complaining that their husbands do not do their fair share of housework and childcare.

Both of these can lead to conflicts in the relationship. Other common reasons for conflicts can be over: money, jobs, a new baby or kids, in-laws, and work stress. In this chapter, we will discuss a wide range of proven and effective strategies that you can use to help you communicate better in your relationship.

Are Having Arguments a Sign Of Non-Compatibility?

The short answer is no. As strange as it sounds, numerous research studies have consistently shown that having arguments in a relationship is not a red flag in itself. It is also not necessarily a sign that the relationship is in trouble or is doomed to fail. Arguments and disagreements will come, no matter how strong the relationship bond is. What matters is that a couple patiently work out together the best ways to resolve their differences. However, if a couple have constant arguments before getting married, they are likely to continue having them after marriage, even though they may love each other very much.

Making Time to Listen To Your Partner

When a husband gets home from work, because of the stresses of the day, he may want to have some time for himself to unwind, relax and settle down for a bit before dealing with any family problems. This could involve switching on the TV and watching the news or some sport. After he has relaxed, he is ready to engage with his wife and any concerns that she may have and want to discuss. However, we feel this is the wrong way round, and we believe strongly that a husband's leadership is demonstrated by putting his wife's emotional needs before his own, and this must start the very moment he steps in the front door. The first thing he should do is ask his wife about her day and be prepared to go deeper than the surface. This means he needs to ask her follow-up questions. Once she has unloaded her day, he can unwind in whichever way he feels he needs to. This strategy is very effective for maintaining marital well-being and happiness. It is also easy for men to employ. Let's take a look at an example, and then we'll discuss a powerful and effective technique on how this can work in practice.

In John Gray's book, *Men are from Mars, Women are from Venus*, he suggests how men and women can view resolving things differently to each other. He argues that men like to fix and solve things, but ladies may feel the best way of 'fixing' a problem they may have at times is simply for men to listen to them talk about it. He gave an example that regularly happened early in his marriage. He would often get home from his relationship counselling work of having eight clients a day, feeling totally exhausted, and nothing else left to give. The effect from this meant that his wife felt emotionally ignored and abandoned. In order to resolve this, Gray dropped the last appointment of the day and treated his wife as the most important client of the day, so he could be more responsive to her and his family's needs. She then became his eighth client. He found by doing this he was gradually being loved more, became more relaxed, and to his surprise, both his relationship with his wife and his work flourished.²¹⁴ Most people cannot pick and choose the work they could drop at the end of the day, especially if they are an employee or a contractor involved in deadline-driven projects. So here is a solution that we came up with for men to adopt.

Creatively visualise yourself as a smartphone. Whatever happens during the day, be determined to ensure you have at least 15% charge left on your battery. This means learning how to pace yourself emotionally throughout the day. If your levels are running low, learn to relax on the way home by playing music or listening to a podcast or motivational talk. Make sure that when you turn that key to open your front door, you still have at least 15% emotional battery charge left to listen to your partner. After doing this, you can then attend to your own needs to unwind. It absolutely works! If in the bad chance, you find yourself in a place where you feel you only have about 2% emotional battery life left within you, then you still need to listen first to your partner before doing your own thing. Our advice, in these circumstances, is to listen and do not respond. You do this by saying to your partner that you love her, that your day has been particularly challenging and all you can do right now is just to listen to her, and that you will definitely respond within the hour if still required to do so. As she shares with you what she wants to say, make sure you show her attentiveness, and repeat back to her what she says and how she told you she feels about it. This demonstrates empathy, and that you value and respect her. This is a highly validating technique. If an important sports game is on TV, then you may have to forgo some of it. This solution is the best way to avoid potential conflict issues building up and simultaneously demonstrates your deep love, affection, concern and commitment to her.

For this technique to be effective, it must be done as part of your regular daily routine. To repeat, you need to do this every day! The other benefit of doing this daily is that it can alert you to any issues that could become big problems later on if not dealt with much earlier. When a husband asks his wife, "How are you?" and "How's your day been?" it reminds her that she is greatly loved and appreciated and that he is also highly committed to her emotional well being. When Stephen first started to do this, Ebun was quick to mirror it, by asking him how his day went before he had a chance to ask her. However, the important thing is to ensure the man consistently asks his lady how her day went the moment he gets in.

There is another reason, why men should use this technique. Research has shown that if a wife works, and she feels strong dissatisfaction in her workplace, this is also extremely likely to be translated into having dissatisfaction in her marriage. Which will lead to a higher proneness for divorce if care is not taken.[215] If a man appreciates his wife working, like many husbands do,[216] then this strategy is an absolute must in order to preserve your marriage.

How to Listen

Listening is a skill that requires patience, calmness and lots of practice. This includes not interrupting until the other person has finished speaking. As the Bible wisely says, "Everyone should be quick to listen, slow to speak, and slow to get angry." (James 1:19.) In any difficult discussion, it therefore pays to be patient, calm and respectful with each other. Also, showing attentiveness in your listening demonstrates that you value and sincerely care about your partner's thoughts, feelings, opinions and views. Consistently doing this will in time lead to more peaceful and constructive dialogue. Which in turn will lead to a higher likelihood that issues can be amicably resolved.

Empathy

Empathy is a vital relationship skill to have for a happy marriage. Women are generally better at empathy than men.[217] Empathy, takes listening skills to another level, because it also involves putting yourself in another person's shoes to feel what they feel and see points of view from their side. In practice, genuine empathy works when three things happen together:
1. <u>Listening and interpreting</u> – This is about listening carefully to someone and reading their body language to understand their feelings better. Sometimes, what a person says and how they behave may not be consistent. This may be because they are afraid or don't feel they are free to open up about their feelings, or they may be hiding something. If they are not saying anything, it could mean that they feel so emotionally overwhelmed with frustration or anger that they close down, and this makes it difficult for them to be able to talk.
2. <u>Validating</u> – This involves assuring a person that the feelings they are experiencing are relevant and understandable. This validates their feelings, and also feeds into affirming their value in the relationship.
3. <u>Identifying</u> – Being able to mentally and emotionally identify with what the other person has experienced as if you were the one going through it. This is what is meant by putting yourself in another person's shoes, to feel what they feel and see things from their perspective.

If only the first two points are followed with enough sensitivity, this will mimic empathy, even if a person lacks natural empathy skills. Other proven ways to develop empathy can be by participating in volunteer person-facing charity work, like helping at a food bank, a homeless person's shelter, a local hospital, or a hospice.

Having Your Very Own Relationship 'Business' Meeting

It is never good to put off discussions about things that are really important to either of you. However, at times, when there is not enough time to talk properly about problems or issues that affect the relationship it can make sense for a couple to agree a set time every week for a meeting to talk about them. It is a bit like having your very own business meeting; to discuss the challenges in the relationship, to plan ahead or perhaps even to brainstorm for ideas and work out a solution on a problem together. We recommend that once the date and time has been agreed, then a clipboard with a sheet of paper and a pen is used to make up the agenda points for your meeting. The numbered point list below is just an example for the kind of things that could be put on an agenda for your meetings. When you add an item on your agenda, also write a short description. This helps to prepare your partner's mind that a particular item will be discussed at the meeting.

Example Agenda
1. Matters arising from the previous meeting
2. Conflicts (describe the issue)
3. Unresolved issues (describe the issue)
4. Behaviours (describe the issue)
5. Children (describe the issue)
6. Finances (describe the issue)
7. Moving home (describe the issue)
8. Work and career (describe the issue)
9. Business plans (describe the issue)
10. Holidays (describe the issue)
11. Family events, etc. (describe the issue)
12. Any other business

The list will form your agenda items for your meeting. If it turns out that an issue that is listed for discussion is really 2 or 3 separate points, then consider taking each point separately. This is because mixing many points together, unless they are directly related, would make it impossible to get a proper resolution on them. For example, making a complaint about a partner's constant failure to put dirty clothes in the wash basket, not putting the cap back on the toothpaste tube, and not paying the bills on time would not be wise to treat them together. While all these points may be true, it would be better if they were separated into their own individual agenda items.

It is important to agree a set time for how long your meeting should last, and trying to stick to it. If the meeting does need extra time, for example, by extending the meeting by an extra 30 minutes, this should be agreed by both of you. However, if it is not possible to deal with every agenda item, then you will need to agree to carry over the undealt with items to the next meeting. The reasons why it is important to have a set time for how long a meeting should last is to:

- Respect each other's time.
- Keep the meeting focused.
- Avoid a partner from feeling over tired, frustrated, or being emotionally overwhelmed.

If one partner ends up agreeing to a decision because they either feel fed up or they feel they are not being listened to anyway or feel repeatedly nagged into agreeing that defeats the purpose of the meeting. In that event, it may be better to put off that agenda point to the next meeting, because the purpose of the meeting is to seek win-win outcomes for both partners. Also, it makes sense to try to allocate a specific amount of time to deal with each agenda item. This will just act as a guide only, but will help to keep the overall meeting time on track.

Don't worry, if at the first meeting, there seems to be around 10 to 15 plus items on your list to discuss or things go a bit chaotic at first. As you consistently do this, the agenda items for subsequent meetings will become less and more focused. Finally, please remember, this meeting is between the two of you, and therefore all opinions should be considered as being highly valued. Therefore, to get constructive and positive outcomes from your meeting, it is vital that both of you will need to be patient, respectful, considerate and polite to each other throughout.

Raising a Point of Order

At times, in a meeting, a partner may want to raise a point on how a particular item on the agenda should be treated first before discussing the subject itself. This is generally called raising a 'point of order'. The purpose of taking time out to discuss a point of order would be, for example:

- To gain further clarification on understanding the agenda item.
- Whether an agenda item should be broken up into smaller points and discussed separately.
- For some other reason involving the process of the meeting or how it is conducted.

Each point of order will need to be discussed and agreed on its own merits before it will be possible to discuss the relevant agenda point.

Strategies for Dealing with Conflicts

Below, we have outlined a range of useful conflict resolution tips and strategies that you may wish to adopt for yourselves. All of them have been proven to work and are highly effective.

1. Plan When to Have Your Discussion

It is not wise to have discussions to resolve disagreements, either within one hour of getting in from work or within one hour of the time for normally going to bed. If the time you want to have the discussion is not convenient, for example, because a partner is feeling tired, then try to agree a time that is acceptable to both of you on another day.

2. Be Time Conscious

Always try to agree a specific time limit for closing the discussion and, if necessary, agreeing another time when the discussion can be continued. Doing this does not lessen the importance of needing to discuss an issue. However, if tensions are high, it may make sense to take time out for about 20 minutes to collect your thoughts. Recognise if you are having a discussion that has no chance of reaching a satisfactory resolution. In this case, it may be better to suspend it for now and come back to it another time. See the section below on Overcoming Gridlocks.

3. Be a Good Listener

Listen carefully to each other's point of view. Make notes if you feel it would be helpful. Doing this can help you to see more clearly what the other person is saying. Also, writing down what the other person has said, can help you to see and identify more clearly the areas of frustration they are experiencing. Repeat back what you have heard. This powerfully proves that you have listened to them and may already bring you halfway to resolving the disagreement.

4. Keep Cool & Calm

Always speak in a low, slow speaking and calm voice. When high pitches or angry tones in voice are used, it can make it very difficult to listen effectively and respond positively. If you get easily angry, reflect on what triggered your anger and how you could have handled it differently. Try taking deep breaths or counting five seconds before each response. It will allow the brain some thinking time, rather than responding in the split second of the moment. If necessary, take a short break to allow time to collect your thoughts. Also, repeating back what a partner says, can help give you some important seconds to collect your thoughts together, to give a more considered response.

5. Keep Discussions Simple

Don't mix different problems together, but rather stick to one issue at a time. It is easier to discuss multiple or complex issues by first of all breaking them down into separate parts, and then systematically going through each part. If it seems difficult to do this, try sitting down with a piece of paper and look at the problem logically. Firstly, write down the problem or issue. Then break down the problem into separate parts. For example, a partner's complaint might be: "When we go out I feel that you do not give me enough attention." There are two things here: (1) possibly not going out enough and (2) not giving enough attention. Which is the real problem here? It could, of course, be both.

6. Getting Your Facts Fight First

Don't make assumptions by trying to psychoanalyse or mind-read how your partner feels about something. It is more respectful to patiently seek clarification of what they mean if it is not clear what they are trying to say. If they find it difficult to express themselves, try helping them by breaking down the issue into smaller parts to seek out what can be understood by both of you.

7. Ask Open Questions

Always start discussions by asking open ended questions,

beginning them with: Who, What, When, Where, Why and How. This demonstrates high levels of interest and validation for the other person's thoughts, feelings, ideas and opinions. You could use a soft opening question like: "How was your day?" or "How do you think/feel about...?"

8. Avoid Blaming

Be direct and say how you feel but avoid blaming or insulting behaviour. Avoid attacking your partner when addressing their unwelcome behaviour or attitude. For more information, please see the section below: How to Address Each Other's Faults

9. Communicating Respectfully

Be very kind, gracious, respectful, and validating with your words. For example:

- "I am glad you are sharing that with me."
- "I disagree with you because it does not take into account..."
- "I also know that you are not satisfied with ..."
- "Is there a compromise we can agree on?"
- "What about this compromise, which takes into account what you said you feel about ..."

10. Be Willing to Say Sorry

Always be humble by being quick to admit your mistakes and apologise when you are in the wrong. Doing so shows maturity, great respect and loving behaviour.

11. Be Forgiving

Don't use the admission of mistakes to score points. This wastes time, is disrespectful and highly frustrating. Instead, be gracious and forgiving. There is real power in forgiveness.

12. Wait Patiently For a Response

Do not take silence in a discussion as a sign of assent or full agreement. No matter how urgent the matter is. Always wait for responses, rather than assume. If your partner is being silent, it may be either they are not clear about something that has been said to them or they are not sure if the proposed course of action is the right one to take. It could also indicate they are still thinking and processing the issue over in their mind. Therefore, avoid nagging your partner for a response. An alternative way forward could be to ask your partner how far they are prepared to go in the interim before a full response can be expected. You could also ask them to tell you what specific things they may not be comfortable about to make a decision on the matter right now.

Compromise Is About Sacrifice

Sacrificial love is about being able to compromise and often involves going out of your way to do something for your partner that will inconvenience you. Marital conflict resolution often involves negotiating; to obtain a win-win outcome for both partners, or compromising; to agree a neutral position. Care should be taken to avoid one partner feeling disadvantaged, because this could lead to resentment building up in the relationship. Any conflict resolution often involves some form of compromise. Marriage is about sacrifice, and the need at times to compromise illustrates this: to give up something for the sake of harmony or progress in the relationship. When sacrifice is motivated by love, the sacrifice is significantly easier to bear because of the benefit that both, may directly or indirectly get from it. The opposite of sacrifice is selfishness. No marriage will last very long if selfishness is a constant problem. An example of mutual sacrificial love is where a couple have children and both parents share mutual responsibility in their nurturing and care. A similar example could be where one parent does the school run in the morning, and the other does it in the evening or takes the child to some extra activity like scouting or playing a sport.

Writing Love Letters

There are some people who have listening and understanding problems for a number of genuine reasons. To get round this, we suggest that partners may like to try composing short 'love' letters to each other, to explain their point of view, the history behind it and why the issue is important to them. Always end each letter with, "I love you", because this affirms the value you have for your partner, even if it is difficult to 100% feel that way at times. Also, write your letter in a positive way that will encourage your partner to want to read it. For information on how to make a complaint to your partner, please see the section below: How to Address Each Other's Faults.

Of course, you do not need to wait for a problem to arise before writing a love letter to each other. It is also a romantic thing to do. Therefore, try not to forget important dates in the year, such as your wedding anniversary and your partner's birthday, as well as Valentine's Day and Christmas Day. You could use the calendar app on your smartphone to remind you. Getting a card and writing by hand inside it a special message to express your love and appreciation for your partner and what they mean to you, is a powerful gesture of love affirmation. Also, if you feel up to the challenge, you could try writing them a love poem.

How to Address Each Other's Faults

Giving or receiving criticism in a relationship, never mind in any other area of life, can be difficult to deal with. There are two types of criticism: constructive and destructive. In this section we will look at the differences between both of these, and suggest how to make a complaint to a partner in a positive way.

Definitions for the different criticisms:

- *Constructive criticism*: means giving useful feedback and suggestions for improvement. This can include using positive language to encourage change in a person's behaviour or offer positive, alternative ways of doing something for a better outcome.
- *Destructive criticism*: is always harmful and sets out to pull down or undermine a person. In relationships, destructive criticism can be interpreted as being overly critical, judgmental, blaming or trying to shame.

Let's see how the two compare using practical examples. A constructive criticism may start with giving positive feedback and then contain a complaint. This can be done by depersonalising the criticism and starting with "I". For example: "I liked the way you dealt with your parents in telling them not to interfere in our relationship, but I felt you did not back me up when I mentioned about me starting a new job." On the other hand, a destructive criticism will focus on blaming, by starting with the word "you". For example: "You are always too busy for us these days." Using "I feel/felt…" instead of leading with "you", is significantly softer sounding, and less likely to be negatively received or get a defensive reaction. A positive alternative could be: "I liked it when we used to regularly go out nearly every weekend. I realise that you are busy because of work, but our relationship is suffering as a result. Can we urgently make regular time to spend more time together please?" Changing how we communicate can be a bit like learning a new skill. However, the more you practice, the better you will get at it, and the less friction, tension and arguments you will experience in your marriage.

Avoid Miscommunication

Miscommunication in a relationship is when something is being said or expressed but is not received or understood in the way it was meant. Sometimes, things can be said out of hurt or anger by one partner when complaining about the behaviour or attitude of the other. They hope their partner will listen and change their ways immediately. However, their partner's reaction may differ from what they were expecting. Instead, they may react with anger or exasperation or switch off entirely rather than engage with what is being said. Below are two common miscommunication examples, often used by ladies more than men, but still applies to both:

1. "Always"

This word is generally used to express feelings of frustration about an occurrence that has happened more than once. When this word is used, its purpose is to shut down any kind of opposition rather than discussing the issue. Using the word, "always", never resolves anything. Instead, it ends up putting two people in a bad mood. It is better to avoid using it altogether, and opt for a lower calmer voice and slower speech to discuss the issue, and hope the matter can be resolved amicably, with negotiation.

2. "We Need to Talk" (or "I Want Us to Discuss Something")

When this phrase is used, the person is not generally looking for a mutual discussion. For example, they may say this when they feel they need to offload overwhelming feelings of anger and emotional frustration about a particular behaviour of their partner. The purpose is simple. She wants him to accept he has done wrong and immediately change. When these words are used, she is not in the mood to discuss or negotiate. Once he replies, "Yes, okay, what's up?" this response is like giving permission to press a red button and launch a nuclear missile. She will then lay out the charges against him. If he either interrupts or tries to defend himself, this is only likely inflame her anger further. The only thing that her partner can do in this situation is to simply show attentiveness and listen. Better still, to get a pen and paper out and take bullet point notes, as if compiling an agenda for a future meeting. There is little point in responding. It is better for him to say that he is listening carefully to what she is saying and not go beyond that. This type of conflict, ultimately produces no winners, and often leads to a bad night for both partners (or, creating a tense, uncomfortable atmosphere that can last for several days afterward).

The solution to this is simple. When a partner says, "We need to talk," respond to them, "I will only agree to talk as long as you give me the right to respond." If they agree, then follow the advice in the section above: Strategies For Dealing With Conflicts. If they do not agree, then say, "In that case, while it is clear that you want to say something that is very important to you, I will only agree to listen if you agree to give me the right to respond."

A better and less confrontational approach would have been in the first place to ask, "I need to discuss something that has upset me, but it is also important that we do this when you are not tired or busy, so that emotions can be managed on both sides. When can we do this, please?" When your partner responds, "What is it about?" You can tell them the subject but refuse to discuss it there and then. Instead, say, "Not now, because I know you are tired or busy, but tomorrow is fine. What time is best for you?"

Dealing with Stonewalling

Professor John Gottman, American psychologist and researcher of over four decades on divorce prediction and marital stability, came up with what he calls the four horsemen of apocalypse: Criticism, Contempt, Defensiveness and Stonewalling, because of their negative power to damage marriages. In this section we focus on Stonewalling, because it is the most harmful (out of the four) to marital stability and is a very high predictor for divorce if it is not dealt with.[218]

Stonewalling, also known as giving the silent treatment, is a response caused by suppressing intense feelings of anger or frustration instead of venting out or discussing them. This causes the person to close down and become stonewall silent. Gottman, through his research concluded that men are more likely to be stonewallers than women. He believes that the reason for this is because men tend to be more physiologically overwhelmed by marital confrontation situations; causing their pulse rates and blood pressure to rise, and lead to a verbal shut down. However, for the partner of a Stonewaller, it can be very frustrating. If Stonewalling becomes habitual and not dealt with, the relationship will become fragile.[219]

Duana C. Welch, in her book, *Love Actually – For Single Parents*, advises Stonewallers to be aware of when they begin to feel overwhelmed and want to tune out. They should take this as a prompt that they need to take at least a 20 minute break from the situation, until they feel they have calmed down enough to be able to re-engage in the discussion. This is because it can take at least 20 minutes, particularly with men, before pulse rates and blood pressure starts to come down. Before the Stonewalling partner steps away to take a time-out, they should assure their partner of their love for them, and explain to them that they are experiencing feelings of being overwhelmed, and that they just need to take a short break before resuming again.[220][221] Doing this communicates positively to the other partner that they are loved and affirmed in the relationship.

Overcoming Gridlocks

Another relationship communication problem that Gottman's research identified was how couples can deal with 'gridlock' type situations.[222] That is, when a strong issue of disagreement lacks a normal compromise to be found to resolve it. Often times, these issues can reflect compatibility differences around:
- Roles and responsibilities in the relationship.
- Future plans.
- Differences in core values and beliefs.

Some examples of these type of disagreements are:
- Whether or when to have children.
- Whether or not to have a religious ceremony, such as a Christening, to mark the birth of a child.
- Participating in each other's religious festivals. If the couple are from different faith backgrounds or one partner is an atheist, this may be a problem.
- Whether or not to have an elderly relative live in.
- Whether to live in retirement in a quiet coastal town or move to a sunnier climate abroad.

The common thread in all of the above examples is that while they may not be relationship deal breakers, they may not be easy to resolve either. A strategy for ways to overcome gridlock issues is as follows:
1. The couple need to agree that they are dealing with an issue that neither partner are willing to give ground on to resolve it, but are open to at least discussing it.
2. The couple need to agree to discuss the issue positively without hurting each other. Being positive in this instance, is focusing on the "can-do". In other words, don't tell your partner, what you can't do; tell them what you can do.
3. Each partner should open up about:

- Why the issue is important to them,
- What it means to them,
- The history behind why it is important to them, and also (if relevant),
- How it links to their values and beliefs.

4. Try to break down the gridlock issue as much as possible into smaller parts. This helps to define more clearly the common areas that compromise can be reached on, from those that are more difficult and need more time.
5. Positively look for areas of flexibility. This involves a negotiation process to give ground by agreeing on trade-offs between you. For example, one partner may have a dream of doing a degree programme or want to have a holiday home to part rent out and also use as a family retreat, but the other partner is not willing to support using the couple's savings for either of these. The first partner may offer flexibility by saying, "I am prepared to agree to a smaller holiday home than I dreamt of having, and wait a few years to get it if you are willing to get behind the project and work with me on it." This may only be a start to break the deadlock, but at least it could get a conversation going.
6. Try putting yourself in the shoes of your partner, and seeing the problem from their perspective. Does that make you see the problem in a different light?
7. Try reframing your proposed way of going forward by thinking up ways that will specifically benefit your partner.

Dealing with gridlock issues, are likely to be highly emotional and stressful events. Therefore, try not to be overly or unreasonably expectant for a fast solution. It may need quite a number of little sessions to make effective progress in the longer term. When progress is made, no matter how small, acknowledge it with gratefulness and appreciation to your partner, by always saying, "Thank you." Constant politeness, lots of appreciation and always using low soft voice tones go a long way to keeping hearts and minds open for compromises to be made.

When dealing with gridlock issues, a couple need to accept that some issues may never be resolved. If this is the case, the couple are advised to put an invisible fence around it, and only raise it for discussion with the prior agreement of the other partner. This treats the issue as an obstruction that needs to be side stepped so that it no longer has power to dominate the relationship or prevent it from progressing forward. Put simply, these type of issues should be seen as an irritation but not strong enough to define the marriage. But be aware that refusing to discuss something could be regarded as being disrespectful and offensive. Therefore, our advice is to always be prepared to have a discussion even if it is not likely to end up in an agreement.

STEP 4: Getting Engaged

Chapter 15: Getting Engaged

When to Get Engaged

There are no hard and fast principles for when the time is right to get engaged for marriage. Each relationship is different because each partner in that relationship is different with their own level of emotional readiness to take the next step towards marriage. Also, a partner may be resistant to commit to marriage because they feel some areas in their life are not yet in order. Such as not earning enough in their career yet or would rather have enough money saved for a deposit for a first home or a 'fairy tale' wedding. While these aspirations may sound reasonable, the couple should discuss and agree a timeline that will be realistic against other plans they will have, such as taking into account a lady's natural reproductive body clock and when the couple would like to have children. For more information on this, please see Chapter 21: Sexuality & Fertility.

In this chapter, we will provide some guidelines to help you know if your relationship has matured enough for you to take the next step towards getting engaged. We will also discuss what to do if your partner appears to be resisting the idea of getting engaged, as well as useful tips and suggestions to help men prepare and propose to their partners.

How Long Should a Couple Have Known Each Other Before Getting Engaged?

Let's first consider the lengths of time people on average generally will take to get engaged and married. In 2016, the average age in the UK for first marriages for women was 31.5 years and for men was 33.4 years.[223] But in the US for women it was 27.4 years and for men it was 29.5 years.[224] The average age gap is roughly the same of around 2 years. Also, both UK and US couples on average, date for 3.3 years before getting engaged and then get married on average 15 to 18 months later.[225] [226] [227] Of course, these figures are averages only. Many will get engaged and married earlier and for others, it will be later. In respect of age, we would caution against getting married under the age of 21, for the following reasons:

1. The human brain reaches full maturity around the age of 25,[228] and this coincides with psychosocial maturity in young adults.[229] [230] Our psychosocial maturity definition for marriage, in this sense is:
   a) Having an understanding of how to develop and maintain an exclusive committed relationship based on love, trust, kindness, respect and emotional interdependency.
   b) Having a well-balanced understanding to make complex and critical judgments and decisions that directly affect the lives of others.
   c) Accepting responsibility for how a husband or wife's decisions, actions and behaviour can affect the social, emotional and economic wellbeing of their spouse and their family.
   d) Having the capacity to respond and resolve in a

positive way to complex emotions, conflicts, challenges and crisis in the marriage as they arise.
2. The divorce rate is much higher for those who get married before age 20, but significantly drops when people get married after age 20.[231] Most degree level students will have graduated by age 21 to start their career, and therefore are unlikely to be economically stable before then.
3. It can take time for those under 21, and not in college or university or a trade or profession, to establish a career with a high enough income to adequately support a family.

We are not saying that people should not get married before 21, but rather if they do, we advise the couple should have similar cultural values and beliefs,[232] and also ideally be supported by family and pastoral support from a church or other religious community to give the new marriage the best possible chance of success.

Putting age aside, we recommend that before a couple become engaged, they should ideally have been actively dating and courting each other for at least a year beforehand. This would include at least 3 months dating plus at least 6-9 months courtship. This gives the couple time to get to know each other's character and personality, including their flaws, habits and behaviours. It also gives them time to get to know the strength and depth of feeling they have for each other, as well as to make sure that both feel the same way about each other. Being in a close relationship for at least a year will also confirm whether there is enough love and trust between them to have the confidence to place their lives in each other's care. Lastly, one year should be long enough for a couple to align their thinking around their agreed goals, plans and priorities together for the future.

To avoid a lady getting trapped into a long-term relationship that is going nowhere we advise that it is very unwise to cohabitate, unless a she has been proposed to, got an engagement ring on her finger and has agreed a wedding date that is just around the corner. That is, within 3-6 months, but not longer. The reason why many couples take in total around 5 years to get to the altar is because the vast majority of them cohabitated beforehand. In the UK almost 9 out of 10 couples cohabitate.[233] Over a period of 10 years, out of every 100 cohabitating couples, 40% will split up, 50% will marry and 10% will remain together, while those cohabitees that have children 27% will break up before their child is 5 years old.[234] Also, there is a greater chance of divorce if a couple do cohabitate before marriage.[235] [236] [237] That is the reality. Furthermore, it is unwise to cohabitate because in most cases, it is the lady that gets disadvantaged. Typically, after a lady has given 5 or 6 years of her life in a failed cohabitation relationship, she finds herself back on the shelf, significantly older, and has to start again. So does the man, except that he does not have to deal with a ticking maternal body clock. It therefore makes sense to ensure a relationship is intentional and going somewhere to save the trauma of being in a time wasting relationship.

What about Whirlwind Romances?

Whirlwind 'Hollywood' type romances seldom work, because in real-life, it takes time to get to know someone properly. If a couple want to get married too quickly, it substantially increases the risk of missing major character flaws in someone. In other dating and relationship books, the dating and relationship stages are sometimes characterised as seasons of the year to exemplify the different stages a couple's relationship passes through in its growth to maturity. At the beginning of the romance, like spring and summer, things can feel new, fresh, warm, and exhilarating. However, like autumn and winter, relationships can have stormy crises and challenges that must be managed and overcome. All relationships naturally have their ups and downs, but when challenges and crises occur, each partner will see the other's character strengths and weaknesses. If the couple can adapt and overcome a challenge or crisis, they are more likely to grow in their love, trust, and emotional interdependency for each other. If the couple does not perform well in dealing with the challenge or crisis, it may cause at least one of the partners to lose confidence in the relationship which may lead to its break up. This is why we strongly advocate that couples should not try to shortcut the time period necessary to naturally get to know each other. What a couple is not willing to learn by choice before marriage will have to be learned the hard way during the marriage. No marriage is immune from this learning principle. Learning in the classroom of courtship is far better preparation than having to learn the lessons of non-compatibility and non-suitability in the real world of marriage. This is why it is better to have a reasonable amount of time to get to know each other before getting engaged. To avoid wrong matches being made, and marriages ending up in divorce.

Dealing with Excuses

Marriage is not meant for everyone, and not everyone in a relationship wants to get married. For example, some people, in our experience usually men, who are in a long-term relationship, having witnessed their parents or other close family members or friends get divorced, may be reluctant to get married. This inevitably means their partners, usually women, who want to get married end up wasting years of their lives in relationships that are not going anywhere. In our experience, the reality is that from as early as six months to a year into the relationship, men know their future plans and whether they hope to include the lady they are dating in them. If a man has not intimated his long-term feelings about his lady after a year of courting, then she needs to ask him what his intentions are and where he thinks the relationship is going. Common excuses people give for refusing to commit to getting married are, they:

- Do not feel they are ready.
- May feel they are too young.
- Don't want to settle down right now.
- Want to focus on their career or studies right now.
- Have not emotionally moved on from a previous bad relationship.
- Don't want to feel tied down with just one person.
- Feel that marriage is old fashioned.
- Feel that marriage is just a piece of paper.
- Are anxious about the high divorce rates.

All of these excuses suggest that the partner who does want to get married did not ask early on in the dating and courtship stages about the future plans of their partner and whether they were featured in them.

Ladies: If, after a year in a relationship, your man has avoided bringing up the subject of marriage and the future or has been saying things like "not now," then you have a right to ask him where he thinks the relationship is going. You can simply ask him, "I've been enjoying our time together, but what are your intentions to where you see this relationship going?" If he responds that he will propose soon, it may make sense to clarify what "soon" means to him by asking him for a timeline of his plans for the next 2, 3, and 5 years. If you are not directly included in them, you will know how he feels about the relationship. You may also need to remind him that you are a bit old-fashioned and think it is reasonable to always be intentional with relationships. If your man is emotionally invested in you, being confronted this way will not scare him off. On the other hand, if he is not giving you a clear direction regarding his plans, it means he is not likely to be marriage-minded, at least not with you. In this instance, you will need to take the following steps:

1. Let him know calmly that you are not happy with the lack

of direction in the relationship.
2. Stop having sex immediately and withdraw the amount of time you spend with him.
3. Wait and be patient to see how he reacts.

If after doing this and your man has not changed his attitude towards where the direction of the relationship is going, then be prepared to walk away from the relationship and do not call him. If he does not call you after eight weeks, it means he has gotten over you and moved on. In this case, you need to do so as well.

If a lady is engaged and already cohabitating, but still has not got a date for marriage one year after her man had proposed to her, then she needs to ask him about his intentions. If he cannot or will not give her a date, she should tell him she needs some space. For example, she could say to him that she learned about a place that is about to be rented out. If he asks from where she can tell him she saw it on a property rental website or heard about it from a friend. But she will need to be prepared to follow through with this. Otherwise, he may not take her seriously. Perhaps some space apart may help him to make up his mind on what he really thinks about her. If a man has proposed and there is still no agreed wedding date a year later, this is a clear sign of lack of commitment. It is very likely in this scenario that even if a wedding were to take place, there is a very high risk that the marriage would end in failure.[238]

Men & Proposals

It's a huge thing for a man to propose to his lady. Men generally want their marriage proposal to be romantically done and, if possible, as a complete surprise to their lady when they do it. This means men are prepared to wait and wait while looking for that romantic moment, and they don't mind taking their time to carefully plan it to be that way. A lady may have to be patient with how her man chooses to do this. Getting engaged has significant consequences, and most men need to feel in control of how it is done. Delays could also be linked to fears of proposal rejection and also how the lady's family may react.

Men: When you propose, have a rough date timeline in mind that you know you can realistically aim for. Ideally, it should be within a year to avoid the risk of unplanned pregnancies or wasting your lady's time. You do not have to agree on the exact date when you propose, but it is good to have this in mind because she may naturally ask. Also, the actual date may still have to be agreed with the families on both sides. It is not good to prolong wedding dates, especially if you would like to have children at some point.

Talking to the Prospective Bride's Parents

In some traditions, a man is expected to ask a lady's father for permission to propose. Many families of ladies appreciate this respectful gesture. This is because it gives honour to those who have been responsible for caring and investing in a lady's development and achievements to the point of when the man first met her. If a man needs permission from his lady's father to propose, it makes sense for the man first of all to ask his lady if she is likely to accept. If a man is from a different culture to his lady, he should do his homework regarding standard etiquette for how a marriage proposal from her culture is normally done.

The ideal expectation is that parents from both sides will welcome and accept the new member into their respective families. However, this is not always the case, and it is not uncommon for couples to get married without a family's blessing (including key family members refusing to come to the wedding). When there is a lack of acceptance for marriage from one or both families, and the wedding goes ahead anyway, the consequences could be that a family may hold back their social or economic support to the couple. Whichever way a couple chooses to do things, they should seek the involvement of their respective families, as much as possible. This includes awareness of cultural sensitivities, customs, and traditions that may need to be observed.

Proposal Suggestions

Once the time feels right for both partners to desire to get married to each other, the man traditionally begins planning a marriage proposal. Here are some of our own marriage proposal ideas for men:

- Propose With Poetry: Write a love poem or use an existing one to express your feelings before you make your proposal. There are plenty of examples of love poems on the internet.
- Holiday Proposals: Propose during a special celebration day such as Christmas, Valentine's Day or your lady's birthday.
- Creative Proposals: If many of the traditional proposal methods don't seem right for you, research online for creative proposal suggestions. There are many creative ways to propose that range from arranging for a plane flying in the sky with a banner attached to it, or spelling out the proposal in flower petals or going up in a hot air balloon and then proposing.
- Memorable: This could be as romantic as a quiet restaurant dinner with just the two of you, or up a mountain or on a picnic or dinner with friends.

"Will You Marry Me?"

To help men plan what they may want to say as a lead up to their marriage proposal, here are some suggestions that they can include.

1. Tell your lady about the exact moment you realised they were the One for you. There may be a defining moment for you that took your partner from being a significant other to being the One for you.
2. Mention what it is most that you love about them. Make a list of the reasons why you love them. It can be as simple as loving their smile, their laugh or sense of humour, or how you have been personally touched by them, or how they have made you a better person.
3. Talk about how you see your future together.

Don't worry, if you think you will not remember everything you want to say. Just write it down on a piece of paper and read it to her. Your lady knows you and will be just as touched in the exact same way as if you had remembered every word off by heart.

Buying the Engagement Ring

Some men like to propose with a ring already in their pocket, because they feel it will symbolically enhances the romantic moment for them. However, engagement rings are expensive, and there are risks of getting one in advance of the proposal. For example:
- Trying to ensure the correct ring size.
- Getting a metal (and colour) that a lady actually wants.
- Getting the type of stones that a lady prefers.
- If the lady rejects the proposal or she does not like the ring, returning the ring to the jewellers will mean not getting a full refund, because it will be viewed as used or pre-owned immediately after leaving the shop.

To get the right sized ring in advance of a proposal, a man could buy a low cost ring sizer gauge either through Amazon or Ebay. A ring sizer gauge is a ring measuring tool with approximately 30 different sized plastic or metal rings attached to it. He can then use this to measure his lady's ring finger and then buy the ring. However, if a man wants to measure his lady while she is not noticing, then it is best to do this with a vernier caliper and say to her that he wants to measure her ring finger on her right hand because he wants to buy her a dress ring. (It may not be a complete truth but is not entirely an untruth either.) A vernier caliper is a measuring gauge that can discreetly go over a lady's ring finger without her hardly even feeling it, and is also available from either Ebay or Amazon. The man can then use this to compare the width against the different rings sizes on the ring sizer gauge. But you will need to take into account that rings on the ring size gauge are thin and you may need to go up a size (or two) if the width of the ring you want to buy is quite wide.

When you are having your discussions with your lady about your future plans, we suggest you could also informally discuss with her what kind of ring she would like. Or, better still, when the man is out shopping with his lady, they can pass by a jeweller, and then she can show him the kind of rings she likes and even get her ring finger professionally measured there. Although, doing this will raise her expectations very high, and she will undoubtedly be very disappointed if this is not followed up by action.

Ladies: If an engagement ring is important to you and your man still has not given it to you after 6 months of his proposal, you may need to challenge him about this to make sure he is still serious about the relationship. If there are exceptional financial circumstances, then you both could consider getting a low cost fabulous looking imitation ring as a temporary solution. Money can also be saved by buying a second hand ring from an antique jewellery auction. However, if you decide to buy a second hand ring through an auction, you may still need to take it to a jeweller to get it professionally resized, which will still be cheaper than buying a brand new one.

How to Make Sure Your Man Is Right For You

Ladies: Both men and women usually know if their partner is the right One for them or not. However, if your man proposes but you have doubts or are not sure he is the One, then definitely you should say, "No". Here is a check list to help you with making up your mind. Can you say yes to all of these?

- [ ] Do I love him?
- [ ] Do I see him as the One I want to share the rest of my life with?
- [ ] Would I be proud to introduce him to others, "This is my husband"?
- [ ] Do I think that our future plans are compatible with each other?
- [ ] Do we have enough interests, beliefs and values that are compatible with each other to make a marriage work?
- [ ] Do I like to kiss him?
- [ ] Do I like the way he shows affection to me?
- [ ] Do I like the way he treats me?
- [ ] Does he show kindness and respect to me?
- [ ] Is he always calm and patient with me?
- [ ] Can I wake up with him next to me for the rest of my life?
- [ ] Do I like his voice?
- [ ] Is he open about his finances?
- [ ] Do I trust him with finances?
- [ ] Do I trust him with children around?
- [ ] Do I like him as a person?
- [ ] Do I like the way he treats and respects both his and my family and friends?
- [ ] Do I like the way he treats people whose job it is to serve, like waiting staff or cab drivers?
- [ ] Do I think he is calm and patient with other road users when he is driving?
- [ ] Does he show he cares about me with the

following:
- ( ) Opens doors for me.
- ( ) Buys me gifts.
- ( ) Does things all the time for me.
- ( ) Asks me how I am and how my day went.

Changing Your Mind

If after accepting or giving a proposal, you later change your mind, it is better to pull out than making a mistake of getting married to the wrong person. If you have any doubts at any time, even at the altar on the wedding day itself or any time beforehand while you go through all the planning, booking, and paying for everything, stop and pull out. Don't feel guilty or embarrassed. Weddings are for one day. However, marriage is a serious lifelong commitment. It is one thing to get butterflies in your stomach because of nerves. It is completely different if you have doubts in your mind about whether your feelings for each other are deep enough to be bound together for the rest of your lives. If there was constant arguing, or your partner was abusive and disrespectful to you before you are married, then this will 100% continue in your marriage.

Prenuptial Agreements

Our readers would be right to question what the subject of prenuptial agreements is doing in a book on love, dating, and marriage. However, many people these days will not get married without having one in place. Suffice to say, we are not fans of prenuptial agreements, but can understand why people would consider them. They can sometimes offer a solution to get around difficult issues, where either one or both partners already have significant assets and income beforehand, or there is inheritance issues to consider, for example, because of children from a previous relationship.

A survey carried out by Savanta ComRes for the Marriage Foundation, concluded that 1 in 5 couples marrying for the first time, now enter into a prenuptial agreement. 44% of these were unsurprisingly from higher income earning managers and senior executives. Also, prenups were most likely to be considered by couples who had attended some form of marriage preparation class.[239][240]

Whether the motive for having a prenup is founded on distrust or over-cautiousness is impossible to say. However, given the high levels of divorce, it could be arguable to suggest there does appear to be some fear motive for deciding to go down this route. If one partner feels the need for a prenuptial agreement but the other objects, the way to break the deadlock is to agree to have a limited life prenuptial agreement. This could be, for example, that the agreement would be done away with after 5 or 10 years.

If a couple wish to take out a prenuptial agreement, independent legal advice for each partner is absolutely essential, but doing this is not cheap. The fees for getting a professionally drawn up agreement by lawyers, can easily start at £5,000 for each partner. If the agreement is not drawn up by lawyers and the couple end up getting divorced, there is a high risk that a judge may rule that the prenuptial agreement is void on the grounds that a former spouse could not understand the full legal implications of what they agreed to.

Chapter 16: Safeguarding Your Marriage

In this chapter, we will look at the kind of things that can go wrong in a marriage and discuss various prevention strategies that can be put in place to reduce the chance of a relationship being vulnerable to breaking down. We have mainly focused on infidelity, which is the number one reason for divorce. Also, before sexual betrayal takes place, there are often other areas in a relationship that may not have been going well. We hope to deal with as many of these underlying factors as possible in this chapter. There can never be any justification for infidelity or any kind of bad behaviour in marriage. To be clear, wrong is wrong, and infidelity, whatever the reason, is wrong. We hope that by dealing with the underlying causes of relationship failure and how these can be prevented, it will help our readers know how to safeguard and protect their marriage. We all want to have an emotionally rewarding, lifelong, happy marriage. Building your marriage with structures already in place to deal with problems before they arise is the best way to safeguard it from failure. Just like building impenetrable castle walls, it takes a lot of time, hard work, and effort to ensure the structure of the marriage is sufficiently robust enough to withstand attack.

Common Reasons for Relationship Breakups

There are many reasons that can cause marriages to fail and end up in divorce. The number one cited reason for divorce is infidelity, and potentially a hidden number two reason is infertility. There is a third common reason, cruelty, which includes violent, abusive or controlling behaviour (normally by a husband).[241] [242] [243] [244] Other major contributors to divorce, but in no particular order:

- Lack of commitment.[245]
- Conflicts and arguments.[246]
- Growing apart. That is, no longer having anything in common.
- Sexual problems, including feeling sexually unfulfilled.
- Unemployment or other economic hardships.
- Debts out of control or spending financial assets without agreement.
- Addiction problems including drinking, smoking, drugs misuse, gambling or pornography.
- Mental health and depression.
- Not having the same religious practices, beliefs and convictions as each other.
- Interference by in-laws.

If any of the above issues involve struggles you are personally trying to deal with, and you are concerned, it could jeopardise a new relationship, it is advisable before looking for a new partner to first seek suitable professional therapeutic assistance. In the meantime, please continue reading because it will also help you positively focus your mind to know what you should do once you have received the help you might need.

Why Do Men (& Women) Cheat?

There are many reasons why men cheat. Though, for men, the question in the headline of this section may feel rhetorical because in many cases, they already know why. But when these reasons are presented to women, they may find it difficult to accept because, as far as a woman is concerned, no man who truly loves and cares about his wife (or partner) would want to hurt her by cheating on her. Recognising the causes of marital unfaithfulness will hopefully help people to put the necessary prevention strategies in place to lessen the chance of a sexual betrayal from ever happening. Before we begin, it should be noted that both men and women can and do cheat. Over the past hundred years, numerous research studies have consistently shown that men are between 20-40% and women are between 20-25% unfaithful in marriage.[247]

The following list consists of the most common reasons for marital unfaithfulness based on both our research and our experience. Except for the first two, they are mentioned in no particular order. Also, the list of reasons apply to both men and women.

1. Sexual Unfulfilment

Reason: A partner believing that their sexual needs are not being fully met in the relationship. This can also be because of limited or no sexual access to their partner.

Prevention: Discuss with each other openly and look for different ways to meet each other's sexual needs. For example, when women are in menopause, hormonal changes can make it difficult for them to get close sexually with their partners. Also, if a man has erectile dysfunction problems, this can make him feel of lesser manly worth. Look for alternative ways to give sexual satisfaction to each other. Do research together and have a positive open discussion on your findings. Also, consider seeking professional medical or therapeutic help. For more information on overcoming sexual problems, please see Chapter 20: Sexuality & Fertility.

2. Emotional Unfulfilment

Reason: Feeling emotionally neglected. Emotional needs not being sufficiently met. Feeling of being taken for granted. Lack of empathy shown. Lack of physical affection. Lack of emotional support. Lack of sensual and verbal care and attention.

Prevention: Cuddle and kiss each other in the morning and evening. Ask how each other's day went so that any emotional issues or stress from the day can be dealt with. Learn to be a good listener, and if necessary, repeat back what you have heard to demonstrate to your partner that you have listened to them. Make time at least once a week to have a planned meeting to deal with problems that are too complex to deal with there and then. Make time for regular dates, as well as taking short breaks of one or two nights away.

3. Opportunity

Reason: This is about time and circumstance. Maybe he or she didn't mean it to happen, or it was planned ahead of time. The opportunity for infidelity can be through deliberate deception by arranging a secret rendezvous at a hotel or by chance or circumstances through a planned work event such as a conference or other out-of-town commitment.

Prevention: Always be accountable to each other. Allow access to each other's smartphones and passwords. Have a home screen photo of both of you on your smartphones. Always talk about your spouse to strangers of the opposite sex. Talk to your spouse openly about your feelings and problems.

4. Anxiety Driven

Reason: A partner may be experiencing depression by feeling they are not progressing in life the way they expected or feeling they have been overlooked in their career progression at work. Also, they may be experiencing overwhelming feelings of frustration or depression about getting behind on bills and rent or mortgage payments, with no solution in sight, which can also be accompanied by feelings of a low sense of self-worth.

Prevention: Always talk to each other about things that may be causing mental distress and threaten the integrity of the relationship, family, home, and work. Try to take a positive "can-do" attitude in coming up with plans that create a way out of the problem. Sometimes, getting a sheet of paper, writing the problem down, and then coming up with random out-of-the-box solutions can fire up the creativity from within to come up with ideas to resolve the dilemma. If it is money, look at agreeing on a budget together. If the problem appears greater than the couple are able to deal with themselves, then do not be afraid to seek outside help. Seeking outside pastoral or couple therapy intervention to help when people are in mental crisis can be like letting light come into a very dark place. Also, there are charities that specialise in helping people free of charge with their financial problems. Your local library or the website of your local authority will usually advertise what free money advice services are available in your area.

5. Thinking They Can Get Away With It

Reason: Arrogance is next to pride, and pride always precedes destruction. It's in the Bible (Proverbs 16:18). When a partner gets caught, they may say they did not mean to do it. But these types of cheaters generally get caught out sooner or later. It is only a matter of time. There are very few so-called perfect crimes, and this is definitely not one of them. A woman's intuition or a man's suspicions may be enough for them to launch a personal investigation or even hire a private detective to spy on their spouse.

Prevention: In the courtship stage of the relationship, have a no-secrets agreement. This involves being accountable to each other by each partner telling the other where they are at all times. Always make regular phone and video calls to each other, especially when one partner has travelled. Before the wedding, make sure you follow each other on all social media platforms. After the wedding, consider sharing passwords on smartphones and computers. However, if a spouse is financially irresponsible, we advise you do not give access to your bank account or other assets.

6. Love Grown Cold

Reason: This is when the initial fire in the relationship has gone out. There may be arguments. Sex may no longer be attractive with a partner. Emotional attachment feelings have either significantly reduced or disappeared for each other. In short, the emotional connection a couple once had, may now be low to almost non-existent. The couple do not share enough things in common. Feelings of dissatisfaction or discontent in being in the relationship may also be strongly felt.

Prevention: Create opportunities for regular once-a-week (or at least once a fortnight) dates. Join in and actively participate together in clubs and associations that appeal to the passion in both of you. Also, consider regularly going together to a place of worship. Consider giving up some of your free time by being active together in voluntary community projects like food banks or homeless persons' shelters. Look for opportunities to do things together, such as recreational activities, or regularly go to different places of interest. Use these suggestions as an opportunity to fall in love all over again, to re-ignite the passion you had in the beginning of the relationship for each other. Also, remember what it was in the first place that drew you both to each other. Think about the great memories you had together, and the things that you achieved together. For more ideas, tips and suggestions to keep the flames of passion alive in your marriage, please see Chapter 13: How to Have a Happy Marriage.

7. Taken for Granted (Similar to Emotional Unfulfilment above)

Reason: Lack of understanding of each other's needs. Lack of politeness. Lack of empathy towards each other. No longer feeling being listened to. Feeling undervalued and underappreciated in the relationship.

Prevention: Always say an abundance of pleases and thank yous to each other. If it is impossible for you to get bored of hearing, "thank you", then you should never get tired of saying, "please". Always ask how each other's day went. Make sure you always embrace each other in the morning and evening with a cuddle and a kiss. Make sure your spouse knows where you are at all times.

8. Feeling Disrespected

Reason: A partner feels disrespected or unappreciated in their relationship. They may also feel constantly humiliated or undervalued in front of others. They may feel undermined in the relationship or constantly being nagged or whined at by their partner. They may be the victim of an abusive relationship. If a male partner is not doing their fair share of house chores and child care, the female partner may take this as being disrespected in the relationship, and register this also as a lack of commitment to the relationship.

Prevention: Always make the habit of ensuring that all communication between you is positive and demonstrates kindness and respectfulness for each other (even when at times it might be difficult to do this). Openly share your feelings with each other. Always use positive and constructive language with each other. Always be kind, appreciative and polite to each other at all times. Men should make sure they do their fair share of the house chores and child care responsibilities, especially when their partner is also a co-breadwinner with them.

9. Beware of 'Mate Poachers'

Reason: Mate poachers are stealers of partners in committed relationships. They may be looking for non-committal casual sex from a married person because it lessens the likelihood that the other person will want to be emotionally attached to them. Alternatively, if they are looking to be the next Mr or Mrs of a person who is already married, they may try to break up that relationship by luring the person away from it.

Prevention: Always make sure your wedding ring is in clear view wherever you go. When in the company of someone of the opposite sex, regularly bring out photos of your partner (and children) from your wallet. Have a picture of you and your partner on your smartphone's home screen. Your partner should also do the same. Besides reminding you that you are in a committed relationship, a photo of both of you on your smartphone may help to safely return your phone to you in the event it goes missing. If you find yourself in a conversation with someone you feel you are getting attracted to, talk about your spouse, and take out photos of them. Always avoid being in places on your own. Always be accountable to your partner on your whereabouts.

10. Addictions & Neurotic Behaviour Traits

Reason: A significant contributory reason for sexual unfaithfulness in relationships is when a person has either an addiction problem or neurotic condition or has ADHD or displays controlling or other types of abusive behaviour. All of these have a higher risk of infidelity and unstable relationships associated with them.

Prevention: Seek outside specialist help from a therapist trained in the specific area of concern. If you have addiction problems, such as drugs, alcohol, gambling, or pornography, there may be no cure. However, a person can receive help to break free with the assistance of an outside organisation, such as a local group of Alcoholics or Gamblers or Drugs Anonymous. These provide group mentoring support and essential accountability. For problems with pornography, many online organizations provide accountability software, where an accountability partner monitors a person's online usage. In some cases, counselling and therapy should be considered as well. For neurotic conditions such as mental health problems, anxiety or depression, specialised therapy such as Cognitive Behavioural Therapy may be of help. However, before any kind of treatment programme can begin, a person needs to face up and fully accept that they have a problem and are willing and committed to deal with it. Also, people with addictions and neurotic behaviours have sometimes found comfort and help by being active in a local religious faith community. For further information, please see our bonus chapter on: Dating & Mental Health.

In closing this section, couples should be vigilant for things that can drive a spouse away and, worse still, into the arms of another. Love, respect, and trust are inevitable causalities in a relationship when infidelity occurs. If the relationship survives betrayal, then love, respect, and trust will have to be rebuilt from scratch. If a relationship has suffered deterioration that a couple feel has gone beyond repair they should, before involving lawyers, immediately seek the assistance of pastoral support or professional couple therapy, to see if it is still possible to save the marriage.

Handling Sexual Betrayal

The way that men and women react to extramarital affairs by their partners is slightly different.

- <u>Men</u> place a very high value on sexual loyalty and faithfulness. They take infidelity committed by a partner as a personal humiliation and shame on their ego, especially if the community they belong to publicly finds out about the affair. Also, many men find it difficult to control feelings of jealousy, and in some cases these can turn violent[248] or immediately cause them to walk out of the relationship altogether. If a man seems to take no action, he is still likely to feel highly humiliated, and may even emotionally withdraw into himself for a time.
- <u>Women</u> are likely to view sexual infidelity by their men through a more emotional lens. They are more likely to feel threatened by a rival if some form of emotional attachment is involved.[249] For example, a lady might confront her partner by asking, "Do you love her?" An example of this was in Sybil's story. Sybil shared with us that she found out one day her partner, John, had committed infidelity because of seeing on his smartphone, websites advertising prostitutes. She confronted him and he confessed that he only went with a prostitute once. She said because it was a prostitute, there was no emotional attachment and that he promised he would not do it again. She decided to forgive, let it go, and try to forget about it by remembering why she loved him. It has to be accepted not everyone can do this.

The Power of Forgiveness

Forgiveness is uniquely, a human species quality and a powerful tool to use in a relationship. It is also one of the most important contributors to a healthy relationship. When a partner withholds forgiveness and refuses to let go of an offence, it risks feelings of resentment and bitterness taking hold of them. Lack of forgiveness even has the power to break up a relationship. When offence happens, it can seriously diminish trust levels, especially when it comes to infidelity or constant lying behaviour. This is because choosing to forgive is different from forgetting about the offence. Some offences are easier to dismiss than others. For example, suppose a partner forgets to put the washing in the machine by a set time because a clothing item is needed to wear for an important event. In that case, it is likely to make their partner very upset and let down, but in a short time, the incident will be let go of and eventually forgotten. However, if the offence is linked to secretly wasting the couple's life savings on an addiction problem, that would be more difficult to forgive and overlook.

When one partner commits an offence against the other, it causes emotional pain and hurt. Some emotional wounds heal faster than others. If an emotional wound is particularly deep, like a betrayal of trust or infidelity, it can take a very long time to heal and recover from this fully. Some emotional wounds may never be fully healed. This is why forgiveness is not always easily possible without substantial healing having first taken place. It is one thing to forgive a person intellectually and quite another to forgive from the heart when the heart is still broken and recovering from betrayal. Being financially dependent upon a spouse may compel a person to forgive out of necessity. An example of this could be a man's wife and children being economically dependent on him, and breaking up their marriage could reduce the household to a state of poverty. But forgiving out of financial dependency is not true forgiveness.

Forgiveness should ideally be linked to genuine remorsefulness of the actions committed by the offender, but this may not always be forthcoming. At times, when a murder trial is over, and even though the murderer has shown no remorse, the family of the victim, because of their religious faith, may somehow find the courage and strength to forgive the murderer so that they can find peace and move on.

Some offenders in a relationship are not even sorry for their behaviour, and may even justify their bad behaviour by blaming their victim partner instead. This would suggest that the relationship is toxic. For more information on what to do if a partner is in a toxic relationship, please see Chapter 21.

"Can Infidelity in a Marriage Be Forgiven?"

Yes, absolutely. However, for a marriage to move past an act of infidelity, it will require a lot of work and commitment from both spouses. First of all, the offending spouse will need to demonstrate full remorsefulness and contrition. There also needs to be willingness to make themselves fully accountable to their spouse in every area of their life and do whatever it takes to reform their own attitudes and behaviour. In such circumstances, saying, "I am very sorry and I will never do it again," would sound clichéd and lack value. Only actions over time will be able to satisfactorily prove otherwise. Even then, for some people, it may not be enough. This is because there needs a willingness of the victim spouse to forgive and stay in the relationship, as well as a desire to work through the problems as a couple in facing the issues of what led to the infidelity in the first place.

It is often difficult for couples seeking repair in their marriage to do this alone. Therefore, we would always suggest they seek couples therapy through either pastoral support if they are part of a religious community or seek the help of a professionally trained couples therapist. Sometimes couples may need to go through several couples therapists until they meet the right one for them.

Further Reading

For further reading to learn more about relationship and marriage repair, we recommend, *Hold Me Tight* (Dr. Sue Johnson), and *The 5 Love Languages* (Gary Chapman).

Chapter 17: Let's Talk About MONEY

Money Matters

Money affects every aspect of a marriage and raising a family. Money may not always bring happiness, but financial hardship can bring huge unwelcome stress and anxiety in a marriage. A key principle to building a successful and happy marriage is the need for financial transparency and accountability in decision making. In this chapter, we will explore different ways that couples can choose to arrange and handle their finances.

Being Married Makes Financial Sense

First of all, let's start this chapter by looking at the financial wealth benefits of marriage, by answering the question, "Does being married make financial sense?" Ohio State University's Center for Human Resources certainly believes it does. Their research found that married people had 93% higher wealth per person than singles.[250] The reasons for this can include:
- Lower living costs.
- Higher credit score rating due to married status and

therefore access to lower cost credit.
- More likely to get promoted and enjoy greater salary increases at work.
- Sharing and transferring tax benefits (as relevant).
- Tax free lump sum gifting to each other.
- Upon the death of one spouse, the surviving spouse is normally entitled to receive the transfer of:
    - Property, investments, shares and other assets free of inheritance tax, and
    - Former spouse's pension entitlement.

Financial Transparency

Until a couple are legally married, each partner is legally regarded as being single, and are treated that way in all their financial affairs. If the relationship ends, then apart from property that may have been bought or rented in both names, both can effectively walk away. However, married couples cannot do that as easily because only a court of law can end a marriage. As part of the divorce proceedings, financial obligations and assets will be declared and decided upon. This is very important to understand because when two people get married, their debts, other financial obligations, and any assets brought into the marriage may have to either be merged or managed together. As an engaged couple begin looking towards both their wedding and their new lives together as husband and wife, forward planning in the area of finances will now take on a new significance.

The things you need to disclose with each other ideally before or soonest after you get engaged are:
- Any issue that can affect your credit score rating.
- Outstanding debts and other financial obligations.
- Former spousal and or child support (from previous relationships).

- Bankruptcy, court judgments, voluntary debt arrangements
- Personal bank and savings accounts.
- Business bank accounts and financial health of the business, including assets and liabilities.
- Pensions, savings, stocks and shares, and other investments (both in your country of residence and abroad).
- Property assets (national and international).
- Life insurance.
- Wills already in place.

We are not suggesting at this stage sharing financial passwords, etc. That would be up to the couple to decide after they get married.

The above list can seem a bit overwhelming, especially if finances are not in a good order right now. However, we suggest that you have this conversation in two parts. Firstly, casually, before a proposal is made. This is where you can keep things light but gently asking about debts, salaries, business interests and property. This can also include regular giving to a religious organisation or a charity or a political party or other membership organisation. Besides anything else, what a person financially gives to reveals deeply their values, beliefs and concerns. But remember not to get too heavy, because privacy should be respected if no proposal has been made yet. Once a proposal has been made and accepted then it is appropriate for a full open disclosure to take place.

Dealing with Debts

Soon after a marriage proposal has been accepted, a full disclosure of assets and liabilities need to take place. It is no longer about this is your debt and this is my debt, because once you are married, debts will jointly affect the financial outgoings and disposable income for both of you. If the debts of one partner are too much for the couple to bear for a new marriage to cope with, the marriage date may need to be postponed or put off altogether. Money issues can put a huge strain on marriages and families. Fortunately, there are a number of organisations that can assist with giving highly qualified advice for free. Your local library or the website of your local authority will usually advertise what free money advice services are available to you in your area. In the UK, there is also the charity, National Debtline. There telephone number is: 0808 808 4000, and website address: www.nationaldebtline.org.

Paying off a Partner's Debts

It is not uncommon for there to be a stronger financial partner in a relationship. However, we advise caution before considering paying off a partner's debts. But if a partner feels strongly they want to do this, they should wait till after the couple are married and not before. This is because if the relationship fails, it is very unlikely that any money would be paid back, even if there was already a formal written agreement in place.

Buying Versus Renting

Whether you want to get a mortgage to buy your first home together or rent a place, you need to ensure that your credit rating is satisfactory. Buying makes sense, because it means that you get your foot on to the property ladder. If a couple are in a fortunate position to buy a property, we would strongly encourage them not to buy before they are engaged. Having said that, buying a property and getting a mortgage together is not proof that the relationship is heading towards marriage. Only a marriage proposal, an engagement ring on a ladies ring finger and a marriage date that is just round the corner (that is, getting married within the next 3 to 6 months), can prove that. If a couple need to rent, it may make sense to move somewhere small on the outskirts of town, where renting will be cheaper, or consider moving in with a parent. This will help to save money for a deposit and also keep costs down. However, before using a letting agency, we suggest you do an internet search on them for reviews to learn from the experience of other client renters who have used them before. If you are renting for the first time, you may need a rent guarantor. In the UK, if you cannot provide a guarantor, there are private companies that will step in for a fee. You can find them through an internet search, but check first with the letting agent or landlord to ensure they will accept a company as a rent guarantor, because not all of them do.

Working & Having Children

Up to the 1970s, men were traditionally seen as the principle breadwinner, protector, and provider. However, as we discussed in Chapter 4, in the section called: Hunter Warriors & Care-Giver Co-Breadwinners, such ideal notions no longer square up with financial realities in the 21st century. In practice, although married men do earn more than women,[251] to keep the household finances healthy it often requires wives to also pitch in as a full-time co-breadwinner. When the couple also have children to care for, this can put a strain on the marriage if childcare and housework is not fairly managed between them. When one spouse does not do what the other perceives as their fair share of the childcare and housework, it will be interpreted as showing a lack of commitment to the relationship. If not addressed, it will most likely lead to the inevitable failure of the marriage.[252][253][254][255] These considerations are difficult topics for couples that are not yet married to think about, but nonetheless, need to be thoroughly discussed before marriage.

Bank Accounts

You will need to discuss whether to have joint or individual bank accounts. Having a joint savings account when you are engaged can be a great way of saving together for the wedding as well as also begin saving for a deposit for you to purchase a property together. However, if one partner is not very good with money, we would suggest that after the marriage, the couple may need to continue using separate bank accounts, and have a joint savings account that requires both signatures to withdraw money from.

Budgeting

How a family chooses to organise their finances is very important. Before marriage, the partners were only responsible for themselves, but once they are married, they are legally and financially responsible and accountable to each other. Therefore, it is sensible to decide how a couple should run their finances before they get married. This helps to avoid misunderstandings and conflicts later on. Gary Chapman, bestselling author of the *5 Love Languages* book series, suggests couples adopt a "10-10-80 Plan". The first 10% of your joint income for saving and investing, the second 10% for charitable giving, and the remaining 80% for mortgage or rent, bills, and other household and family costs.[256] Whether you agree or disagree with Chapman's budgeting suggestions, the important key point for couples here is that they need to create an agreeable budgeting plan for their finances. You can find lots of creative and highly effective ways to save money by searching for 'money saving hacks' on the internet. It is also a good idea to have at least one of you responsible for tracking the money that comes in and goes out to ensure all bills and debts are paid, and that money is also set aside for holidays, rainy days, pension, insurance, and savings.

If one or both partners like to gamble, smoke, or regularly go to the pub or club, these should be budgeted for and agreed upon in advance. Many women, because of pregnancy, may give up alcohol or smoking for the sake of the health of the baby they are carrying. Likewise, many men who were heavy drinkers, before marriage, may either quit or significantly reduce their alcohol consumption because their priorities have suddenly changed. However, there is no guarantee that either spouse in the relationship will reduce or give up gambling, smoking or drinking after marriage. What is certain, carrying on with these habits will reduce the amount of disposable income the family will be able to rely on.

The Cost of Addiction Problems

Addictions are often linked to alcohol or drug dependency, gambling, pornography, etc. Addictions cannot be cured, they can only be managed. Sometimes, the temptation to give in to addiction can be significantly reduced as a consequence of a person adopting a radical lifestyle change. This could be as a result of finding faith in God, or finding spiritual connection and meaning or purpose another way. Addictive behaviour that is not managed will put a heavy financial and emotional strain on a relationship. Also, agreements to curb these problems without proper outside accountability in place are unlikely to be honoured. If debts have been accumulated as a result of an addiction problem, then a wedding may need to be postponed to address both the debts and the addiction problem. If a partner has ever had to deal with an addiction problem in the past, then the couple should openly discuss this, including agreeing on how to deal with a relapse if it should occur in the future. For example, it may be wiser for each spouse to have a separate bank account, and one spouse to be responsible for paying bills, rent or mortgage etc., and the other spouse to pay part of their monthly salary into their spouse's bank account.

Summary

In marriage, a couple's finances should be regarded as a single economic unit. It is, therefore, not about "my money" or "your money" but "our money". Marriage, provides an excellent way of managing shared income, household expenditures and accumulating family wealth. In the first few years of marriage, it may not feel that way when finances are very tight with possibly a new mortgage or having to provide for a young family, but as the years go by, managing your family finances will get easier.

STEP 5: Marriage – Getting Ready to Say, "I Do"

Chapter 18: Wedding Preparation Ideas

Congratulations to you both, if by now you are already engaged. Obviously, everyone has their own ideas on how they would like their wedding to go. These days, there is also a huge amount of information on the internet to help couples to plan their special day. Given the high cost of weddings, sometimes £20,000 upwards, we wanted to share our own ideas with you on how to reduce the cost of yours. We are not here to tell anybody how to spend their money, but would encourage our readers to be realistic in their goals and aspirations regarding their wedding day, so that they focus more on the joys of their married life together afterwards. As a starter, a simple search on the internet, 'planning a low cost wedding' will throw up lots of pages with useful ideas. Whatever kind of wedding you are planning, we hope this chapter will give you a few ideas you had not previously thought about before.

Our Story

Ebun and Stephen met at the same church in London. At the time, Ebun was a student doing her Master's. In time, they fell in love and developed strong emotional attachment feelings for each other. However, once Ebun's studies were completed, she moved back to Nigeria. She did not want to get married in the UK, because she wanted her family to be present. Therefore, Stephen had to travel to Nigeria. Also, dealing with the cost of a wedding abroad was not easy. Besides the wedding costs, we also had to set apart money for Ebun's UK spouse visa application, which we prioritised as the most essential cost. If you know of people who have had to go through this experience and also what it takes to get married abroad, then you will know there are no cheap options. Once, a date had been agreed with Ebun's family, Stephen, then ran around crazily getting everything needed for the wedding before going to Nigeria. Ebun took charge of all the arrangements in Nigeria and got family and friends to rally around. With no little amount of stress involved, we have no hesitation in saying that God greatly helped us, including getting all the documentation together to make a successful visa application for Ebun, so that she could join Stephen in the UK. The visa was granted and Ebun was back in the UK within 3 months of being married.

What Do You Want For Your Wedding?

The wedding day is an important and special moment for the bride and groom. It is a public event where you will openly declare your legal marriage vows in front of your family, friends, and well-wishers. It also gives you your first happy memories together as a newly wedded couple. You may want an expensive dress, chauffeur-driven limousine, expensive rings, full banquet reception, as well as a top band and DJ to dance till late. Alternatively, you may be looking at having a destination wedding abroad to an exotic location. The planning of a wedding, no matter how large or small can be very stressful. However big or small you would like your wedding to be, still requires a budget along with a realistic timeline to have everything ready for the day.

Therefore, the first thing that needs to happen, is to agree a realistic budget along with a buffer zone (say, no more than 10%) and keep strictly within it to avoid costs escalating.

Some Money Saving Ideas

Make a list of what kind of things you feel you will need. Be prepared to happily save money on things that are not so critical. Here are a few of our own suggestions:

- *Invitations* – design it online for free using Canva.com and then send it to your guests through Whatsapp, Signal or other free messaging app.
- *Wedding ring bands* – you could save money by buying your rings through an antique auction listing site such as the-saleroom.com and easyliveauction.com, where up-and-coming auctions are listed all year round. Be sure to consider the current open market gold price and the auction house commission fees. Also find out if they will agree to post your successful bid to you or whether you have to make alternative arrangements through their recommended third-party packing company. If a ring on offer does not seem to be your size, you can buy a ring sizer on either Amazon or Ebay and resize the ring yourself if you are confident enough. You can also buy a ring size measure gauge to measure your finger on Amazon or Ebay. These ring-sizing tools are very affordable. Please remember that these gauges are thin, and you may need to go up a size (or two) if the ring width is wide. As an alternative to traditional gold or other precious metals, you can also buy online different colours of stainless steel wedding bands at low cost.
- *Wedding dresses* – save money by purchasing either a low cost new or second hand wedding dress through apps such as Ebay or Vinted, etc.
- *Bridal accessories* – check online for low cost ideas.

- *Venue* – for an affordable venue, consider using a small hotel, pub, or a community hall.
- *Caterer* – agree on a simple menu, and consider rallying the support of family and friends to help with serving food.
- *Photographer / videographer* – consider using a university student who is studying photography or media.

Your Marriage Vows

Most non-religious wedding celebrants will allow you to consider writing your own wedding vows, and many of them actually encourage it. You can get lots of useful ideas on how to write your wedding vows online. The wording in the vows used by civil registrars for legal ceremonies are dictated by law. However, you may be able to negotiate with them to add to the vows. Most churches and faith denominations have set vows for wedding ceremonies, but some may agree to make minor changes as long as it is in keeping with their marriage service traditions. Our advice is that if you either want your own vows or wish to request slight modifications, to ask anyway. It doesn't cost to ask.

Chapter 19: Marriage Preparation

Preparing For Marriage

We are now at the marriage preparation stage. By now, as a couple, you would have known each other for a minimum of 9-12 months and have decided that you wish to be with each other for the rest of your lives. In this chapter, rather than review what has already been discussed in other chapters (except for re-emphasis), we want to focus on a range of things that will undoubtedly come up in your marriage.

There is a perception that before marriage, couples focus more on their wedding day planning than on marriage preparation. This is probably true and may partly reflect why divorce statistics are so very high. If a 20 or 30 years older version of you could travel back in time and have a conversation with you right now, what would the more senior you advise the younger you? In some cultures, that would be the job of older married family members and elders of the community. They would try to prepare a couple for their new married life together by giving them the benefit of their wisdom and experience. Many couples in recent times now seek out this similar kind of preparation advice by participating in a marriage preparation course. Usually, these courses last around 6-8 weeks. We fully recommend them. What we have written below doesn't replace these types of courses but is offered to at least complement them and prepare you both for your married lives together. As the years go by, in time, you will find yourselves in that privileged position of being that older and wiser parent, aunt, or uncle in the family or community, where your own advice will be sought out to encourage others as they are about to embark on their marriage journey.

The Honeymoon Period

After getting married, couples commonly take a vacation together. This is known as going on a "honeymoon," and is an opportunity for the newly weds to spend time alone and enjoy themselves as they begin their new journey together as "Mr and Mrs". The word honeymoon comes from Old English. "Honey," which means sweet and "moon," which is equivalent to roughly one month. Many people may not be able to afford a honeymoon holiday getaway for as long as that.

However, the "honeymoon period" is different from the newly wedded couples' first vacation together. It is the sweet-as-honey time period from getting married to when the realities of married life start to sink in. During the honeymoon period, the couple may experience heightened feelings of adoration for each other. Slightly similar novel light-headed feelings may be felt by a person who has just started a new job or by someone enjoying an exciting but new experience of something they have never done before.

Having these new feelings is a God-given and uniquely human way for a couple to bond closer and be emotionally interdependent upon each other. Whereas before, you were legally treated as two separate individuals, you will soon be legally attached to each other and also legally and emotionally responsible and answerable to each other. This is why the feelings you experience for each other before you get married will be different from how you will feel about each other after you are married. You will also notice that other people will treat you differently in your new status as "Mr and Mrs". It is right that they should, because you deserve to be accorded the rightful recognition and respect that both society and the community you are part of give to all of its married citizens.

To sum up, the honeymoon period is a novel-driven adjustment phase to allow a couple time to:
- Get to know each other in their new shared legally married status.
- Get used to being called, "Mr and Mrs".
- Get used to sharing the same space as each other.
- Learn how to work together towards shared goals, but this time as a married team.
- Get used to being a legal family unit in their own right.

The euphoric feelings experienced in the honeymoon period usually wane off in time, but not always. They are there for newly marrieds to cope more easily in the transition into married life and living together, and also to help smooth over the inevitable adjustments this would require. In time, these feelings should be replaced by a deeper, more mature love for each other. Research suggests the honeymoon period can last on average 6 months to 2 years.[257] Some couples retain these feelings all their married lives.[258] However, in some cases, these feelings may last only a few short days. If you do not get them at all, it may indicate that there are areas in your relationship that need attention. Notwithstanding, these feelings are not compulsory, and a couple can still grow into a deep mutual love for each other based initially on mutual respect and friendship, as well as sharing similar cultural values and beliefs. This can also be quite common in many arranged marriages.

To enjoy the most out of your marriage you need to:
1. Treat each other with an abundance of love, affection, respect and kindness.
2. Be sensitive and attentive to each other's emotional needs and feelings.
3. Be willing to say sorry or forgive each other when offence has been committed.
4. Learn to compromise and make sacrifices for each other.
5. Support each other in difficult times.
6. Respect each other's opinions, values and beliefs.
7. Be constantly on the look out to safeguard and protect your marriage from attack.

A couple will also need to learn how to deal with and solve problems together and avoid getting fixated on unsolvable ones.[259] We discussed how to deal with difficult and seemingly unsolvable problems in Chapter 14: Let's Talk About COMMUNICATION. What sustains an enduring marriage beyond the 20-year point is a combination of mutual respect, friendship, and support for each other in difficult times. What makes a lasting marriage to be a happy one is when the couple see themselves as an intimate partnership in which both feel secure, valued, and emotionally interdependent upon each other.[260]

The Cohabitation Effect

This is a phrase that social science researchers coined to describe the negative effect that cohabitation can have on marriage in making those who live together before marriage, to be more prone to divorce than those that do not. Research studies dating back over 30 years consistently demonstrate this.[261] [262] [263] For example, Professor Catherine Cohan, from Pennsylvania State University, highlights in her review of research in this area that "compared with those that marry directly, married people who lived together before marriage report:

- Lower marital happiness and satisfaction,
- Poorer marital conflict resolution and social support behaviours,
- A greater likelihood of marital domestic aggression,
- Lower commitment to their spouse, and
- More depressive symptoms, and less life satisfaction."[264]

The reason for raising the above in this chapter and not an earlier one is that many people who get married these days would have already been living together. Given that this is a book about how to get married and stay happily married, it makes sense to discuss this and, hopefully, offer some practical advice to couples in this situation that will give their marriage the best possible chance of success.

Around 15-20 years ago, Stephen would regularly perform marriage blessings for couples, who did not go to church, but nonetheless still wanted to have a Christian marriage service at their wedding. The vast majority of these couples were cohabitating. Often times, because of time and distance constraints to where the couple lived, he would only have a short amount of time to do marriage preparation with them. This would involve asking couples these three questions.
1. How do you know you love your fiancé?
2. How will you keep the fire going in your relationship after you are married?
3. What things do you think will change in your relationship after you are married?

All of these questions have been dealt with elsewhere in this book. However, because this chapter is about marriage preparation, we felt it would be helpful to give more attention to question number 3, 'What things do you think will change in your relationship after you are married?' If you look at the question carefully, you may be able to tell that it looks like a bit of a 'loaded question', and you would be right to think that. In other words, the correct response should be, "Everything will change!" However, the majority of cohabitating couples that Stephen asked this question were ready to respond with, "nothing would change". If this is you, this would be a mistake. In which case, one would begin to rightly ask a rhetorical question, "Why did these couples want to get married if they feel nothing will change after they get married?" A possible appropriate answer could be that a couple may want to formally define their love for each other in their relationship, and marriage is a public and legal way to do this. Marriage publicly affirms that two people who have entered into this institutional union have decided to forgo their independent single-person status rights. Instead, they have chosen to be legally and exclusively bound to each other, as well as being accountable to and responsible for each other. They now want to take their relationship to the next commitment level: the public societal status of being known as "Mr and Mrs".

Let's look at some of the things that will change in your relationship once you are married:
1. You will be known as "husband" and "wife" and be formally addressed to by others as "Mr and Mrs".
2. Your family, friends, and society at large will treat you both different than before.
3. Your social relationships will change. Many of your friends before you were married will drift away, and new friends will come to replace them, and will now only ever know you as a married couple.
4. You will be legally, physically, and emotionally responsible for each other's health and well-being.
5. As husband and wife, you will have exclusive sexual access to each other.
6. Your moral faithfulness and accountability to each other will be underpinned by your promissory marriage vows to each other.
7. You will both be focused on your family's wealth creation:

to give your children the best possible start in life, and to financially plan and protect both of you in your latter years and retirement.
8. You will have legal rights with regard to joint parental responsibility and next of kin decisions.
9. In the event of a spouse's death, the surviving spouse will have a legal claim to inherit the former spouses assets; such as pensions, investments, and property. This also includes receiving the benefit of 100% exemption from inheritance taxes.
10. Your credit scores as married people will be significantly higher than single people.
11. People will regard that when one of you makes a decision it will have the same equal weight as if both of you made it.
12. Being married means that a relationship breakup is less likely compared with cohabitation. Also, only a judge can legally break up or annul a marriage covenant.
13. You will have the permanent security of being part of a legally binding two-person team.
14. Married men earn considerably more than women and single men. They are also more likely to be promoted in their workplace.
15. Marriage gives you greater assurance of life-long companionship.

Why then, does research consistently show that couples who cohabitate and then get married are more prone to divorce than those who do not? Social scientists are not fully certain why, but they think that in many cases, at least one of the spouses may already have a low expectation for marriage success.[265] In some cases, this can be attributed to the emotional effects a partner may have experienced when seeing their own parents' relationship fail. This might lead to lower commitment from them, or even to withholding from fully fighting for the survival of their own marriage. We also feel there are two other fundamental reasons that could contribute to marriage failure where a couple cohabitated before.

The first is that many marriages collapse simply because one or both spouses feel they no longer have anything in common with each other. In short, they grow apart. This is symptomatic that there was not enough compatibility in the relationship in the first place. It is also a big problem with many relationships today, and not just with those that lived together before marriage.[266] You may recall that when we spoke about compatibility in Chapter 2, we broke compatibility into three main areas: interests, values and beliefs. If there is strong compatibility, then a couple is considerably less likely to grow apart. If you feel there is not enough compatibility before you get married, then you need to discuss this with your partner as a matter of urgency to see if this can be rectified before going ahead with your wedding plans.

The second reason is that when a couple live together before getting married, in our opinion, they are considerably less likely to experience the strong novelty honeymoon period effect that a couple who did not live together before marriage experience. This honeymoon effect is a result of living together for the first time under the same roof. This would not be a new experience for a previously cohabitating couple. The additional risk comes in when at least one or, in some cases, both spouses adopt a 'business as usual' attitude to their relationship because they believed beforehand that nothing would change after marriage.

For those couples who are cohabitating before marriage, our suggested remedies to help them experience the novelty and euphoric feelings of the honeymoon period in their new marriage is that within one month (but not more than three months) on either side of your wedding date, you:
- Move house. The novelty experience of somewhere new to live will be excellent for relationship bonding and team

building.
- Actively participate in new social groups and activities together.
- Actively participate in a local charity or community project you both can be passionate about.

"Is Having Conflicts A Bad Sign?"

If you are having conflicts with your spouse and you both want to stay in the relationship, it means you both are very much in love and emotionally invested in each other. However, immediate action is required the moment a couple recognise they have started to take each other's feelings for granted. This could be a sign that a couple are beginning to grow apart. Another sign of a struggling relationship is when either one or both spouses are avoiding conflicts or refusing to sort out disagreements between themselves. In both of these situations a couple will need to work out where things began to slide away and also work hard to rebuild the love and connection they previously had in the relationship. Also, the importance of continuously saying, "I love you," "how are you?", "how is your day?" are all assuring and affirming to hear, especially when a couple are also going through tense or challenging times. If a couple feel that a relationship has deteriorated to the point that they are finding it too difficult to resolve matters between themselves, we strongly advise they seek help from either pastoral support from their religious community or a couples therapist. Do not despair if the first couple therapist you try doesn't fit well with you. It may be that a couple might need to try out two or three before they are able to find one that they both feel comfortable with. The key to finding the right couple therapist is that they should be positive in their attitude, fair and unbiased in their treatment to both of you, and always take a "can-do" approach regardless of how bad things seem to be.

Avoid Raising a Disagreement Late at Night

Are you or your spouse a morning or a night person? If it is late at night, and one spouse has something that they are upset about and want to raise with the other, it would be wiser to agree another time when both spouses are not feeling too tired and can concentrate on what is being said. Trying to deal with disagreements late at night when at least one spouse's body clock is not up to the task will most certainly lead to conflicts becoming worse than they should, and is also likely to lead to an unpleasant atmosphere in the home lasting for several days afterwards. Therefore, we strongly advise that it is not wise to have discussions to resolve disagreements (no matter how pressing or urgent) within one hour of either of you getting in from work or within one hour of either of you normally going to bed. Chapter 14: Let's Talk About COMMUNICATION, offers lots of effective strategies on how to handle conflicts in relationships.

Spontaneity & Romance

Some people get their enjoyment from planning out things in great detail. That is how they get their personal satisfaction. However, an occasional dose of spontaneity can cause a small but healthy dopamine surge, which thrives on the excitement of doing new things. Even if the couple have to book a time together in advance, it does not have to be the normal typical dinner or theatre date. Try new things together, like doing an escape room experience, secret cinema, and interactive period drama, visiting a stately home, castle, or other fun events near you. The takeaway is to avoid getting fixated on when or what fun things should happen. Spontaneity can be fun, even for people who don't normally like surprises. A little excitement every now and then is not only very healthy for the marriage but also very good for the fire of romance in the relationship to keep burning. Additionally, it is essential to keep the passion going by being affectionate with each other daily and at every opportunity, such as regularly kissing, cuddling, and holding hands. Having sexual intercourse with each other also adds strength to the emotional bond between you.

Sensual Sex

A woman's sexual pleasure is more linked to her emotional needs than physical needs. By contrast, the man's sex drive is more physically based. This is why a man can still experience an orgasm even if the couple have had an intensely heated argument an hour before. It takes a little more effort for a woman to gain enough sexual arousal for penile penetrative sex because emotional tenderness plays a higher role in women than men. Therefore, for women to enjoy sex and increase the potential for an orgasm, they first of all need to be in a relaxed emotional state. They are better able to experience this when there is intimacy and foreplay beforehand, such as gentle touching and caressing, and hearing softly spoken sensual words to heighten their sexual arousal.

Sexual Performance

Most people feel that sex is a fundamental part of a happy marriage. In many ways this is true, but not always. First of all, as we get older, our ability to perform may be hampered by hormonal changes, such as menopause for women and reduced levels of testosterone in men. These play a critical role in a person's sex drive (libido). However, both of these, in most instances, can be treated. Secondly, as people get older, unforeseen health problems can arise and affect their capacity to perform sexually. We explore some of these issues in greater detail in Chapter 20: Sexuality & Fertility.

Watch Out For Jealousy

Jealousy is a sign of mate guarding, especially by males. But it can also signify insecurity by one partner in a relationship. At its extreme, it could be a sign of a potentially toxic and unhealthy relationship. Couples place a tremendous amount of love and trust in each other for the well-being and sustainability of the relationship. Spouses should be wise and sensitive not to test the trust between them by having friends of the opposite sex too close. Otherwise, the risk is that one spouse may erroneously think that a genuine plutonic friend of the other is more than just a friend. Also, other things that can cause jealousy and insecurity are when relatives (such as in-laws) or friends are allowed to take precedence over a spouse for attention. Examples of this can be spending too much time with friends or constantly letting people that are not mutually welcomed into the family home. If one partner feels their status in the marriage is being challenged by unwanted feelings of jealousy then this urgently needs to be discussed and the other partner should seek to understand these feelings with empathy and respectfulness. If feelings of jealousy are leading to violent, controlling or other abusive behaviour, then please see Chapter 21: How to End Toxic Relationships, for information and advice about this.

Saying Sorry

We all get things wrong every now and then. We also make mistakes and sometimes costly ones. We can make errors of judgment or even bad decisions. The quicker an apology is made, the faster and easier it will be to move on. It is often said, "It takes a strong person to say sorry." Some people just don't seem able to say sorry, no matter what. They may view saying sorry as a sign of weakness. This could not be further from the truth. When saying sorry, it must be meant and accompanied with genuine feelings of remorse. Saying sorry also is highly affirming and places a high value on the person that has been offended. If the apology is sincerely meant, it is a sign that the offender values the relationship.

Laughter

Laughter in marriage brings couples together. Laughter makes people happy, and happy couples enjoy each other's company more. Being able to laugh at yourself or using irony with wordplay can help to release tension from awkward moments or a crisis. Everyone's sense of humour is different, but the type of humour to avoid is sarcasm because it is used to mock, humiliate and demean others. Laughing at your mistakes or mishaps can also be healthy. For example, over-baking a cake or forgetting your glasses or mistakenly wearing the wrong shoes or socks when you go out.

Affirmation

We already discussed the importance of words of affirmation and praise in Chapter 13: How to Have a Happy Marriage. Here, we would like to re-emphasise its importance in making each partner feel loved and adored by the other. This is because it sends a profound message to each spouse that they are highly valued by the other. For example, partners like to be constantly reminded that they are loved by receiving compliments and appreciation from each other. Wives particularly appreciate receiving regular tender embraces of affection and kisses from their husbands, as well as compliments on their appearance; especially noticing when they have a new hairstyle or wearing a new garment. Also, in marriage, the spouse who cooked appreciates being given a "thank you" and receiving positive feedback on their culinary skills, such as being told that the food was "delicious". Men like being appreciated for fixing and doing things, even if it is something they regularly do or are good at doing anyway. It does wonders for their egos and also helps to keep their testosterone levels high. Complements and affirmation always make people work harder, go further and do more for others.

Chapter 20: Sexuality & Fertility

Sexuality is a very broad term and covers things like sexual identity, attraction, experiences, and behaviours. There is a debate of how much of our sexuality is influenced biologically, such as through our genes and hormones before birth, and how much is influenced by our environment, such as the society and culture we were raised up in. While it is difficult to say with certainty which has greater influence, as we stated in Chapter 3, both have a role to play. In this chapter we will focus on sexuality and fertility because both are intrinsically linked to a couple's high expectations in their marriage, particularly with regard to sexual intimacy and satisfaction as well as also possibly hoping to have children.

SEXUALITY

Sexual Intimacy

Is sex all that most people seem to think about? Yes, but obviously not all the time.[267] However, sex in marriage is regarded as sacred because of its association with exclusivity and monogamy. Sexual intimacy cannot produce emotional intimacy, but emotional intimacy can intensify sexual intimacy. Emotional intimacy also leads to closeness and emotional bonding. Sex in marriage:

- Can improve well being and self-confidence.
- Strengthens the emotional bond, connection and commitment the couple have to each other.
- Is more pleasurable because a couple are usually more relaxed around each other, and as a result are under less pressure to perform well every time.

It is possible that cohabitation can also provide these benefits. However, until a couple are married, then such a relationship will lack the legal protections and privileges that marriage has to offer. This also includes on a social level enjoying the benefit of having a lifelong companion, close confidant, supporter and close ally.

Sexual Problems

Sexual problems can equally affect both men and women, but in different ways. When dealing with any type of sexual problem in a relationship it should first of all be openly discussed before sex actually takes place. There may also need to be precautions in place, such as using condoms, to either prevent the spread of a sexually transmitted infection or to avoid an unplanned for pregnancy. Let's now discuss some of the common sexual issues that may arise in a marriage, as well as looking at some suggestions on how to deal with them.

Vaginal Dryness

Usually, in pre-menopausal women, the vaginal passage is slightly moist and this generally indicates a healthy vagina. When a woman is sexually aroused the vaginal passage gets lubricated through the glands in the vaginal wall, this prepares the vagina for penile penetration. In addition to this, her cervix will release

mucus just before ovulation (the time when the egg from one of her ovaries is released). If a woman is not sexually aroused enough for her vaginal passage to naturally lubricate, having sexual intercourse is likely to be painful. This also risks tearing the skin in her vaginal passage. Sexual foreplay is therefore an important element of sexual arousal for women, and helps them to relax and be in the mood for sex. Sexual foreplay can include:
- Massaging.
- Caressing sexually sensitive areas, including: breasts, vaginal area, buttocks, inside the arms and thighs, neck, ears, waist and navel area, spine and lower back.
- Spending time hugging and caressing with gentle kissing.
- Sweet talking.

However, when a woman experiences problems with getting sexually aroused as well as coping with vaginal dryness, there could be a range of reasons to explain this.[268] We cover three of the more common reasons here:

1. Perimenopause

Perimenopause usually affects women from age 45 and over, but can also affect 1% of women under the age of 40.[269] The common symptoms of perimenopause are: irregular periods, hot flashes and night sweats, sleeping problems, mood changes decreasing fertility, urinary and vaginal infections, and loss of lubrication in the vaginal passage.[270] When a lady is in the perimenopausal stage of her life, her estrogen levels significantly reduces.[271] Estrogen increases blood flow in the vaginal area, which vitally contributes to naturally lubricating it.[272] 19.4% of women are affected by vaginal dryness during the perimenopausal stage and 34% after menopause.[273]

2. Polycystic Ovary Syndrome (PCOS)

PCOS is a high cause of infertility and sexual dysfunction in women, due to hormonal imbalance – usually because of high testosterone and low estrogen. While it is hard to get accurate figures, in the UK, it is estimated that 10% of women are affected by PCOS.[274] Not all women who have PCOS will have these problems. Some become pregnant naturally, and others with the aid of assisted reproduction, such as in vitro fertilisation (IVF). However, according to research, around half of women with PCOS are also likely to experience lack of sexual arousal and vaginal dryness.[275] There are many treatments available to alleviate the effects of PCOS, which a medical professional will be able to assist with.[276]

3. Endometriosis

Endometriosis affects 1.5 million women in the UK. (That is 1 in 20.) Endometriosis is a condition where tissue similar to the lining of the womb grows in other places, such as the ovaries and fallopian tubes. This condition can affect fertility and can cause pain during and after sex, as well as many other issues. Also, hormone treatments can cause vaginal dryness. Endometriosis can affect ladies of any age, from puberty to menopause. However, with the right endometriosis treatment, these along with other issues can be addressed, and the symptoms of endometriosis made more manageable.[277] [278] Our readers can find lots of suggestions for overcoming sexual problems with this condition, by making an internet search for: 'endometriosis sex tips'.

Vaginal Lubricants

Fortunately, there are a whole range of over the counter vaginal lubricants available in pharmacies and through online stores to assist with vaginal dryness. If having a baby is a couple's desire and a lady experiences vaginal dryness, she may need to consider a fertility friendly lubricant, which will replicate the cervical mucus and allow the sperm to travel much more easily to meet and fertilise the egg. Other vaginal lubricants may have spermicide gel in them. Which can block or slow down the sperm from reaching the egg. However, as a pregnancy prevention method, spermicidal lubricants only offer around 72% (widely reported) effectiveness, and does not give any protection against sexually transmitted infections.

Menopause

The average age for menopause is 51 (but can happen much earlier). Menopause is reached when a lady has not had a period in 12 months. Common perimenopausal and menopausal symptoms can be hot flushes, difficulty sleeping, reduced sex drive, mood swings, higher levels of anxiety, and it can also cause dryness in the vaginal passage.[279] If having penetrative sex hurts a woman, then she may need to get professional medical advice. She may be recommended to take some form of Hormone Replacement Therapy (HRT), because her ovaries have either reduced or stopped producing estrogen and progestogen hormones. However, HRT has known potential risks associated with developing cancer later on. A woman may also be recommended by a specialist used to dealing with menopause to take soy isoflavones supplement or including soya or tofu in her diet, because soy isoflavones can bind to the estrogen receptors and is reported to counter some of the side effects of menopause.[280] Our readers are strongly encouraged to make their own research enquiries and also seek medical specialist opinion before engaging in any kind of treatment.

Female Breast & Nipples Discomfort

Sometimes women can experience breast and nipples being either extra sensitive or feeling sore or achy just before a period. Other common reasons for this can be during pregnancy or breastfeeding. If a lady is not sure about a pain or discomfort she is experiencing or she feels a lump in her breast, she should immediately seek professional medical advice.

Erectile Dysfunction

Erectile Dysfunction is not uncommon in men from age 40 plus. The major reasons for this could be:
- *Psychological* – Going through depression, anxiety or other stress.
- *Medications* – There are many medications that can cause side effects of erectile dysfunction. The most commonly reported are antidepressants, which are prescribed to counter the effects of depression. However, these can also cause levels of the serotonin hormone to increase and thereby reduce the sex drive (libido). Some medications can also delay or inhibit ejaculation in men. Men will be able to understand any potential side effects from their medication by reading the leaflet that came with it, or they can look up the name of their medication and information about it online.
- *Diabetes & heart disease* – Either high or low blood pressure can cause erectile dysfunction due to insufficient blood being able to enter into the penis to achieve an erection.
- *Prostate cancer treatment* – If a patient has undergone treatment and they have experienced erectile dysfunction, then it is advised that they seek professional medical advice.

In many cases erectile dysfunction can be treated. Below are common widely reported treatment methods. This is given for information purposes only and should therefore not be taken as a recommendation. If a reader has any concerns, they should do their own research and seek appropriate professional medical

advice.
- Vitamin D supplement may help to boost lower levels of testosterone.
- Healthy eating.
- 30 minutes exercise every day.
- Lose weight, if there is also an obesity problem.
- Cut down on alcohol.
- Stop smoking.
- Request a change of medication. If it is suspected that a prescribed medication may be the cause of erectile dysfunction then the patient may need to seek professional medical advice about the possibility of switching to alternative treatments.

Erectile dysfunction is often an early warning sign of potentially serious underlying health issues to do with the organs of the body. If a man experiences erectile dysfunction, a medical practitioner may suggest any of the following treatments. All of which should allow for male orgasm by ejaculation:
- *Viagra & Cialis* - However, these type of medications are widely reported not to be safe if you have low blood pressure.
- *MUSE* - Medicated Urethral System for Erection. Pellet inserted into the urethra; the opening of the penis.
- *Penis vacuum pump* – This is a plastic tube that fits over the penis, and is used to draw blood into the penis to create an erection.
- *Surgical penile implants* - Either an implant pump or malleable prosthesis.
- *Alprostadil* – A prescription medicine that is administered either via penile injection or cream application.

If a man feels there are no viable solutions for his erectile dysfunction problems, a couple can still enjoy the pleasure of each other by caressing, massaging, kissing and cuddling each other. Also, it is still possible for a male, to achieve orgasm and ejaculate even without having a full erection.

Oral Sex - Good or Bad?

Our own view is that what a consenting couple choose to do between the sheets is entirely their own business. We left out oral sex from the foreplay list above because of the links associated with the higher risk of contracting the sexually transmitted infection, human papillomavirus (HPV) in the mouth and throat. HPV does not directly give a person cancer, but it causes changes in the cells it has infected, and these cells can then become cancerous.[281] Other sexually transmitted infections that can be passed on through oral sex are gonorrhoea, genital herpes and syphilis.[282] As we have previously said, before a couple engage in any sexual activity both of you should ensure you are free from any sexually transmitted infections.

Night & Day Body Clock

Circadian rhythms are governed by the body's master clock in our brain and affects our sleeping pattern.[283] Everybody is different, but essentially when it is dark, our brain is telling us it is time to sleep, and when it is light, to wake up and get up. However, some people are morning types (early bird risers) and like to go to bed early. Others are happy to stay up very late but don't like to get up too early. When a couple have different body clocks it can present challenges for when sexual activity can take place. For example, if one spouse wants to go to bed at 10 pm there is no point in expecting a strong sexual performance from them at 1 or 2 am in the morning. It may be better to plan to come together at 10 pm instead. Men like sex when it is time for them to go to bed, because once they ejaculate it causes their body to completely relax and generally makes them doze off within a very short time. By contrast to this, men's highest levels of testosterone is early in the morning because testosterone is produced throughout the night.[234] With all this in mind, having sex does not need to be spontaneous. Instead, it can be beneficial for a couple who have busy lives to plan when they may want to have sex.

Sexual Fetishism

Sexual fetishism is where a person receives sexual gratification from a particular object, like an item of clothing or part of the body or doing an activity, such as dressing up, role playing, etc. It is very difficult to get reliable data on how many people engage in these type of sexual activities. This is because the data is very inconsistent. In short, nobody really knows. However, what is widely reported in the public domain would indicate that such activities are more common than most people realise. If either of you have any sexual fetishes that are important to you, then it is better you talk about this before getting married. Always be respectful. Do not try to force your partner to accept a sexual fetish they find either unappealing or unpleasant. If the other partner is not comfortable about it, they may be willing to agree a compromise, but this may not always be the case. Seeking consent applies to everything sexually done in the marital bed, not just with sexual intercourse.

When Sexual Attraction Wanes

For some males in a long-term relationship, if care is not taken, they can feel a sense of overfamiliarity with their partner. This is because the dopamine and the testosterone hormones used to fire off the sex drive for passionate love making (including foreplay) may not be as exciting as before. The reason for this is that, although he may deeply love his wife, he may no longer see her as a novel sexual attraction. We know that many ladies reading this may be surprised by this. So let's try to explain this with an interesting story.

The Coolidge Effect – The story goes (no known attributable source) that Calvin Coolidge, 30th President of the United States (1923-29) and his wife Grace went to visit a government run farm. They briefly were separated and Mrs Coolidge, on passing the chicken coops noted that the rooster was vigorously mating with a hen. She asked one of the attendants how frequent the rooster did that. He replied, "Dozens of times." Mrs Coolidge then asked the attendant to mention that to the President when he passes by. The attendant did so, and the President then asked him, "With the same hen?" To which he replied, "Oh no, with a different hen each time." The President then said, "Please tell that to Mrs Coolidge".

The Coolidge effect is widely cited and documented in anthropology, biology and psychology research to illustrate how widespread the dopamine novel attraction of new females is to males in the animal kingdom. That is, males preferring to copulate with different (novel/new) females.[285] Professor of Psychology, David M. Buss, refers to the Coolidge effect in his book, *The Evolution of Desire*, as a compelling reason for why after the first month of marriage, the frequency in sexual intercourse decreases to roughly half after the first year and steadily declines thereafter.[286] The best way of countering the risk of sexual attraction waning is to have a change of environment. For example:
- Often go for short breaks away.
- Look for a good Airbnb cottage or cabin with a log fire. Don't forget to pack a couple of spare blankets for the floor!
- When the house is empty the couple can come together in other rooms of the house.
- Going on regular dates, and enjoy new thrilling experiences.

- Go for a husband and wife make-over. Lose weight, adopt a healthy lifestyle, change your hairstyle, go for a wardrobe overhaul, etc.

How to Raise Oxytocin Levels in Your Relationship

To raise the oxytocin levels and increase the bonding between both of you, and also to counter the risk of either sexual activity or sexual attraction waning, here is a list of strategies that husbands can use. A husband can:

- Show his affection to his wife through holding hands, kissing frequently and putting his arm around her waist.
- Give his wife a warm embracing hug at least once a day, and kiss her at least twice; before leaving for work and when he gets home.
- Constantly remind her that she is beautiful, (including noticing and positively commenting on new her hairstyle and how well she is dressed and looks,) and most importantly, constantly reminding her that he loves her very much.
- Immediately upon returning from work, first of all ask how his wife's day went and discuss any immediate concerns or issues she has before concentrating on his own needs.
- If returning home late or have to travel out of town, always remember to at least once or twice a day give his wife a call.
- Carry a photo of his wife on the home screen of his mobile smartphone. Wives can also do the same, because when both spouses do this, it triggers the release of oxytocin, the bonding hormone in each of them to perceive their spouse as increasingly attractive and rewarding compared with other women.[287] [288]

When a husband does all these things, then even with limited foreplay in the bedroom, his wife's oxytocin levels are likely to remain high and be more openly embracive towards him to make sex significantly easier and more intimate for her. After all, if the only time a husband tells his wife he love her is just immediately preceding to having sex with her, it is unlikely to relax her or convince her that he is being sincere.

Sex Drive

Everyone's sex drive, the desire for sex, is different. If a husband says that he wants sex once a day (or every other day) and his wife only wants it once a week, they need to discuss and negotiate between them and try to agree to come together maybe every second or third day. In the same way, if one demands oral sex or the lights should be on, but the other doesn't like it, be respectful to each other and look for alternatives for satisfaction and pleasure. Also, planning for sex; making scheduled appointments for when a couple come together for sex can add to the expectation of excitement. Compromising is an essential prerequisite for a happy, balanced, and sexually satisfying marriage.

It can be healthy for a wife at times to say, "No" to sex when she is not up for it, because it can reflect positive confidence about herself. However, it is not good to say, "No" all the time! According to female sex therapist, Susan Kay Preslar, it is better for a wife to say, "No, not now, ..." and then give a promise at the same time of when. For example, "Not now, but looking forward to Saturday morning." She says in her book, *Fanning The Female Flame*, that when a wife gives a promise like this, it is very important that she keeps it. Otherwise, it is likely that resentment in her husband will build up due to lack of availability of sex.[289]

Preslar, in referring to research, states that as many as 40% of all women, around the world, are affected by low libido, that is, their sexual desire is low.[290] [291] While there may be many reasons for low sexual desire in women, such as those mentioned above, it is something that she believes, many women can positively change. Although, Preslar's book, *Fanning The Female Flame*, is quite explicit, we recommend it because it offers clear strategies that may help many women who are bothered by their low sex drive and want to also hold onto the sexual intimacy in their relationship.

FERTILITY

The Cost of Delaying Marriage

There are many reasons why people have fertility issues. Probably the most common and predictable reasons are getting married later in life and planning to start a family late. There could, of course be many other reasons, and we will touch on some of these below.

In the mid-1970s, the average age of first married women was 22.8 years. Around 40 years later, by 2016, this had increased to 31.5 years.[292] That is a huge 9-year age rise, and also probably explains why more couples than ever before are seeking IVF as a possible solution for them to have a baby. According to the Human Fertilisation & Embryology Authority:

> "In 1991 there were around 6,700 IVF cycles recorded at licensed fertility clinics in the UK. By 2019, the number of cycles had increased tenfold to over 69,000. ... [Also,] in 2019, live birth rates for patients under 35 were 32% per embryo transferred, compared to below 5% for patients aged 43+ when using their own eggs."[293]

If a couple are planning to have a family, putting off marriage because one or both partners do not feel they are ready could be very expensive later on, with IVF costing around £5,000 plus per cycle.²⁹⁴ It is common for women to need on average, 3 cycles of treatment to achieve success, because after each cycle of treatment a review will take place and learnings for that will then form recommendations for the next treatment cycle (and so on). Some women go through as many as 12 cycles and still do not have any success with it. IVF, therefore, offers no guarantees, but what is clear is, the earlier the treatment begins, the greater the chance of a successful outcome.

How Soon To Plan For A Baby

If you are hoping to have children naturally, then we would ask you to consider planning to have children sooner rather than later. Fertility problems for those of reproductive age affects just over 14% of couples in the UK[295] and around 15% of couples worldwide.[296] Infertility affects both men and women almost equally.[297] Fertility problems increase with age in both men and women, but is more evident in women, because by the time they reach age 35, they are about half as fertile as they were in their early 20s. Overall, male fertility does not appear to be affected before the age of 50.[298] However, it should also be pointed out that sperm counts have declined sharply among men from all over the world. Data extracted from research studies have shown that during 1973–2018, sperm counts in men have declined at a rate of 1.4% per year with an overall decline of around 50-60%, and no evidence of a levelling off.[299]

The reason why women who are age 30s plus are more affected by fertility issues is because they have fewer eggs left, of lesser quality, and there is increased risk of having a child with a genetic abnormality.[300] Also, as a woman gets older this adds to the risk of miscarriage. In women:
- Under 30, 10% of pregnancies will end in miscarriage.
- Aged 35 to 39, up to 20% of pregnancies will end in

miscarriage.
- Over 45, more than 50% of pregnancies will end in miscarriage.[301]

When women are born, they already have all the potential eggs they will need. In fact, at birth a female human will have around 1-2 million follicles. By the time of puberty, that number will drop to around 300,000. Usually, every monthly cycle one follicle will have grown and attained sufficient maturity into an egg, and then it is released. However, during a female reproductive lifetime, the vast majority of follicles will deteriorate. By the time a woman is 37 years old, she may have only 25,000 follicles remaining. Although, rapid decline of available follicles normally happens around age 35.[302]

Male fertility also suffers as men grow older. As a man approaches 50, the number, quality and motility of his sperm significantly decreases. This means that the chances of conception becomes more difficult, and also, because of lower sperm quality, the risk of miscarriage goes up. Also, as stated above, since the 1970s, sperm count in men have decreased by more than half. Though we cannot make specific recommendations, there are some things that men can do to increase their own sperm fertility rates. The list below are widely reported suggestions that may help, but cannot replace seeking advice from a suitably qualified medical professional:
- Do not smoke.
- Cut down on alcohol consumption.
- Make sure your body mass weight is good.
- Ensure plenty of exercise.
- Eat a balanced diet.
- Make sure any medication that is taken does not affect sperm quality.
- Seek advice about taking vitamin supplements C, D and

Zinc (but keep within the daily recommended limits).

We would always recommend that men have a sperm analysis done before getting engaged. This can be done through either their local general medical doctor or at relatively low cost through a private fertility clinic who in many cases will also provide the result the same day. Take a look at the result and then see what needs improving.

"Is IVF The Answer?"

For some couples, the answer is yes, but unfortunately, not for everyone. In vitro fertilisation (IVF) is unfortunately not a silver bullet solution for all infertility problems. The process involves a lady taking intensive daily hormone drug therapy. This is given to her to ensure that the normal number of monthly released follicles (usually around 20) produce as many mature eggs as possible that can be harvested. These are then put in a dish with the sperm for natural fertilisation or a single sperm maybe taken and injected into the egg by an embryologist. Sometimes at this stage, eggs do not fertilise. Then the IVF cycle comes to an end and then the IVF cycle will have to begin again from scratch. Sometimes, one or more eggs may fertilise and become embryos but the cells do not split sufficiently, leading to low grade embryos. When this happens, they may not be strong enough to go to blastocyst stage (a natural process that happens after 5-6 days where the embryo leaves the egg sack). In which case, they cannot be used for embryo transfer (natural embedding into the womb) for pregnancy to be made. If the embryo is successfully placed inside the womb, it may or may not embed itself in the lining for pregnancy to take place. If the grade of the embryo is high and the woman is aged 32, there is a 30% chance of a live birth. The older the woman the lower the chance of a live birth. As you can see, it can be a physically and emotionally demanding experience, as well as financially intensive, and with no guarantees at the end of it.

Conclusion

People are getting married later and also having children much later as well. The perfect age to have children is when a married woman is in her early 20s.[303] However, the younger the couple, the less money and resources they may have to rely on. So, a balance needs to be found between the timing for acting on a couple's desire for children and the resources necessary for a growing family. Not many people are privileged to start off in their married life with well-paid jobs. Science may be able to assist to a degree to help couples with having children, but it does have its limits. The hope is that reading all of the above puts into full perspective the reason for justifying why relationships need to be intentional if the focus is for the couple to be married and start a family. Delaying or allowing time to be wasted is likely to be costly later on, with fertility treatment having no guarantee of success and incurring the risk of losing out on having a natural birth family. The important takeaway for couples from the above information is that the earlier you try for a baby, the better your chances for success. Likewise, the earlier you try, the earlier you are likely to discover if there is a problem. If there is a problem, and it is spotted early enough, you have a greater chance of successfully dealing with it.

And Finally ...

Chapter 21: Dealing With Toxic Relationships

Domestic abuse and violence are not always treated in dating and relationship books. We took the view to include the topic just in case someone reading our book realises that they are entangled in an abusive relationship and may need a few pointers to help them to know what to do. Also, by providing this information we felt that our readers would feel better prepared to help their family members or friends who may be caught up in an abusive relationship.

What Is Domestic Abuse?

Domestic abuse-related offences are defined under British law (and paraphrased) as any incidence of threatening or violent behaviour or other abuse which consists of any of the following: physical; sexual; controlling; coercive; economic; psychological; or emotional; and is between people who are aged 16 years and over, and who are personally connected to each other.[304]

Up to March 2021, the police recorded 845,734 domestic abuse related crimes in England and Wales. This was a 6% increase from the previous year, and every year domestic abuse crime has consistently increased. However, no-one actually knows the true numbers, because for the most part, it is a hidden and under reported crime. Although both women and men can be subject to domestic violence, it is in the vast majority of cases women that are the victims. This is exemplified by data from the UK's Office of National Statistics, which indicate that the number of domestic homicides that occurred three years up to March 2020 and who were killed by either a partner or ex-partner was 247. Of these, 214 (that is, 87%) were female victims, but by contrast 33 (that is, 13%) were male victims.[305]

What Is A Toxic Relationship?

Constantly having arguments in a relationship doesn't make it toxic. However, if one partner in a relationship does not always feel safe from physical, sexual, mental, financial or emotional abuse from the other, no matter how slight, then they are in a toxic and abusive relationship.

Let's take a look at some examples of toxic and abusive relationships:

- One partner may use controlling and coercive behaviour through physical violence and intimidation against the other.
- An abusive partner may even try to blame their victim for their bad behaviour.
- An abusive partner may steal money from his or her victim, by using their ATM card to withdraw cash without permission, or use the victim's credit card without their free-will consent.
- Alternatively, a victim may feel that it must be their fault for their partner's bad behaviour to them.
- In some cases, a victim may want to leave their toxic relationship, but feel they cannot, because they either fear

there may be hostile or violent repercussions for doing so, or because they fear they may be unable to cope on their own.
- An abusive partner, fearing that they have gone too far with their bad behaviour, may say sorry and ask for forgiveness so that the relationship can continue. However, after things have quietened down for a bit, they will return again to their controlling and violent behaviour.
- Other kinds of abuse can be:
    - Outbursts of uncontrolled anger and rage.
    - Controlling, manipulative, intimidating behaviour.
    - Jealousy (see below).
    - Gaslighting (see below).
    - Constant "jokes" that aren't really jokes. They are said with the intention to demean and humiliate.

If you recognise yourself in any of the above examples, then you are definitely 100% in a toxic, unhealthy and abusive relationship. You are a human being and deserve to be treated so much better. You should immediately end your relationship, and do not look back. This is because, if a partner uses any kind of abuse, no matter how small, it is considerably likely they will do it again, and again. Sometimes, the only way to be free of an abuser is with the help of the police or courts. If either you or your family are in danger, you should always call the police.

If you feel your relationship is in trouble and you or other members of your family are not in physical, sexual, psychological, emotional, or financial danger, and you want to try to save your relationship then you may need to seek outside intervention through relationship counselling or pastoral support. However, if either you or your family are at risk of physical, sexual, psychological, emotional, or financial harm or danger then you need to leave the family home as soon as possible or arrange for legal action through police and the courts to get a restraining order to be placed upon your partner.

Jealousy

Feeling a bit jealous in a relationship can be a normal and healthy thing. After all, the whole point of exclusivity in a relationship is an unwillingness to share the intimate sexual and emotional connections a couple has for each other with an outsider. However, when normal protectiveness feelings cross the line into controlling or violent behaviour that is totally unacceptable, regardless of the circumstances. When a partner shows a consistent pattern of jealousy, this is also likely to include other bad behaviours. For example:
- Controlling behaviour, such as one partner refusing to allow the other to talk to anyone of the same or opposite sex, or a partner demanding that the other must not leave the house or go anywhere without being escorted. This can also include threats, coercion and intimidation.
- Violent behaviour, including physical and verbal abuse, as well as damage to property.

If jealousy becomes a persistent problem in a relationship, but the jealous partner does not use the type of controlling or violent behaviour as described above, then the couple should immediately seek outside help for relationship advice and guidance. However, if the victim, including their family, do not feel safe, they should look for ways to immediately end the relationship altogether.

Gaslighting

Gaslighting is trying to convince someone to believe something that is not true. We are not talking about the odd occasion of forgetfulness. Rather gaslighting is a sustained psychological manipulation that is meant to make a victim doubt their sanity, judgment, and memories. The phrase, "gaslighting" originated from a play called Gaslight, written in 1938 by Patrick Hamilton. The play was later made into two movies in 1940 and 1944 with the same title. The latter was more successful and starred Ingrid Bergman and Charles Boyer. The films are about a husband who turns the gas lights in the attic on, to reduce the gas pressure and make the lights downstairs dim. He does this to try to make his trusting and adoring wife no longer trust in her own perception of reality. Gaslighting always comprises of control and manipulation through deception and lies. Gaslighting is a serious breach of emotional trust. If you believe this is happening to you, you should immediately break off the relationship. We then suggest you seek out family and friends who know you very well to ensure you are emotionally supported, while you regain your self-esteem and confidence back.

Planning an Exit from a Toxic Relationship

If either you or other members of you family are in immediate danger, then you need to end the relationship immediately. Do not go back to collect clothing, documents or other personal items. These are replaceable; you are not. Call the police. They can then arrange for you to collect your things. If you are a lady, then you may be able to get assistance from a domestic violence support service in your area. Many local authorities provide such a service in conjunction with local charities who have expertise in this area, including access to a domestic violence refuge centre.

If it is possible (and safe to do so), document the abuse through photos, videos, audio recordings, emails, screenshots of text messages, etc. Also, consider keeping a diary. Store the evidence in a safe place or consider sending the evidence to a trusted friend for safe storage. This evidence may be needed later on, if it becomes necessary for legal action to take place.

If you are planning to leave but are afraid to let on to your partner that you are going to leave them, here is a list of things to help you plan ahead of time, but this depends on whether you can. Your safety has to be absolutely paramount. Leaving a partner is never financially easy, but it is not wise to stay and risk being permanently injured or killed.

- Limit the number of people to the absolute minimum and who you trust with your plans to leave.
- Find out what help, advice and services are available in your area from your local authority and other charities for victims of domestic violence and other abuse. You may also need legal advice if you are either already married or have children. This can be obtained from a local law centre or a family law firm in your area. Also, in the UK, the National Domestic Abuse Helpline can be contacted in confidence, 24-hours a day, and are free to call on: 0808 2000 247. Their website for further information is: www.nationaldahelpline.org.uk.
- Accommodation planning:
  - Check with your local authority to find out if they provide a domestic violence refuge shelter. This type of service is generally provided for women and their children only, but some may also provide support for men as well.
  - Check with family or friends, if they can put you up temporarily.
  - If necessary and as soon as it is safe to do so, find out from your local authority how to declare yourself homeless with them. They are obliged to legally help you if you have children or you are an adult who is regarded as being vulnerable (for example, a person with a disability).
  - Alternatively, you may be able to find somewhere to rent privately.

- Some people use hotels in the first instance, but this can be expensive.
- Budget the costs of your plan. Remember, though, financial cost is always second to your health, safety and life.
- If you think you have time to plan, then consider opening up a bank account (either online or from a high street bank). If you choose to open an online bank account and you are worried that your partner can get access to your smartphone, then delete the app and any emails or texts relating to it from your smartphone once you have opened the account. You can then reinstall it whenever you need to. Then, every now and then transfer some money into it. Let the money in the account build up until you feel you have reached enough money to leave. But don't wait to leave if it is not safe to remain.
- Make a list of things you need to take with you for when you plan to leave. This could be clothing and personal documents. For example: birth certificate, passport, driving licence, education certificates, financial statements, health and other family records, etc.
- Arrange for your personal mail to be redirected to an alternative address that is not going to be the one you will be staying at. Otherwise, if it is not safe for you to stay, don't worry, because this can still be done after you have left. Royal Mail, in the UK, state that it takes up to 3 weeks to put a mail redirection order in place. This service can easily be arranged online with the Royal Mail through their website.
- Plan your leaving date when your partner will not be at the address for a few hours. For example, because they have gone to work.
- Plan where you are going to store your property. Either with a family member, friend or storage unit. If you are going to use a storage unit, check availability with them,

and what the shortest time in advance you need to book a unit with them.
- If necessary, create a plausible reason to leave the house.
- On the day of leaving:
  - If you feel either you or your family's life is in danger, then call the police in advance to see if it is possible to arrange for a police officer to be in attendance.
  - Have a family member or a friend with you.
  - Have your list ready and pack everything you will need to take with you in the space of less than half the time that your partner said they will be returning, to give yourself plenty of time to leave.
- Book a van in advance, or the moment you are ready, order an XL (extra-large – 7 seater) private hire car. If this is not possible for you to do, try to get a member of your family or one of your friends to help to arrange and book this for you.

Moving On

After you have left an abusive relationship and are now safe, part of the moving on with your life process may involve the need to consider therapy or counselling. This is important, because therapy can help you to:
- Understand that the abuse you received was not your fault.
- Come to terms with the need for emotional closure regarding the relationship.
- Receive the necessary psychological support and emotional healing to deal with and overcome the trauma, hurts and pain that you experienced in the relationship.
- Deal with any issues of low self-esteem or lack of self-worth. This will help you to avoid the chance of getting into a similar type of bad relationship in future.

Without going through this kind of reflective therapy, it will be difficult to fully trust again in a new relationship. We advise you to only get involved in a new relationship once sufficient healing has taken place. You will begin to sense when the time is right to start a new relationship, when you feel happier and secure in yourself and your confidence and self-esteem appear to have increased. This means that you are mentally in a safe place to start dating again. If you are married, you should only start a new relationship once you are legally free to marry again. For more information and advice on this, please see our bonus chapter: Divorced, Widowed, or Was in a Long Term Relationship.

Online Bonus Chapters (Access Password Here)

List of online Bonus Chapters:

1. Dating & Single Parenthood
2. Divorced, Widowed, or Was in a Long Term Relationship
3. Dating For Over 50s
4. Dating & Disabilities
5. Dating & Mental Health
6. Interracial & Interethnic Relationships
7. Age Differences
8. Faith & Beliefs

To access the Bonus Chapters, please visit our website at the following link, or use the QR code.

https://lovedimensions.co.uk/bonus-dating-chapters/

The password is: **marriage**

Thank You

Dear Reader

Thank you for allowing us to come into your life to share the valuable information in this book.

If you enjoyed this book, please kindly consider recommending it to others. So that they can be helped with their own love journey. Also, please help by spreading the message in the book about marriage by gifting a copy of it to others. We also, fundamentally believe in the concept 'each one, teach one'. By sharing with others the knowledge and ideas in this book, it will help to re-enforce that knowledge for yourself.

At Love Dimensions, we offer dating and relationship for marriage coaching. We also provide dating and relationship conferences and seminars. For more information about any of our services, or to be added to our Newsletter mailing list, please visit our website: www.lovedimensions.co.uk. We would love to hear from you.

Best wishes.

Stephen and Ebun Hammond

Acknowledgments

This book took almost four years to research and write. The goal we set ourselves was to put into one compendium all the resources that a person would need to find the right lifelong marriage partner for them. Also that married couples could have a ready resource to know exactly what they need to do to enjoy lifelong and emotionally satisfying companionship with each other. We hope this book has accomplished these aims. To this end, we thank God Almighty for giving us the inspiration to carry out this assignment, as well as the grace to complete it. We also thank you, our reader for joining us on this journey, and hope that you will be inspired by this book to pass on to others what you have learnt from it.

We wish to say thank you to all the professors around the world who responded to our requests, answered our questions, and as relevant, sent us their research work. In particular, we would like to thank:

Professor Sir Simon Baron-Cohen, University of Cambridge
Professor Eric Bressler, Westfield State University
Professor Susan Case, Case Western Reserve University
Professor Catherine L Cohan, Pennsylvania State University
Professor Andrey Korotayev, HSE University

Professor Sandra Langeslag, University of Missouri - St. Louis
Professor Ragini Verma, University of Pennsylvania

To the many hundreds of people, we have either helped directly or conversed with about our work, and being able to test out many of the ideas presented in this book, we pay special tribute to you and thank you.

Finally, we lovingly acknowledge and deeply appreciate Stephen's father, Charles Hammond, for putting up with nearly four years of talking about almost nothing else except dating and relationships. His patience was amazing, as was his comments, ideas and suggestions.

References

If a reference is shown in *italics*, it means that the full reference has already been cited above it.

References

1. Fisher, Helen., (2023, Accessed on: 17 February). HelenFisher.com, Romantic Love: Can It Last? https://helenfisher.com/romantic-love-can-it-last/
2. Sissons, Claire., (2022, 23 August). MedicalNewsToday, Typical testosterone levels in males and females, https://www.medicalnewstoday.com/articles/323085
3. Mongeau, Paul A., Hale, Jerold L., Johnson, Kristen L., Hillis, Jacqueline D., (1993). Who's Wooing Whom? An Investigation of Female Initiated Dating, Chapter 4, Interpersonal Communication (Ed. Pamela J Kalbfleisch), Psychology Press (p51-68).
4. Mongeau, Paul A., and Carey, Colleen M., (1996). Who's wooing whom II? An experimental investigation of date-initiation and expectancy violation, Western Journal of Communication, 60:3, 195-213, DOI: 10.1080/10570319609374543.
5. Stripe, Nick., (2019, 1 April). Office For National Statistics, Married by 30? You're now in the minority, https://blog.ons.gov.uk/2019/04/01/married-by-30-youre-now-in-the-minority/
6. United States Census Bureau., (2020, December). Historical Marital Status Tables (Median Age of First Married, https://www.census.gov/data/tables/time-series/demo/families/marital.html
7. Buss, David M., (1994, 2016). Basic Books (Perseus Books), The Evolution of Desire (2016, p48, 93).
8. Johnson, Matthew D., (2016). Wiley Blackwell, Great Myths of Intimate Relationships (p48).
9. *Buss, The Evolution of Desire* (2016, p54).
10. Amato, Paul R., Booth, Alan., Johnson, David R., Rogers, Stacy J., (2007). Harvard University Press, Alone Together: How Marriage in America Is Changing (p24).
11. Gordan, Amie, M., (2020, 25 September). Psychology Today, Does Similarity Matter in Relationships? https://www.psychologytoday.com/gb/blog/between-you-and-me/202009/does-similarity-matter-in-relationships
12. Hewitt, Rachel., (2020, 7 March). Higher Education Policy Institute, Mind the gap: gender differences in higher education, https://www.hepi.ac.uk/2020/03/07/mind-the-gap-gender-differences-in-higher-education/
13. Erudera College News., (2021, 20 September). Women Outnumber Men In US Colleges – Nearly 60% Of Students In 2020/21 Were Women, https://collegenews.org/women-

References

outnumber-men-in-us-colleges-nearly-60-of-students-in-2020-21-were-women/
14. Buss, *The Evolution of Desire* (2016, p34-36).
15. Amato, et al., *Alone Together* (p194).
16. Skoulding, Lucy., (2022, 26 April). Save The Student, This is how much your degree will earn you in 10 years, https://www.savethestudent.org/graduates/this-is-how-much-your-degree-will-earn-you-in-10-years.html
17. GOV.UK., (2019, 25 April). Department for Education, Graduates continue to benefit with higher earnings, https://www.gov.uk/government/news/graduates-continue-to-benefit-with-higher-earnings
18. Szalay, Jessie & Dobrijevic, Daisy., (2022, 25 February). Live Science, Chromosomes: Facts about our genetic storerooms, https://www.livescience.com/27248-chromosomes.html
19. Arnold, AP., (2017, 2 January). A general theory of sexual differentiation. J Neurosci Res.; 95(1-2):291-300. doi: 10.1002/jnr.23884. PMID: 27870435; PMCID: PMC5369239, https://onlinelibrary.wiley.com/doi/10.1002/jnr.23884
20. Wizemann TM, Pardue ML., (2001). Institute of Medicine (US) Committee on Understanding the Biology of Sex and Gender Differences; editors. Exploring the Biological Contributions to Human Health: Does Sex Matter? Washington (DC): National Academies Press (US); 2001. 3, Sex Begins in the Womb. https://www.ncbi.nlm.nih.gov/books/NBK222286/
21. NHS., (2019, 15 August). Differences in sex development, https://www.nhs.uk/conditions/differences-in-sex-development/
22. Faculty of Sport and Exercise Medicine UK., (2020). Disorders of Sex Development. [Summary information is based upon the Consensus statement on management of intersex disorders.] International Consensus Conference on Intersex. Pediatrics. 2006 Aug;118(2):e488-500 and Global Disorders of Sex Development Update since 2006: Perceptions, Approach and Care. Horm Res Paediatr 2016;85:158-180, https://www.fsem.ac.uk/wp-content/uploads/2020/02/Disorders-of-Sex-Development-brief-statement.pdf
23. Rosalind Franklin University of Medicine and Science., (2021, 29 March). "Massive study reveals few differences between men's and women's brains: Neuroscientists conduct meta-synthesis of three decades of research." ScienceDaily, , www.sciencedaily.com/releases/2021/03/210325115316.htm

References

24. Goldman, Bruce., (2017, Spring). Standford Medicine, Two minds - The cognitive differences between men and women, https://stanmed.stanford.edu/2017spring/how-mens-and-womens-brains-are-different.html
25. Pawlowski, B., Atwal, R., & Dunbar, R. I. M., (2008). Sex Differences in Everyday Risk-Taking Behavior in Humans. Evolutionary Psychology, 6(1). https://doi.org/10.1177/147470490800600104
26. Brown, Lauren., (2019, 23 April). People Management, Men more likely to ask for a pay rise – and get more when they do, https://www.peoplemanagement.co.uk/news/articles/men-more-likely-ask-pay-rise-and-get-more-when-they-do#gref
27. Lewis, Warren., (2021, 7 December). Financial Reporter, Gender pay gap sees men receive 57% more than women in pay rises, https://www.financialreporter.co.uk/gender-pay-gap-sees-men-receive-57-more-than-women-in-pay-rises.html
28. Ingalhalikar, Madhura., Smith, Alex., Parker, Drew., Satterthwaite, Theodore D., Elliott, Mark A., Ruparel, Kosha., Hakonarson, Hakon., Gur, Raquel E., Gur, Ruben C., and Ragini Verma., (2013, 2 December). Sex differences in the structural connectome of the human brain Proceedings of the National Academy of Sciences, 111 (2), https://doi.org/10.1073/pnas.1316909110
29. *Ingalhalikar, et al., Sex differences in the structural connectome of the human brain.*
30. Gerrits, Robin., Verhelst, Helena., and Vingerhoets, Guy., (2020, 8 June). Mirrored brain organization: Statistical anomaly or reversal of hemispheric functional segregation bias? Proceedings of the National Academy of Sciences, 117 (25) 14057-14065, https://doi.org/10.1073/pnas.2002981117
31. Corballis MC., (2014, 21 January). Left brain, right brain: facts and fantasies. PLoS Biol. 2014 Jan;12(1):e1001767. doi: 10.1371/journal.pbio.1001767. PMID: 24465175; PMCID: PMC3897366, https://www.ncbi.nlm.nih.gov/pmc/articles/PMC3897366/
32. Beaty, Roger E., Kenett, Yoed N., Christensen, Alexander P., Rosenberg, Monica., Benedek, Mathias., Chen, Qunlin., Fink, Andreas., Qiu, Jiang., Kwapil, Thomas R., Kane, Michael J., and Silvia, Paul J., (2018). Robust prediction of individual creative ability from brain functional connectivity, Proceedings of the National Academy of Sciences, 115 (5) 1087-1092,

References

https://doi.org/10.1073/pnas.1713532115
33. Amalric, Marie., and Dehaene, Stanislas., (2016, 11 April). Origins of the brain networks for advanced mathematics in expert mathematicians, Proceedings of the National Academy of Sciences, 113 (18) 4909-4917, https://doi.org/10.1073/pnas.1603205113
34. *Sissons, Typical testosterone levels in males and females.*
35. Epstein, Randi Hutter., (2018, 27 March). The New York Times, The Highs and Lows of Testosterone, https://www.nytimes.com/2018/03/27/well/live/testosterone-supplements-low-t-treatment-libido.html
36. Wein, Harrison., National Institutes of Health, Understanding How Testosterone Affects Men (Article dated: 23 September 2013), https://www.nih.gov/news-events/nih-research-matters/understanding-how-testosterone-affects-men
37. Herbert, J., (2017). Oxford University, Testosterone: The Molecule Behind Power, Sex and the Will to Win.
38. Losecaat, Vermeer AB., Krol, I., Gausterer, C., Wagner, B., Eisenegger, C., Lamm, C., (2020). Exogenous testosterone increases status-seeking motivation in men with unstable low social status. Psychoneuroendocrinology. 2020 Mar;113:104552. doi: 10.1016/j.psyneuen.2019.104552. Epub 2019 Dec 19. Erratum in: Psychoneuroendocrinology. 2020 Feb 10;:104586. PMID: 31884320.
39. van Anders, Sari M., Steiger, Jeffrey, and Goldey, Katherine L., (2015, 5 November). Effects of gendered behavior on testosterone in women and men. Proc Natl Acad Sci U S A.;112(45):13805-10. doi: 10.1073/pnas.1509591112. Epub 2015 Oct 26. PMID: 26504229; PMCID: PMC4653185.
40. Galea LAM, Frick KM, Hampson E, Sohrabji F, Choleris E., (2017). Why estrogens matter for behavior and brain health. Neurosci Biobehav Rev. 2017 May;76(Pt B):363-379. doi: 10.1016/j.neubiorev.2016.03.024. Epub 2016 Mar 31. PMID: 27039345; PMCID: PMC5045786. https://www.ncbi.nlm.nih.gov/pmc/articles/PMC5045786/
41. Thomas, Liji., (2018, 15 November). News Medical Life Sciences, Estradiol Measurement, https://www.news-medical.net/health/Estradiol-Measurement.aspx
42. Stanczyk, Frank Z., Clarke, Nigel J., (2014). Measurement of Estradiol—Challenges Ahead, The Journal of Clinical Endocrinology & Metabolism, Volume 99, Issue 1, 1 January

References

2014, Pages 56–58, https://doi.org/10.1210/jc.2013-2905
43. Chadid, Susan., Barber, John R., Rohrmann, Sabine., Nelson, William G, Yager, James D., Kanarek, Norma F., Bradwin, Gary, Dobs., Adrian S., McGlynn, Katherine A., Platz, Elizabeth A., (2019). Age-Specific Serum Total and Free Estradiol Concentrations in Healthy Men in US Nationally Representative Samples, Journal of the Endocrine Society, Volume 3, Issue 10, October 2019, Pages 1825–1836, https://doi.org/10.1210/js.2019-00178
44. Dhindsa S, Furlanetto R, Vora M, Ghanim H, Chaudhuri A, Dandona P., (2011). Low estradiol concentrations in men with subnormal testosterone concentrations and type 2 diabetes. Diabetes Care. 2011 Aug;34(8):1854-9. doi: 10.2337/dc11-0208. Epub 2011 Jun 29. PMID: 21715518; PMCID: PMC3142021, https://www.ncbi.nlm.nih.gov/pmc/articles/PMC3142021/#s5
45. Rosner W, Hankinson SE, Sluss PM, Vesper HW, Wierman ME., (2013). Challenges to the measurement of estradiol: an endocrine society position statement. J Clin Endocrinol Metab. 2013 Apr;98(4):1376-87. doi: 10.1210/jc.2012-3780. Epub 2013 Mar 5. PMID: 23463657; PMCID: PMC3615207, https://www.ncbi.nlm.nih.gov/pmc/articles/PMC3615207/
46. Gillies, GE., and McArthur, S., (2010). Estrogen actions in the brain and the basis for differential action in men and women: a case for sex-specific medicines. Pharmacol Rev. 2010 Jun;62(2):155-98. doi: 10.1124/pr.109.002071. Epub 2010 Apr 14. PMID: 20392807; PMCID: PMC2879914.
47. Schulster M, Bernie AM, Ramasamy R., (2016). The role of estradiol in male reproductive function. Asian J Androl. 2016 May-Jun;18(3):435-40. doi: 10.4103/1008-682X.173932. PMID: 26908066; PMCID: PMC4854098, https://www.ncbi.nlm.nih.gov/pmc/articles/PMC4854098/
48. World Health Organisation, Gender and health (2022, Accessed on: 3 August), https://www.who.int/health-topics/gender#tab=tab_1
49. Case, Susan S., and Oetama-Paul, Angela J., (2015). Brain Biology and Gendered Discourse, Applied Psychology 64(2), DOI:10.1111/apps.12040, https://www.researchgate.net/publication/269287751_Brain_Biology_and_Gendered_Discourse
50. *Case and Oetama-Paul, Brain Biology and Gendered Discourse.*
51. Tannen, Deborah., (2017, 28 June). Time, The Truth About How

References

Much Women Talk — and Whether Men Listen, https://time.com/4837536/do-women-really-talk-more/

52. Baron-Cohen, Simon., (2003). Penguin Books, The Essential Difference (p57-58).
53. Lutchmaya, Svetlana., Baron-Cohen, Simon., Raggatt, Peter., (2002). Foetal testosterone and eye contact in 12-month-old human infants, Elsevier Science Inc, Infant Behavior & Development 25(3):327-335, DOI:10.1016/S0163-6383(02)00094-2
54. Lutchmaya, Svetlana., Baron-Cohen, Simon., (2002). Human sex differences in social and non-social looking preferences, at 12 months of age, Elsevier Science Inc, Infant Behavior & Development 25(3):319-325, DOI:10.1016/S0163-6383(02)00095-4
55. Connellana, Jennifer., Baron-Cohen, Simon., Wheelwrighta, Sally., Batkia, Anna., Ahluwalia, Jag., (2000). Sex differences in human neonatal social perception, Elsevier Science Inc, Infant Behavior & Development 23(1):113-118, DOI:10.1016/S0163-6383(00)00032-1
56. *Baron-Cohen, The Essential Difference* (p58).
57. Johnson, Sue., (2014). Piatkus, The Love Secret (p68).
58. *Johnson, The Love Secret* (p70).
59. Plaister, Natasha., (2021, 17 September). FFT Education Datalab, Which A-Level subjects have the best (and worst) gender balance? https://ffteducationdatalab.org.uk/2021/09/which-a-level-subjects-have-the-best-and-worst-gender-balance/
60. Adams, Richard., (2021, 13 August). The Guardian, Girls overtake boys in A-level and GCSE maths, so are they 'smarter'? https://www.theguardian.com/education/2021/aug/13/girls-overtake-boys-in-a-level-and-gcse-maths-so-are-they-smarter
61. Adams, Richard., (2019, 22 August). The Guardian, GCSE results: girls fare better than boys under more rigorous courses, https://www.theguardian.com/education/2019/aug/22/gcse-results-more-rigorous-courses-appear-to-benefit-girls
62. STEM Women, (2022, 22 June). Women in STEM Statistics, https://www.stemwomen.com/women-in-stem-percentages-of-women-in-stem-statistics
63. Sander, Paul & Sanders, Lalage. (2007). Gender, Psychology Students and Higher Education. Psychology Learning and Teaching. 6. 33-36. 10.2304/plat.2007.6.1.33.
64. Research Works Limited / Office for Students, (2020). Male

References

Participation in Nursing and Allied Health Higher Education Courses, https://www.officeforstudents.org.uk/media/1abedca0-a27f-4ee9-a419-15ef5c9eba4b/male-participation-in-nmah-research-report.pdf

65. Prediger, D. J., (1982). Dimensions underlying Holland's hexagon: Missing link between interests and occupations? Journal of Vocational Behavior, 21(3), 259–287. https://doi.org/10.1016/0001-8791(82)90036-7
66. Career Smart, (2021). Which Jobs Do Men And Women Do? Occupational Breakdown By Gender, (Source: Working Futures 2021,) https://careersmart.org.uk/occupations/equality/which-jobs-do-men-and-women-do-occupational-breakdown-gender
67. Stewart-Williams, Steve and Halsey, Lewis G., (2021). Men, women and STEM: Why the differences and what should be done? European Journal of Personality, 13 January 2021, https://doi.org/10.1177/0890207020962326
68. Su R, Rounds J, Armstrong PI., (2009). Men and things, women and people: a meta-analysis of sex differences in interests. Psychol Bull.;135(6):859-884. doi: 10.1037/a0017364. PMID: 19883140.
69. Su, Rong and Rounds, James., (2015). All STEM fields are not created equal: People and things interests explain gender disparities across STEM fields, Frontiers in Psychology (6), DOI=10.3389/fpsyg.2015.00189, ISSN=1664-1078
70. Núñez, F., Maraver, M.J. & Colzato, L.S., (2020). Sex Hormones as Cognitive Enhancers?. J Cogn Enhanc 4, 228–233, https://doi.org/10.1007/s41465-019-00156-1
71. Clint, Edward K., Sober, Elliott., Garland, Jr Theodore., and Rhodes, Justin S., (2012). Male Superiority in Spatial Navigation: Adaptation or Side Effect? The University of Chicago Press Journals, The Quarterly Review of Biology Vol 84, 4, December 2012, https://doi.org/10.1086/668168
72. Baskaran C, Cunningham B, Plessow F, Singhal V, Woolley R, Ackerman KE, Slattery M, Lee H, Lawson EA, Eddy K, Misra M., (2017). Estrogen Replacement Improves Verbal Memory and Executive Control in Oligomenorrheic/Amenorrheic Athletes in a Randomized Controlled Trial. J Clin Psychiatry. 2017 May;78(5):e490-e497. doi: 10.4088/JCP.15m10544. PMID: 28297591; PMCID: PMC6445541
73. Karlsson, Sara., Henningsson, Susanne., Hovey, Daniel., Zettergren, Anna., Jonsson, Lina., Cortes, Diana S., Melke,

References

Jonas., Laukka, Petri., Fischer, Håkan., Westberg, Lars., (2016). Social memory associated with estrogen receptor polymorphisms in women, Social Cognitive and Affective Neuroscience, Volume 11, Issue 6, June 2016, Pages 877–883, https://doi.org/10.1093/scan/nsw010

74. Baron-Cohen, *The Essential Difference* (p8).
75. Baron-Cohen, *The Essential Difference* (p2, 23-25).
76. *Tannen, The Truth About How Much Women Talk.*
77. *Case and Oetama-Paul, Brain Biology and Gendered Discourse.*
78. Baron-Cohen, *The Essential Difference* (p3, 63-66).
79. *Plaister, Which A-Level subjects have the best.*
80. Nicholson, Christie., (2012, 1 October). Scientific American, The Humour Gap, https://www.scientificamerican.com/article/the-humor-gap-2012-10-23/
81. Grammer, K., and Eibl-Eibsfeldt, I. (1990). "The ritualisation of laughter," in Die Natürlichkeit der Sprache und der Kultur, ed W. A. Koch (Bochum: Brockmeyer), 192–214.
82. Provine, Robert R., (2000). Faber and Faber Limited (UK), Laughter: A Scientific Investigation (p32-34).
83. Bressler, Eric R., Martin, Rod A., Balshine, Sigal., (2006). Production and appreciation of humor as sexually selected traits, Evolution and Human Behavior, Volume 27, Issue 2, 2006, Pages 121-130, ISSN 1090-5138, https://doi.org/10.1016/j.evolhumbehav.2005.09.001
84. Bressler, Eric R., Balshine, Sigal., (2006). The influence of humor on desirability, Evolution and Human Behavior, Volume 27, Issue 1, 2006, Pages 29-39, ISSN 1090-5138, https://doi.org/10.1016/j.evolhumbehav.2005.06.002
85. *Nicholson, The Humour Gap.*
86. Herbert, Joe., (2018). "Testosterone, Cortisol and Financial Risk-Taking." Frontiers in behavioral neuroscience vol. 12 101. 16 May. 2018, doi:10.3389/fnbeh.2018.00101; https://www.frontiersin.org/articles/10.3389/fnbeh.2018.00101/full
87. *van Anders, Effects of gendered behavior on testosterone in women and men.*
88. Caprino, Kathy., (2016, 12 May). Forbes, How Decision-Making Is Different Between Men And Women And Why It Matters In Business, https://www.forbes.com/sites/kathycaprino/2016/05/12/how-decision-making-is-different-between-men-and-women-and-why-

References

it-matters-in-business/?sh=1fbdcf144dcd
89. Irrera, Anna., (2018, 14 June). Wall Street wants more female traders, but old perceptions die hard, https://www.reuters.com/article/us-banks-trading-gender-idUKKBN1JA0DF
90. Canadian Women & Sport., (2020, June). The Rally Report: Encouraging Action to Improve Sport for Women and Girls, https://womenandsport.ca/wp-content/uploads/2020/06/Canadian-Women-Sport_The-Rally-Report.pdf
91. Kay, Katty & Shipman, Claire., (2014, May). The Atlantic, The Confidence Gap, https://www.theatlantic.com/magazine/archive/2014/05/the-confidence-gap/359815/
92. Rostron, Claire., (2015, 8 September). Open University, How testosterone affects risk taking behaviour, https://www.open.edu/openlearn/science-maths-technology/science/biology/how-testosterone-affects-risk-taking-behaviour
93. Sissons, *Typical testosterone levels in males and females.*
94. *Buss, The Evolution of Desire* (2016, p270-271).
95. *Buss, The Evolution of Desire* (2016, p316).
96. Wei-Haas, Maya., (2020, 4 November). National Geographic, Prehistoric female hunter discovery upends gender role assumptions, https://www.nationalgeographic.com/science/article/prehistoric-female-hunter-discovery-upends-gender-role-assumptions
97. United States Census Bureau, Current Population Survey 2017 Annual Social and Economic (ASEC), Table FG3. Married Couple Family Groups, https://www2.census.gov/programs-surveys/demo/tables/families/2017/cps-2017/tabfg3-all.xls
98. Office for National Statistics, Ethnicity within marriage or cohabiting mixed-sex relationship, UK, 2018 (Release date: 28 August 2020), https://www.ons.gov.uk/peoplepopulationandcommunity/birthsdeathsandmarriages/marriagecohabitationandcivilpartnerships/adhocs/12186ethnicitywithinmarriageorcohabitingmixedsexrelationshipuk2018
99. *Mongeau, et al., Who's Wooing Whom?* (p51-68).
100. *Mongeau and Carey, Who's wooing whom II?*
101. *Mongeau, et al., Who's Wooing Whom?* (p51-68).
102. Kendrick, S., Kepple, N.J., (2022). Scripting Sex in Courtship:

References

Predicting Genital Contact in Date Outcomes. Sexuality & Culture 26, 1190–1214. https://doi.org/10.1007/s12119-021-09938-2

103. Kelley, K., Pilchowicz, E. & Byrne, D., (1981). Response of males to female-initiated dates. Bull. Psychon. Soc. 17, 195–196. https://doi.org/10.3758/BF03333710
104. *Mongeau, et al., Who's Wooing Whom?* (p51-68).
105. Facebook Data Science., (2021, 12 March) From Classmates to Soulmates, https://www.facebook.com/notes/10158927999853415/
106. Taylor SE, Klein LC, Lewis BP, Gruenewald TL, Gurung RA, Updegraff JA., (2000). Biobehavioral responses to stress in females: tend-and-befriend, not fight-or-flight. Psychol Rev. 2000 Jul;107(3):411-29. doi: 10.1037/0033-295x.107.3.411. PMID: 10941275.
107. Marazziti D, Baroni S, Mucci F, Piccinni A, Moroni I, Giannaccini G, Carmassi C, Massimetti E, Dell'Osso L., (2019). Sex-Related Differences in Plasma Oxytocin Levels in Humans. Clin Pract Epidemiol Ment Health. 2019 Mar 26;15:58-63. doi: 10.2174/1745017901915010058. PMID: 31015856; PMCID: PMC6446474.
108. Rilling JK., Young LJ., (2014). The biology of mammalian parenting and its effect on offspring social development. Science 345(6198):771–776.
109. Post, C., Leuner, B., (2019). The maternal reward system in postpartum depression. Arch Womens Ment Health 22, 417–429 https://doi.org/10.1007/s00737-018-0926-y
110. *Taylor, et al., Biobehavioral responses to stress in females.*
111. Kuperberg, Arielle., and Stone, Pamela., (2022, 20 April). Gender & Society, Mord Dads Are Home Taking Care of Children Than Ever Before - Are Views About Gender and Work Changing? https://gendersociety.wordpress.com/2022/04/20/more-dads-are-home-taking-care-of-children-than-ever-before-are-views-about-gender-and-work-changing/
112. Klein, Wendy., Izquierdo, Carolina., and Bradbury, Thomas N., (2013, 1 March). The Difference Between a Happy Marriage and Miserable One: Chores, https://www.theatlantic.com/sexes/archive/2013/03/the-difference-between-a-happy-marriage-and-miserable-one-chores/273615/
113. Department of Labor (US)., (2022, 20 April). Bureau of Labor

References

Statistics, https://www.bls.gov/news.release/pdf/famee.pdf

114. Murphy, Rhian., Dennes, Matt., Harris, Ben., (2022, 22 July). Families and the labour market, UK: 2021, https://www.ons.gov.uk/employmentandlabourmarket/peopleinwork/employmentandemployeetypes/articles/familiesandthelabourmarketengland/2021
115. Newkirk K, Perry-Jenkins M, Sayer AG., (2017). Division of Household and Childcare Labor and Relationship Conflict Among Low-Income New Parents. Sex Roles. 2017 Mar;76(5):319-333. doi: 10.1007/s11199-016-0604-3. Epub 2016 Mar 11. PMID: 28348454; PMCID: PMC5365149.
116. Gottman, John M., and Silver, Nan., (1999, 2015, 2018). Seven Dials (The Orion Publishing Group Ltd.), The Seven Principles for Making Marriage Work, (2018, p218).
117. *Gottman and Silver, The Seven Principles for Making Marriage Work* (2018, p213, 218).
118. Scott, SB., Rhoades, GK., Stanley, SM., Allen, ES., Markman, HJ., (2013). Reasons for Divorce and Recollections of Premarital Intervention: Implications for Improving Relationship Education. Couple Family Psychol. 2013 Jun;2(2):131-145. doi: 10.1037/a0032025. PMID: 24818068; PMCID: PMC4012696.
119. Norman, H., Elliot, Mark., Fagan, Collette., (2018). Does Fathers' Involvement in Childcare and Housework Affect Couples' Relationship Stability?, SOCIAL SCIENCE QUARTERLY, Volume 99, Number 5, November 2018, DOI: 10.1111/ssqu.12523.
120. Ruppanner, L., Brandén, M., & Turunen, J., (2018). Does Unequal Housework Lead to Divorce? Evidence from Sweden. Sociology, 52(1), 75–94. https://doi.org/10.1177/0038038516674664.
121. Harvey, Steve., (2009, 2014). HarperCollins Publishers Act Like a Lady, Think Like a Man (p65).
122. *Herbert, Testosterone: The Molecule Behind Power.*
123. *Case and Oetama-Paul, Brain Biology and Gendered Discourse.*
124. *Johnson, The Love Secret (*p65).
125. O'Neill, Olivia., and O'Reilly, Charles., (2011). Reducing the backlash effect: Self-monitoring and women's promotions, Journal of Occupational and Organizational Psychology, 84(4):825-832, DOI:10.1111/j.2044-8325.2010.02008.x.
126. Bowles, H. R., & Babcock, L., (2013). How Can Women Escape the Compensation Negotiation Dilemma? Relational Accounts

References

Are One Answer. Psychology of Women Quarterly, 37(1), 80–96. https://doi.org/10.1177/0361684312455524.

127. Baron-Cohen, *The Essential Difference* (p12).
128. Baron-Cohen, *The Essential Difference* (p2, 23-25).
129. Baron-Cohen, *The Essential Difference* (p3, 63-66).
130. Hetherton, Mavis. E., & Kelly, John., (2002). WW Norton and Company, For Better Or For Worse (p47).
131. Peplau, Letiticia Anne., (2003). Human Sexuality: How Do Men and Women Differ?, Current Directions in Psychological Science, , Vol 12, 2, pages 37-40, https://peplau.psych.ucla.edu/wp-content/uploads/sites/141/2017/07/Peplau-2003.pdf
132. *Buss, The Evolution of Desire* (2016, p146).
133. *Buss, The Evolution of Desire* (2016, p147, 321).
134. *Buss, The Evolution of Desire* (2016, p80, 323).
135. Allen, Patricia., and Harmon, Sandra., (1994, 1995). Avon, Getting To "I Do" – The Secret to Doing Relationships Right! (p116).
136. Hyde, Matt., (2018, 4 October). Third Sector, Matt Hyde: Why charities must champion empathy to bring communities together, https://www.thirdsector.co.uk/matt-hyde-why-charities-champion-empathy-bring-communities-together/volunteering/article/1494810
137. Welch, Duana, D., (2015). LoveScience Media, Love Factualy – 10 Proven Steps from I Wish to I Do (p62-63, 66).
138. Cohan, C. L. (2013). The Cohabitation Conundrum. In M. A. Fine & F. D. Fincham (Eds.), Handbook of family theories: A content-based approach (pp. 105–122). Routledge/Taylor & Francis Group.
139. *Johnson, Great Myths of Intimate Relationships* (p99).
140. Chalabi, Mona., (2014, 9 October). FiveThirtyEight, Dear Mona, Does Living Together Before Marriage Increase The Risk Of Divorce? https://fivethirtyeight.com/features/does-living-together-before-marriage-increase-the-risk-of-divorce/
141. Moore, Monica M., (1985). Nonverbal Courtship Patterns in Women - Context and Consequences, Elsevier Science, Ethology and Sociobiology 6:4:237-247, ISSN 0162-3095.
142. *Allen and Harmon, Getting To "I Do"* (p98-99).
143. National Golf Federation., (2021). Golf Industry Facts, https://www.ngf.org/golf-industry-research/
144. International Tennis Federation., (2021). ITF Global Tennis Report, http://itf.uberflip.com/i/1401406-itf-global-tennis-report-

References

2021/7?

145. Perry, Mark J., (2018, 16 November). American Enterprise Institute, Sorry, Feminists, Men Are Better at Scrabble (and Geography and Math), https://www.aei.org/carpe-diem/sorry-feminists-men-are-better-at-scrabble-and-at-geography-and-math/#:~:text=Nor%20are%20there%20misogynist%20gatekeepers,25%20to%2054%20are%20female
146. Losee, Stephanie., and Olen, Helaine., (2007). Adams Media, Office Mate (p. xviii, 13-14).
147. *Losee and Olen, Office Mate* (p9).
148. *Facebook Data Science, From Classmates to Soulmates.*
149. NHS., (2021, 12 July). What infections can I catch through oral sex? https://www.nhs.uk/common-health-questions/sexual-health/what-infections-can-i-catch-through-oral-sex/
150. Tsevat DG, Wiesenfeld HC, Parks C, Peipert JF., (2017). Sexually transmitted diseases and infertility. Am J Obstet Gynecol. 2017 Jan;216(1):1-9. doi: 10.1016/j.ajog.2016.08.008. PMID: 28007229; PMCID: PMC5193130.
151. *Buss, The Evolution of Desire* (2016, p17, 33).
152. Williams, Lawrence E, and Bargh, John A., (2008). "Experiencing physical warmth promotes interpersonal warmth." Science (New York, N.Y.) vol. 322,5901: 606-7. doi:10.1126/science.1162548.
153. *Allen and Harmon, Getting To "I Do"* (p116).
154. The Knot Worldwide., (2021, 2 December). Outdoor Marriage Proposals Skyrocket in 2021, According to The Knot 2021 Jewelry & Engagement Study, https://www.theknotww.com/press-releases/2021jewelryandengagementstudy/
155. Eharmony Editorial Team., (2021, 18 March). eharmony, 10 Online Dating Statistics You Should Know, https://www.eharmony.com/online-dating-statistics/
156. Shashkevich, Alex., (2019, 21 August). Stanford News, Meeting online has become the most popular way U.S. couples connect, https://news.stanford.edu/2019/08/21/online-dating-popular-way-u-s-couples-meet/
157. Sky News., (2019, 27 November). Finding love online: More than half of couples set to meet via the internet, https://news.sky.com/story/finding-love-online-more-than-half-of-couples-set-to-meet-via-the-internet-11871341
158. Dating Zest., (2022). Tinder Statistics 2022 & Fun Facts That You Didn't Know Before, (Accessed: 22 November 2022) https://datingzest.com/tinder-statistics/

References

159. *Dating Zest, Tinder Statistics 2022.*
160. *Dating Zest, Tinder Statistics 2022.*
161. Wakefield, Jane., (2021, 10 February). BBC News, Romance fraud on rise in coronavirus lockdown, https://www.bbc.co.uk/news/technology-55997611
162. Peachey, Kevin., (2019, 10 February). BBC News, Women 'victims in 63% of romance scams', https://www.bbc.co.uk/news/business-47176539
163. *Harvey, Act Like a Lady, Think Like a Man* (p147-159).
164. Berger, Tia., (2019, 29 January). Atlanta Black Star, Steve Harvey Rehashes His 90-Day Rule, Says Women Should View Men as on Probation Before a Sex 'Benefits Package'. https://atlantablackstar.com/2019/01/29/steve-harvey-rehashes-his-90-day-rule-says-women-should-view-men-as-on-probation-before-a-sex-benefits-package/
165. *Harvey, Act Like a Lady, Think Like a Man* (p150)
166. de Munck, V. C., Korotayev, A., de Munck, J., & Khaltourina, D. (2011). Cross-Cultural Analysis of Models of Sexual Love Among U.S. Residents, Russians, and Lithuanians. Cross-Cultural Research, 45(2), 128–154. https://doi.org/10.1177/1069397110393313
167. De Lacey, Martha., (2013, 7 March). Daily Mail Online, When WILL he say 'I love you'? Men take 88 days to say those three words - but girls make their man wait a lot longer (Article dated 7 March 2013), https://www.dailymail.co.uk/femail/article-2289562/I-love-Men-88-days-say-girlfriend-women-134-days-say-boyfriend.html
168. Clift, Courtney., (2020, 14 February). Elemental Medium, This Is Your Brain In Love, https://elemental.medium.com/love-can-make-you-high-14eaa6bcec5d
169. Wu, Katherine., (2014, 14 February). Science in the news (Harvard University), Love, Actually: The science behind lust, attraction, and companionship, https://sitn.hms.harvard.edu/flash/2017/love-actually-science-behind-lust-attraction-companionship/
170. Cappelletti M, and Wallen K., (2016, February). Increasing women's sexual desire: The comparative effectiveness of estrogens and androgens. Horm Behav.;78:178-93. doi: 10.1016/j.yhbeh.2015.11.003. Epub 2015 Nov 14. PMID: 26589379; PMCID: PMC4720522.
171. Zeki, S., (2007). The neurobiology of love, FEBS Letters, 581,

References

doi: 10.1016/j.febslet.2007.03.094.
172. Clift, *This Is Your Brain In Love.*
173. Zeki, *The neurobiology of love.*
174. Herbert, *Testosterone: The Molecule Behind Power.*
175. Losecaat, et al., *Exogenous testosterone increases status-seeking motivation in men.*
176. van Anders, *Effects of gendered behavior on testosterone in women and men.*
177. Nickerson, Charlotte., (2022, 16 March). SimplyPsychology, Instrumental Aggression: Definition & Examples, https://www.simplypsychology.org/instrumental-aggression.html
178. Gillies and McArthur, *Estrogen actions in the brain.*
179. Zeki, *The neurobiology of love.*
180. Andersen, Christopher., (2012). The Robson Press, MICK the Wild and Mad Genius of JAGGER (p226).
181. Roper, Matt, (2019, 17 February). Mirror, Mick Jagger, 75, 'tamed' by 31-year-old girlfriend after bedding 4,000 women, https://www.mirror.co.uk/3am/celebrity-news/mick-jagger-75-tamed-31-14013130
182. Cleveland Clinic., (2022, 27 March). Norepinephrine (Noradrenaline), https://my.clevelandclinic.org/health/articles/22610-norepinephrine-noradrenaline
183. Wu, *Love, Actually: The science behind lust.*
184. Fisher, Helen., (2009). A Oneworld Book, Why Him? Why Her? How to Find and Keep Lasting Love (p126-127)
185. Zeki, *The neurobiology of love.*
186. Marazziti, et al., *Sex-Related Differences in Plasma Oxytocin Levels in Humans.*
187. Carter, C. Sue., and Perkeybile, Allison M., (2018). The Monogamy Paradox: What Do Love and Sex Have to Do With It?, Frontiers in Ecology and Evolution (Vol 6, 29 Nov 2018, p202), DOI=10.3389/fevo.2018.00202, https://www.frontiersin.org/article/10.3389/fevo.2018.00202
188. Burnham TC, Chapman JF, Gray PB, McIntyre MH, Lipson SF, Ellison PT., (2003). Men in committed, romantic relationships have lower testosterone. Horm Behav. 2003 Aug;44(2):119-22. doi: 10.1016/s0018-506x(03)00125-9. PMID: 13129483.
189. Grebe NM, Sarafin RE, Strenth CR, Zilioli S., (2019). Pair-bonding, fatherhood, and the role of testosterone: A meta-analytic review. Neurosci Biobehav Rev. 2019 Mar;98:221-233. doi:

References

10.1016/j.neubiorev.2019.01.010. Epub 2019 Jan 9. PMID: 30639674.
190. Farrelly, D., Owens, R., Elliott, H. R., Walden, H. R., & Wetherell, M. A., (2015). The Effects of Being in a "New Relationship" on Levels of Testosterone in Men. Evolutionary Psychology, 13(1). https://doi.org/10.1177/147470491501300116
191. Carter, Sue C., (2017) The Oxytocin–Vasopressin Pathway in the Context of Love and Fear, Front. Endocrinol., 22 December 2017, Sec. Neuroendocrine Science, https://doi.org/10.3389/fendo.2017.00356
192. *Carter and Perkeybile, The Monogamy Paradox.*
193. Hammock, Elizabeth A D, and Larry J Young., (2006). "Oxytocin, vasopressin and pair bonding: implications for autism." Philosophical transactions of the Royal Society of London. Series B, Biological sciences vol. 361,1476: 2187-98. doi:10.1098/rstb.2006.1939.
194. *Carter and Perkeybile, The Monogamy Paradox.*
195. *Hammock, et al., Oxytocin, vasopressin and pair bonding.*
196. Young LJ., (2003). The Neural Basis of Pair Bonding in a Monogamous Species: A Model for Understanding the Biological Basis of Human Behavior. In: National Research Council (US) Panel for the Workshop on the Biodemography of Fertility and Family Behavior; Wachter KW, Bulatao RA, editors. Offspring: Human Fertility Behavior in Biodemographic Perspective. Washington (DC): National Academies Press (US); 2003. 4. Available from: https://www.ncbi.nlm.nih.gov/books/NBK97287/
197. Fisher, Helen., (1992, 2006, 2016) WW Norton, Anatomy Of Love (2016, p164-165).
198. *Young, The Neural Basis of Pair Bonding in a Monogamous Species.*
199. *Buss, The Evolution of Desire* (2016, p301-303).
200. *Carter and Perkeybile, The Monogamy Paradox.*
201. Walum, Hasse., Westberg, Lars., Henningsson, Susanne., Neiderhiser, Jenae M., Reiss, David., Igl, Wilmar., Ganiban, Jody M., Spotts, Erica L., Pedersen, Nancy L., Eriksson, Elias., and Lichtenstein, Paul., (2008). Genetic variation in the vasopressin receptor 1a gene (AVPR1A) associates with pair-bonding behavior in humans. Proceedings of the National Academy of Sciences, Sep 2008, 105 (37) 14153-14156; DOI: 10.1073/pnas.0803081105.
202. Ophir, Alexander G., Wolff, Jerry O., and Phelps, Steven M.,

References

(2008). Variation in neural V1aR predicts sexual fidelity and space use among male prairie voles in semi-natural settings, Proceedings of the National Academy of Sciences Jan 2008, 105 (4) 1249-1254; DOI: 10.1073/pnas.0709116105.
203. *Buss, The Evolution of Desire* (2016, p37).
204. Booth, A., & Dabbs, J. M. (1993). Testosterone and Men's Marriages. Social Forces, 72(2), 463–477. https://doi.org/10.2307/2579857
205. Manchester Metropolitan University., (2022, 27 September). News, Lessons learned from domestic homicide reviews must be shared more effectively to strengthen responses, research shows, https://www.mmu.ac.uk/news-and-events/news/story/15375/
206. Alvarez, Sergio Diez., (2020, 22 October). University of Newcastle, Australia, Why men wake up with erections, https://www.newcastle.edu.au/hippocampus/story/2020/male-erections
207. *Hetherton and Kelly, For Better Or For Worse* (p53, 86).
208. *Hetherton and Kelly, For Better Or For Worse* (p78-79).
209. O'Brien, Jodi., (2009). Sage Publications, Encyclopedia of Gender and Society (Volume 1, p169-170).
210. *Gottman and Silver, The Seven Principles for Making Marriage Work* (2018, p223-224).
211. *Gottman and Silver, The Seven Principles for Making Marriage Work* (2018, p18).
212. Gottman, John., (2007). Bloomsbury Publishing Plc, Why Marriages Succeed or Fail And How to Make Yours Last (p57).
213. *Gottman, Why Marriages Succeed or Fail* (p65).
214. Gray, John., (1992). Thornsons (Harper Collins Publishers), Men are from Mars, Women are from Venus (2018, p203-204).
215. *Amato, et al., Alone Together* (p121).
216. *Amato, et al., Alone Together* (p123).
217. Warrier, Varun., Toro, Roberto., Chakrabarti, Bhismadev., the iPSYCH-Broad autism group., Børglum, Anders D., Grove, Jakob., the 23andMe Research Team., Hinds, David A., Bourgeron, Thomas., & Baron-Cohen, Simon., (2018). Genome-wide analyses of self-reported empathy: correlations with autism, schizophrenia, and anorexia nervosa. Transl Psychiatry 8, 35. https://doi.org/10.1038/s41398-017-0082-6
218. *Gottman, Why Marriages Succeed or Fail* (p68-102).
219. *Gottman, Why Marriages Succeed or Fail* (p93-95).
220. Welch, Duana C., (2019). Love Science Media, Love Actually –

References

For Single Parents [& Those Dating Them] (p330-331).
221. Gottman and Silver, *The Seven Principles for Making Marriage Work* (2018, p43).
222. Gottman and Silver, *The Seven Principles for Making Marriage Work* (2018, p236-259).
223. Stripe, *Married by 30? You're now in the minority.*
224. United States Census Bureau, *Historical Marital Status Tables.*
225. Reid, Rebecca., (2017, 20 July). Metro.co.uk, How long is the average couple together before they get married? https://metro.co.uk/2017/07/20/how-long-is-the-average-couple-together-before-they-get-married-6793590/
226. Priceonomics., (2016, 9 February). How Long Do Couples Date Before Getting Engaged? https://priceonomics.com/how-long-do-couples-date-before-getting-engaged/
227. The Knot., (2020). The Knot 2019 Real Weddings Study, https://www.wedinsights.com/report/the-knot-real-weddings
228. Arain M, Haque M, Johal L, Mathur P, Nel W, Rais A, Sandhu R, Sharma S., (2013). Maturation of the adolescent brain. Neuropsychiatr Dis Treat. 2013;9:449-61. doi: 10.2147/NDT.S39776. Epub 2013 Apr 3. PMID: 23579318; PMCID: PMC3621648.
229. *Amato, et al., Alone Together* (p77).
230. Mercurio, Ezequiel., García-López, Eric., Morales-Quintero, Luz Anyela., Llamas, Nicolás E., Marinaro, José Ángel., and Muñoz, José M.., (2020). Adolescent Brain Development and Progressive Legal Responsibility in the Latin American Context. Front. Psychol., 24 April 2020, Sec. Neuropsychology, https://doi.org/10.3389/fpsyg.2020.00627
231. *Amato, et al., Alone Together* (p77-79).
232. *Amato, et al., Alone Together* (p24).
233. Stripe, *Married by 30? You're now in the minority.*
234. Martin, Alec., (2013, December). Relate, Factsheet: Separation and Divorce, https://www.relate.org.uk/sites/default/files/separation-divorce-factsheet-jan2014.pdf
235. DiDonato, Theresa E., (2021, 27 January). Psychology Today, Are Couples That Live Together Before Marriage More Likely to Divorce? https://www.psychologytoday.com/us/blog/meet-catch-and-keep/202101/is-living-together-marriage-associated-divorce
236. *Amato, et al., Alone Together* (p73).
237. *Cohan, The Cohabitation Conundrum.*

References

238. *Cohan, The Cohabitation Conundrum.*
239. Benson, Harry., (2021, August). Marriage Foundation, One in five weddings now start with a prenup. Report: https://marriagefoundation.org.uk/wp-content/uploads/2021/08/MF-briefing-note-on-prenups-FINAL.pdf
240. Marriage Foundation., (2021, 29 August). 1 in 5 couples married since 2000 may have some form of prenup in place, finds first-ever research on the subject, https://marriagefoundation.org.uk/wp-content/uploads/2021/08/MF-press-release-on-prenups.pdf
241. *Scott, et al., Reasons for Divorce and Recollections of Premarital Intervention.*
242. *Buss, The Evolution of Desire* (2016, p276-279).
243. *Fisher, Anatomy of Love* (2016, p85).
244. Betzig, L. (1989). Causes of conjugal dissolution: A cross-cultural study. Current Anthropology, 30(5), 654–676. https://doi.org/10.1086/203798, https://laurabetzig.org/pdf/CA89.pdf
245. *Scott, et al., Reasons for Divorce and Recollections of Premarital Intervention.*
246. *Scott, et al., Reasons for Divorce and Recollections of Premarital Intervention.*
247. *Fisher, Anatomy of Love* (2016, p69).
248. *Hetherton and Kelly, For Better Or For Worse* (p35).
249. *Hetherton and Kelly, For Better Or For Worse* (p34).
250. Anderson, Nancy L., (2013, 7 February). Forbes, 5 Ways Love and Marriage Can Make You Wealthier, https://www.forbes.com/sites/financialfinesse/2013/02/07/5-ways-love-and-marriage-can-make-you-wealthier/?sh=68f5c7be2a74
251. McDonald, Leah., (2018, 23 September). DailyMail.com, Married men earn more than any other demographic in America - while women and single men earn around 25% LESS, report reveals, https://www.dailymail.co.uk/news/article-6198907/Study-reveals-married-men-earn-demographic-America.html
252. *Gottman and Silver, The Seven Principles for Making Marriage Work* (2018, p213, 218).
253. *Scott, et al., Reasons for Divorce and Recollections of Premarital Intervention.*
254. *Norman, et al., Does Fathers' Involvement in Childcare and Housework.*

References

255. *Ruppanner, et al., Does Unequal Housework Lead to Divorce?*
256. Chapman, Gary, D., (2010). Northfield Publishing, Things I Wish I'd Known Before We Got Married (p85-87).
257. Tennov, Dorothy., (1999). New York: Stein and Day, Love and Limerence, (p142)
258. *Fisher, Romantic Love: Can It Last?*
259. *Hetherton and Kelly, For Better Or For Worse* (p263).
260. *Hetherton and Kelly, For Better Or For Worse* (p268).
261. DiDonato, *Are Couples That Live Together Before Marriage More Likely to Divorce?*
262. *Amato, et al., Alone Together* (p73).
263. *Cohan, The Cohabitation Conundrum.*
264. *Cohan, The Cohabitation Conundrum.*
265. *Cohan, The Cohabitation Conundrum.*
266. *Amato, et al., Alone Together* (p24).
267. Zane, Zachary and Razor, Calen., (2021, 9 June). Men's Health, Here's How Often Men and Women Really Think About Sex, https://www.menshealth.com/sex-women/a28483383/how-often-think-about-sex/
268. NHS UK., (2021, 30 December). Vaginal Dryness, https://www.nhs.uk/conditions/vaginal-dryness/
269. NHS Inform., (2023, 31 January), Early and premature menopause, https://www.nhsinform.scot/healthy-living/womens-health/later-years-around-50-years-and-over/menopause-and-post-menopause-health/early-and-premature-menopause
270. Mayo Clinic., (2021, 7 August). Perimenopause, https://www.mayoclinic.org/diseases-conditions/perimenopause/symptoms-causes/syc-20354666
271. Waetjen, LE., Crawford, SL., Chang, PY., Reed, BD., Hess, R., Avis, NE., Harlow, SD., Greendale, GA., Dugan, SA., Gold, EB., (2018). Study of Women's Health Across the Nation (SWAN). Factors associated with developing vaginal dryness symptoms in women transitioning through menopause: a longitudinal study. Menopause. 2018 Oct;25(10):1094-1104. doi: 10.1097/GME.0000000000001130. PMID: 29916947; PMCID: PMC6136974.
272. Munarriz, R., Kim, NN., Goldstein, I., Traish, AM., (2002. Biology of female sexual function. Urol Clin North Am. 2002 Aug;29(3):685-93. doi: 10.1016/s0094-0143(02)00069-1. PMID: 12476531.
    https://www.bumc.bu.edu/sexualmedicine/physicianinformation/b

References

iology-of-female-sexual-function/
273. Waetjen, et al., *Factors associated with developing vaginal dryness symptoms.*
274. NHS., (2022, 11 October). Overview: Polycystic Ovary Syndrome, https://www.nhs.uk/conditions/polycystic-ovary-syndrome-pcos/
275. Eftekhar, T., Sohrabvand, F., Zabandan, N., Shariat, M., Haghollahi, F., Ghahghaei-Nezamabadi, A., (2014) Sexual dysfunction in patients with polycystic ovary syndrome and its affected domains. Iran J Reprod Med. 2014 Aug;12(8):539-46. PMID: 25408703; PMCID: PMC4233312.
276. NHS., (2022, 11 October). Treatment: Polycystic Ovary Syndrome, https://www.nhs.uk/conditions/polycystic-ovary-syndrome-pcos/treatment/
277. NHS., (2022, 5 September). Overview - Endometriosis, https://www.nhs.uk/conditions/endometriosis/
278. Endometriosis., (2023, Accessed on: 8 March). WHAT IS ENDOMETRIOSIS? https://www.endometriosis-uk.org/what-endometriosis
279. NHS., (2022, 17 May). Menopause Symptoms, https://www.nhs.uk/conditions/menopause/symptoms/
280. Harvard TH Chan - School Of Public Health., (2022, Accessed: 22 November). Straight Talk About Soy, https://www.hsph.harvard.edu/nutritionsource/soy/
281. NHS., (2022, 27 May). Human papillomavirus (HPV), https://www.nhs.uk/conditions/human-papilloma-virus-hpv/
282. NHS., (2021, 12 July). What infections can I catch through oral sex? https://www.nhs.uk/common-health-questions/sexual-health/what-infections-can-i-catch-through-oral-sex/
283. Booth, Stephanie., (2020, 21 February). WebMD, Get In Touch With Your Circadian Rhythm, https://www.webmd.com/sleep-disorders/find-circadian-rhythm
284. Carey, Tanith., (2014, 26 June). Mirror, Why do men want sex in the morning while women get frisky at night? https://www.mirror.co.uk/lifestyle/sex-relationships/sex/men-want-sex-morning-women-3765310
285. *Buss, The Evolution of Desire* (2016, p125).
286. *Buss, The Evolution of Desire* (2016, p126).
287. Scheele, Dirk., Wille, Andrea., Kendrick, Keith M., Stoffel-Wagner, Birgit., Becker Benjamin., Güntürkün, Onur., Maier, Wolfgang., and Hurlemann. René., (2013, 23 November).

References

Oxytocin enhances brain reward system responses in men viewing the face of their female partner, Proceedings of the National Academy of Sciences 110(50), https://doi.org/10.1073/pnas.1314190110
288. Langeslag, S. J. E., & Surti, K. (2022, February 3). Increasing Love Feelings, Marital Satisfaction, and Motivated Attention to the Spouse. Journal of Psychophysiology. Advance online publication. http://dx.doi.org/10.1027/0269-8803/a000294
289. Preslar, Susan Kay., (2017). Third Star Press, Fanning The Female Flame (p105-105).
290. *Preslar, Fanning The Female Flame (p11)*
291. Shifren, JL., Monz, BU., Russo PA, Segreti, A., Johannes, CB., (2008). Sexual problems and distress in United States women: prevalence and correlates. Obstet Gynecol. 2008 Nov;112(5):970-8. doi: 10.1097/AOG.0b013e3181898cdb. PMID: 18978095.
292. *Stripe, Married by 30? You're now in the minority.*
293. Human Fertilisation & Embryology Authority., (2021, May). Fertility treatment 2019: trends and figures, https://www.hfea.gov.uk/about-us/publications/research-and-data/fertility-treatment-2019-trends-and-figures/
294. NHS UK., (2021, 18 October). Availability - IVF, https://www.nhs.uk/conditions/ivf/availability/
295. National Institute for Health and Care Excellence., (2013, 20 February). Fertility problems: assessment and treatment, https://www.nice.org.uk/guidance/cg156/chapter/context
296. SingleCare., (2021, 23 September). Infertility statistics 2021, https://www.singlecare.com/blog/news/infertility-statistics/
297. National Institute of Child Health and Human Development., (2018, 8 February). How common is infertility?, https://www.nichd.nih.gov/health/topics/infertility/conditioninfo/common
298. Practice Committee of the American Society for Reproductive Medicine in collaboration with the Society for Reproductive Endocrinology and Infertility., (2013). Optimizing natural fertility: A committee opinion. Fertility and Sterility, (Dated: 26 October 2016), https://www.fertstert.org/article/S0015-0282(16)62849-2/fulltext
299. Levine, Hagai., Jørgensen, Niels., Martino-Andrade, Anderson., Mendiola, Jaime., Weksler-Derri, Dan., Jolles, Maya., Pinotti, Rachel., Swan, Shanna H., (2022). Temporal trends in sperm count: a systematic review and meta-regression analysis of

References

samples collected globally in the 20th and 21st centuries, Human Reproduction Update, Volume 29, Issue 2, March-April 2023, Pages 157–176, https://doi.org/10.1093/humupd/dmac035

300. Centers for Disease Control and Prevention., (2021, 3 April). Reproductive Health, Infertility FAQs, https://www.cdc.gov/reproductivehealth/Infertility/#e
301. NHS., (2022, 9 March). Miscarriage Cause, https://www.nhs.uk/conditions/miscarriage/causes/
302. Alviggi C, Humaidan P, Howles CM, Tredway D, Hillier SG., (2009). Biological versus chronological ovarian age: implications for assisted reproductive technology. Reprod Biol Endocrinol. 2009 Sep 22;7:101. doi: 10.1186/1477-7827-7-101. PMID: 19772632; PMCID: PMC2764709.
303. Watson, Stephenie., (2018, 19 September). Healthline, What's The Best Age To Get Pregnant?, https://www.healthline.com/health/pregnancy/best-age-to-get-pregnant
304. Domestic Abuse Act (2021), https://www.legislation.gov.uk/ukpga/2021/17/contents/enacted
305. Elkin, Meghan., (2021, 24 November). Office Of National Statistics, Domestic abuse in England and Wales overview: November 2021, https://www.ons.gov.uk/peoplepopulationandcommunity/crimeandjustice/bulletins/domesticabuseinenglandandwalesoverview/november2021

www.ingramcontent.com/pod-product-compliance
Lightning Source LLC
Chambersburg PA
CBHW071215080526
44587CB00013BA/1384